UNIX for FORTRAN Programmers

Nutshell Handbooks

Nutshell Handbooks are concise, down-to-earth books on a variety of UNIX topics. Other books of interest are:

Managing Projects with make

83 pages, $12.95

This handbook provides a complete treatment of one of UNIX's most enduring contributions to software development, the *make* utility.

Learning the vi Editor

156 pages, $21.95

This handbook is a complete guide to *vi*, the full screen text editor that is available on most UNIX systems. As one user recently remarked, "This book is the only reason I know for using *vi* instead of *emacs*."

UNIX in a Nutshell for System V or Berkeley

272 and 270 pages, $19.50 each

You may have seen UNIX quick reference guides, but you've never seen anything like *UNIX in a Nutshell*. It goes beyond the list of frequently used commands and options found in most quick references, and includes in addition: shell syntax (*sh* and *csh*), pattern-matching syntax, *vi* and *ex*, *sed* and *awk*, *troff* requests and escapes, *-ms*, *-mm*, and *-me* macros, *tbl*, *eqn*, and *pic* syntax, *adb* and *sdb*, *make* and *sccs*.

For orders or a free catalog of all our books, please contact us.

O'Reilly & Associates, Inc.

Creators and Publishers of Nutshell Handbooks
632 Petaluma Avenue, Sebastopol, CA 95472
1-800-338-6887 • overseas/local 1-707-829-0515
email: uunet!ora!nuts

UNIX for FORTRAN
Programmers

Mike Loukides

O'Reilly & Associates, Inc.
632 Petaluma Avenue
Sebastopol, CA 95472

UNIX for FORTRAN Programmers
by Mike Loukides
Nutshell Series Editor Tim O'Reilly
Copyright © 1990 O'Reilly & Associates, Inc.
All rights reserved.
Printed in the United States of America.

Nutshell Handbook is a trademark of O'Reilly & Associates, Inc.
PostScript is a registered trademark of Adobe Systems, Inc.
Alliant is a registered trademark of Alliant Computer, Inc.
Hypercard is a trademark of Apple Computer, Inc.
UNIX is a registered trademark of AT&T.
Convex is a registered trademark of Convex Computer, Inc.
DEC, VAX, and VMS are registered trademarks of
Digital Equipment Corporation.
8086 and i860 are trademarks of Intel Corporation.
IBM is a registered trademark of International Business Machines, Inc.
Macintosh is a trademark of McIntosh Laboratories, and is licensed to Apple Computer.
Xenix is a registered trademark of Microsoft Corporation.
68000 is a trademark of Motorola Semiconductor Corporation.
SUN, NFS, and SunOS are trademarks of Sun Microsystems, Inc.

Printing History

August 1990:   First Edition.

While every precaution has been taken in the preparation of this book, the publisher takes no responsibility for errors or omissions or for damages resulting from the use for the information herein.

Please address comments and questions in care of the publisher:

O'Reilly & Associates, Inc.
632 Petaluma Avenue
Sebastopol, CA 95472
in USA 1-800-338-6887
international +1 707-829-0515

UUCP: uunet!ora!nuts
Internet: nuts@ora.com

Table of Contents

Figures

Tables

Preface

Why Learn UNIX?
How to Use This Book
A Word About UNIX Versions
Conventions Used in This Handbook

Why Learn UNIX?

UNIX has been around for almost 20 years. For most of that time, FORTRAN programmers have avoided it like the plague. There are many reasons for avoiding UNIX: some good, some better, some not so good. It is impossible to deny that there is a huge base of software that runs on other systems; porting these programs to UNIX would take ages. It is also impossible to deny that the UNIX environment is particularly hostile toward new programmers. While there are many useful tools available (in fact, many more tools than on any other system), the documentation for these tools is poorly written and poorly organized. You may never see the forest for the trees. Finally, it is impossible to deny that the UNIX FORTRAN compiler has historically been weak, although UNIX system manufacturers have recently made great progress in correcting this problem.

But it is possible to deny that UNIX is poorly suited for running scientific applications. Furthermore, the trend from central computing systems to distributed networks of workstations is forcing many users to use UNIX, which is the predominant (in fact, the only) viable operating system in the workstation market. Not only are scientific users being forced to use UNIX, but application developers are now investing the programmer-centuries required to port their packages to UNIX; there are currently few major engineering applications that haven't been ported to at least one UNIX platform. As graphics and visualization become increasingly important to the scientific workplace, UNIX will become even more important.

Therefore, we will readily admit that UNIX has a high cost of entry, but the barriers are not as great as many have supposed. Those who have propagated the UNIX guru mystique have done a grave disservice to the programming community. UNIX is certainly no more obscure than VAX/VMS and much less obscure than many operating systems. In turn, the rewards of using UNIX are great: Why share a mainframe with 50 other users when you can have an equally powerful UNIX workstation on your desktop? And once you become familiar with the UNIX repertoire of tools, you will wonder how you ever accomplished anything in another environment.

With this book, our goal is to break down the entrance barrier to UNIX: to give you enough information to let you become productive as quickly as possible. We assume that you already are an experienced programmer: that you know FORTRAN and that you are familiar with some other operating system. While we will not hesitate to provide basic discussions, we will assume that you already understand concepts like I/O, files, binary executables, etc. We will not assume that you know C (the language in which the UNIX system is written) or have any desire to learn it; in fact, we will avoid C as much as possible. Any UNIX programmer who knows C will be better off, but it is not true that you must know C to do useful work.

Rather than just dragging out a few tools and showing you how to use them, we want to teach you how the UNIX tools fit together; there is some order to this sprawling mass of bits. If you come away from this book knowing how to edit, compile, and run a program but nothing else, we have failed. We also want you to learn how to use **make** to manage compilation, how to use **dbx** and **adb** to debug your programs effectively, and how to use RCS (the *R*evision *C*ontrol *S*ystem) to coordinate team development efforts. We want you to be able to write command files (shell scripts) that can coordinate many smaller tools, including those you develop, so that they can perform much larger tasks. We want you to know *why* UNIX compilers don't produce cross-reference listings: because you can use the **grep** utility to create a custom cross-reference table instantly that is infinitely more flexible than a compiler-produced table could ever be. Once you understand the UNIX approach of building large systems from many small, well-defined tools, you will be able to work with the operating system, rather than struggle against it.

How to Use This Book

There are several ways to use this book, depending on your level of experience with UNIX. If you are completely new to UNIX, you may want to read the first few chapters and save the rest for later. If you already have some UNIX experience but want to learn more, you may want to skip the first few chapters. If you feel comfortable with UNIX as a programmer but want to learn more about managing development projects, you may want to focus your attention on the last few chapters.

To help you to use the book, here is a summary of the material we present in this handbook:

Chapter 1, *Introduction to the UNIX Operating System*, is an introduction to the UNIX shell, covering basic UNIX commands and including some simple shell programming. This material is essential to programmers with no UNIX experience. If you have already worked with UNIX, you may want to skip it.

Chapter 2, *Creating a FORTRAN Program with vi*, talks about **vi**, the standard UNIX editor. Most UNIX systems have other editors available (most often, some form of **emacs**). If you already know an editor that's available, you can skip this chapter. However, any UNIX user should be familiar with **vi**, whether or not you use it often.

Chapter 3, *Compiling and Linking FORTRAN Programs*, covers compiling, assembling, and linking FORTRAN programs. This chapter also covers the standard preprocessor, which may be of use. If you are new to UNIX, please read this chapter.

Chapter 4, *FORTRAN Working Environment*, explains the programming environment. This chapter provides an introduction to UNIX I/O, system calls, and error handling. This material should be of use to anyone who is doing FORTRAN programming, whether or not you are already familiar with the system. Beginners may want to skim this chapter and wait until they are more comfortable with UNIX before giving it a thorough reading.

Chapter 5, *Debugging FORTRAN Programs*, introduces the debuggers **dbx** and **adb**. **dbx** is a source-level debugger that all programmers will find useful. **adb** is a more specialized assembly language debugger.

Chapter 6, *Automatic Compilation with make*, defines the **make** utility for managing compilation. **make** is not essential for new UNIX users, but you should learn about it as soon as possible. It is crucial to managing large development projects.

Chapter 7, *Source Management with RCS*, outlines the RCS source management system. RCS also is not essential for new users. Anyone managing a large development project should be familiar with it.

Chapter 8, *Program Timing and Profiling*, sets forth the timing utilities: **time**, **prof**, and **gprof**. These utilities are important for performance analysis. You do not need to know them if you are new to UNIX or if you are only interested in getting a program running and are not concerned about its speed.

Appendix A, *Extensions and Oddities: UNIX Compatibility Issues*, discusses the features and foibles of the standard FORTRAN 77 compiler for Berkeley UNIX. Many manufacturers have developed their own compilers, but most have started from this base. This chapter will be particularly helpful if you need to port programs from other systems to UNIX.

Appendix B, *Programs Mixing FORTRAN and C*, discusses the FORTRAN-C interface. This is an advanced topic. It is not of interest unless you already know C language.

Appendix C, *Data Representations*, covers the most common binary data representations that you will find on UNIX systems. This is an advanced topic, but one that is important to many FORTRAN programmers.

Appendix D, *UNIX Error Numbers and Signals*, shows standard UNIX error codes.

Like all Nutshell Handbooks, this one is open-ended. If you read this book and feel that we have omitted something important, let us know. If we agree, we'll include your suggestions in the next edition.

A Word About UNIX Versions

While there are many UNIX manufacturers, each with a slightly different version of the operating system, there are fundamentally only two different versions of UNIX: System V, which is developed by AT&T, and Berkeley, which is maintained by the University of California. These competing versions are very similar, but there are significant differences—particularly at the system call level. This book covers the Berkeley version of UNIX, Release 4.3 (the most recent, although Release 4.4 is expected soon).

So far, Berkeley UNIX appears to be dominant among scientific programmers. Berkeley UNIX is almost omnipresent at research institutions. In addition, it is the operating system of choice for 68000-based workstations, which are the mainstay of the scientific programming environment. Sun Microsystems' SunOS is a direct descendant of Berkeley UNIX, although it incorporates some System V features. Manufacturers who use Sun's SPARC architecture will almost certainly use some derivative of Berkeley UNIX. Furthermore, most modern superworkstations (e.g., Stardent, MIPS) and minisupercomputers (e.g., Convex, Alliant) run derivatives of Berkeley UNIX. In the scientific programming market, the manufacturers who have System V-based UNIX implementations are striving to make them Berkeley-compatible.

System V derivatives (of which Xenix is the most common) are most common on computers based on the Intel 80286 and 80386 microprocessors. These do not seem to be as popular for scientific applications, but they are, nevertheless, significant. It remains to be seen which version of UNIX will become dominant on Intel's new i860 processors, which promise to have an exciting impact on high-performance workstations.

What difference does this make to you? Most important commands are common to both systems. Porting a program from Berkeley UNIX to System V is more difficult than porting a program from one Berkeley implementation to another, but not much more. If you are using a UNIX version derived from System V, you will still learn a lot from this book. However, you should expect commands to have different options; you will have to consult your vendor's reference manual more often. For scientific programming, the biggest difference is that a FORTRAN compiler is not usually standard equipment with System V; you will have to buy your own. With Berkeley, a FORTRAN compiler is standard, and very few manufacturers have ever dared to make it an added-cost option.

What does the future hold? At this point, it's hard to say. Two major groups (UNIX International, which consists of AT&T, Sun, and their allies, and the Open Systems Foundation, which consists of IBM, DEC, and their allies) are competing for the future of UNIX. Both should have products out within the next year or two; both are trying to integrate System V and Berkeley UNIX into a single system. Whether they succeed in integrating these two versions, one thing is clear: for the foreseeable future, there still will be two standard versions of UNIX.

Conventions Used in This Handbook

The following conventions are used in this book:

Italic   is used for file and directory names when they appear in the body of a paragraph and is used in examples to show variables for which a context-specific substitution should be made. (For example, the variables *filename* and `option(s)` would be replaced by some actual filename or option(s) to a command.) Italic is also used to highlight comments in an example and to emphasize new terms and concepts when they are introduced.

Bold   is used for command names and excerpts from programs when they appear in the body of a paragraph and is used in examples to show commands and other text that should be typed literally by the user. For example, **rm foo** means to type "rm foo" exactly as it appears in the text or example.

`Constant`   is used in examples to show the contents of files or the output from
`Width`   commands.

lower-case   are used for UNIX command names.
letters

UPPER-CASE   are used for excerpts from FORTRAN code when they appear in the
LETTERS   body of a paragraph.

Quotes   are used to identify system messages that appear in the body of a paragraph.

%   is the UNIX C shell prompt.

The notation CTRL-X indicates use of *control* characters. It means hold down the CONTROL key while typing the character "x". We denote other keys similarly (e.g., RETURN indicates a carriage return).

All command examples are followed by a RETURN unless otherwise indicated.

1

Introduction to the UNIX Operating System

Logging In to UNIX
UNIX Commands
The UNIX File System
Standard Input and Output
Controlling Execution
Shell Programs
Shell Customization
Other Basic Tools
Standard UNIX Documentation

UNIX is an extremely versatile operating system that adapts well to scientific and research applications. It offers a wealth of program development tools, ranging from the mundane, like editors, to the esoteric, like compiler-compilers. Unfortunately, this dazzling array of tools is often cloaked in mystery, particularly to the non-UNIX programmer. Getting to know which tools you need and how to use them is a daunting task. This book is designed to strip away the UNIX mystique. Our goal is to introduce experienced FORTRAN programmers to the operating system and get you up to speed as quickly and easily as possible. After a general introduction to the UNIX command environment, we will take you through the steps of program development: editing, compiling, debugging, performance measurement, and program management. When you have finished this book, you should know what tools are important, why they are important, and the fundamentals of how to use them. We focus on Berkeley UNIX, Release 4.3, but most of this book should be applicable to both Berkeley and System V versions.

To a new user, UNIX is like a package with many layers of wrapping: it has many layers of tools, each interesting in its own right but which can distract you from the most basic (and simple) tools at the center.* Once you have gotten to the center, you can work outward and discover the importance of the individual tools. For a new user, the heart of UNIX is its user interface: a program called the *shell*, which is a command interpreter that handles your keyboard input.

Outside of the shell, there are many basic utilities to list your files, edit, sort, search, etc. The FORTRAN compiler, the debuggers, and the timing utilities are the primary program development tools. Once you have written a program, these tools will help you get it working effectively. The outermost layer is a set of program management tools. They will help you to manage the development of large, complex programs—particularly if many programers are working on the same project.

This chapter provides an introduction to the most basic features of UNIX: it introduces programmers to the syntax of most commands, describes the most commonly used commands, and describes the simplest way to manage input and output (the topics at the center of our diagram). It also provides a simple introduction to shell programming, or writing programs made from UNIX commands commonly called command files on other systems. Finally, this chapter describes the organization of the standard UNIX documentation set: the *UNIX Programmer's Reference Manual*, which is available on-line through the **man** command. Later chapters in this book move from the heart of UNIX to fringes, discussing the powerful tools available for program development and management.

There are many sources for more information about UNIX. "UNIX for Beginners" and "An Introduction to the C Shell," both in the UNIX *User's Supplementary Documents*, are useful. Many books provide more comprehensive introductions to the UNIX system. In particular, we recommend:

- *UNIX in a Nutshell* (O'Reilly and Associates), a desktop quick reference, with different versions for Berkeley and System V UNIX. A Hypercard version is also available for Macintosh programmers.

- *The UNIX Programming Environment* by Brian W. Kernighan and Rob Pike (Prentice-Hall), a standard work on UNIX and its tools.

---

*Purists would insist on showing an innermost layer: the UNIX kernel. The kernel is the core of the operating system. It is the program that is always running, whether or not you are doing anything. It manages I/O, time sharing, memory, and every other aspect of the system. We omit the kernel from Figure 1-1 because it is completely invisible to most FORTRAN programmers. Unless you are doing fairly complex system programming in C, you never interact directly with the kernel. The shell handles all of your commands. But the kernel is always there, watching everything you do.

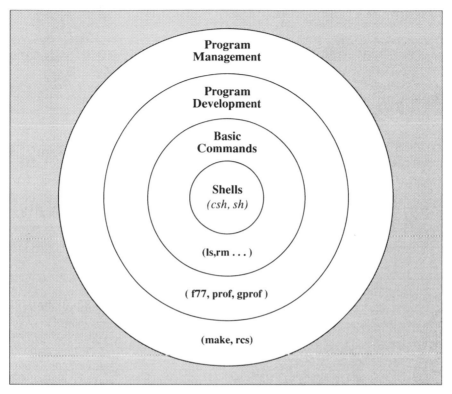

Figure 1-1. The UNIX package

Logging In to UNIX

To log in to a UNIX system, you must have a *username*, which your system administrator will assign. It will typically be your first name, your last name, or your initials. This name is public information. Others, who may not even be users of your system, will use this name to send you messages or mail. Your administrator may also assign a *password*. Always keep your password secret. You can change your password at any time.

When UNIX is waiting for you to log in, it will display the prompt "login:" at your terminal. Respond to this prompt by typing your username in lower-case letters, followed by a RETURN . If you have a password, UNIX will display the prompt "Password:". Respond to this by entering your password. Your password may have upper-case letters and special characters in it. For security reasons, UNIX will not display your password as you type it. If you are dialing in to the system over a telephone line, UNIX may also prompt you for a dial-up password. This is a special password that your system administrator may assign; it ensures that only authorized users can dial in over a telephone line. (Most versions of UNIX do not support dial-up passwords, but you should be aware of the possibility).

A typical login sequence looks like this:

```
login:  joseph          Type your own username
Password:               UNIX doesn't echo the password

This is the message of the day.  It may contain useful
information, like scheduled downtime.  For example:

      system going down at 10 PM for maintenance

%                       UNIX prompt, indicating a successful log in
```

If you log in successfully, UNIX will go through an initialization procedure in which it sets up your terminal and customizes your UNIX environment. This process may or may not require you to do anything; see your system administrator for details. Finally, UNIX will display a message of the day, which may contain useful information about your system's schedule. This is where your system administrator can tell users about any planned maintenance or downtime.

After you have finished working, use the command **logout** to log out of the system. UNIX will respond by displaying the "login:" prompt again:

```
% logout

login:
```

UNIX Commands

When the shell expects you to enter a command on your terminal, it will display a prompt. In most cases, the prompt will be a % (percent sign). At some sites, the prompt may be a $ (dollar sign). The $ indicates that your system is using the *Bourne shell* (**sh**) rather than the *C shell* (**csh**). The most significant differences are: the C shell has much more comprehensive job control features, allowing you to stop a job and continue execution in the background; the C shell has a history facility that lets you recall previous commands; the two shells have different control structures for use in shell programming (writing executable programs from shell commands); and the two shells recognize different shell and environment variables to customize their behavior.

Most of the commands discussed in this chapter are applicable to both shells. We will devote most of our attention to the C shell, except when we discuss shell programming; for this topic, we will focus on the Bourne shell. Although it is the topic of debate, most experienced UNIX users feel that the Bourne shell is preferable for programming, while the C shell is better for interactive work.

At some sites, a few other shells may be available, most notably the *Korn shell* (**ksh**), the *Bourne-Again shell* (**bash**) developed by the Free Software Foundation, and a few other variants. Most of these shells attempt to combine the best features of **csh** with the reliability and speed of **sh**. We will not discuss them in this book, but you should be aware that they exist.

When you see the UNIX prompt, you can enter a command by typing the command name, followed by a RETURN . A UNIX command is simply the name of a file (i.e., the name of a program that the system will load and execute). For example, the command **date** is a program that prints the current date and time on the terminal:

```
% date
Thu Jun  5 10:38:08 EDT 1986
%
```

Many UNIX commands require *arguments*, which are placed after the command name. For example, the **date** command can optionally have the argument **-u**. In this case, it prints the time in Universal time (Greenwich Mean Time) rather than the time in your local time zone:

```
% date -u
Thu Jun  5 14:38:08 GMT 1986
%
```

You may also wish to place some *directive* after the command's arguments; these allow you to redirect the program's terminal input and output. For example, the > (right angle bracket) lets you send output to a file that would normally be displayed on the terminal. Consider the command:

```
% date -u > foo
%
```

This places the current universal time in the file *foo*, creating that file if it does not already exist and overwriting it if it does.

In general, the format of a UNIX command is:

```
% filename   arguments   directives
```

Note that there are many variations in the way commands expect their arguments. Many of these arguments (such as the previous **-u** argument) are called *options*, or *flags*, indicating optional features of the program that you invoke; these typically begin with a - (dash). Many options require their own arguments. For example, the **-o** option to **f77**, the UNIX FORTRAN compiler, lets you specify a filename for the compiled program. This requires an argument:

```
% f77 -o outputfile program.f
```

In this command, the filename *outputfile* serves as an argument to the -o option, while the filename *program.f* serves as an argument to **f77** itself.

Many but not all programs let you combine flags. For example, the **ls** command, which lists the files in the current directory, considers the following two invocations equivalent:

```
% ls -1 -a
% ls -1a
```

If you make a mistake while typing a command, pressing the $\boxed{\text{DELETE}}$ key or the $\boxed{\text{BACKSPACE}}$ key will erase the last letter you typed. On your terminal, one (or both) of these characters should work correctly; if neither works, see your system administrator. To erase the entire line you have typed, enter CTRL-U by holding down the $\boxed{\text{CONTROL}}$ key and typing the letter "u". In the future, this will be abbreviated CTRL-U.

NOTE

Some standard UNIX documentation says that the # (pound sign) is equivalent to delete. This is only the default for obsolete versions of UNIX. If you really want this behavior, use the command **stty -ek**.

The UNIX File System

Files and Filenames

A file is a set of data that has been stored on the system's disk. A file is identified by a *filename*. Filenames may include upper- and lower-case letters, numbers, periods, commas, and underscores. UNIX is case-sensitive: the two filenames *Mine* and *mine* are *not* equivalent. Filenames may not include a / (slash); this is used to separate directories in a UNIX pathname (discussed below). Other punctuation marks, like an ! (exclamation point) and a ? (question mark), are technically legal but will cause problems because these characters have special meanings. There are ways to use these characters if you insist, but you are better off avoiding them. The following table shows some legal, illegal, and troublesome filenames:

Legal	Illegal	Questionable (not recommended)
more_data.dt	*more/data.dt*	*data?dt*
Program.F	*program/F*	*program!F*
2a,std		*2a*std*

In many systems, filename extensions (the part after the period) are considered distinct from the filename. The operating system knows about extensions and handles them separately. This is not true of UNIX. A period is just another character in the file's name. You may have as many or as few as you want.

The File System's Structure

UNIX has a hierarchical, or tree-structured, file system. Each file can be found within a *directory*, as a leaf lives on a twig. Similarly, each directory can be found within a parent directory as a twig lives on a branch, as a branch lives on a bough, and as a bough lives on the trunk of a tree. At the top of this structure is a special directory called *root*. The name of the *root* directory is represented by a / (slash). Figure 1-2 shows, in schematic form, a small part of a typical file system tree.

A directory usually contains files and subdirectories that somehow relate to each other. For example, on most UNIX systems, the directory */usr/local* contains generally used programs that have been developed at that particular site. For development projects currently under way, a directory should contain all the files and subdirectories needed for a given task or subtask. Organizing your files like this will make it easier to use some of UNIX's development tools, like **make**.

As Figure 1-2 shows, there can be any number of directories between a given file and *root*. To specify completely the name of any file or directory, you must enter a full *pathname*, beginning with *root* and listing all the directories between your file and *root*, separated by slashes. For example, the full pathname of *mystuff* is */users/mkl/mystuff*. Complete pathnames are long and cumbersome. Fortunately, they are rarely needed. At any point you are within a current working directory. You can refer to files within this directory without giving a complete path; you only need the filename. When you log in, your current directory is initially the home directory that is assigned by your system administrator. You can change the working directory by using the **cd** command (which we will discuss later). To find out your working directory at any time, enter the present-working-directory command:

```
% pwd
/users/hun/hisstuff
```

This shows that you are currently working in the directory *lusers/hun/hisstuff*.

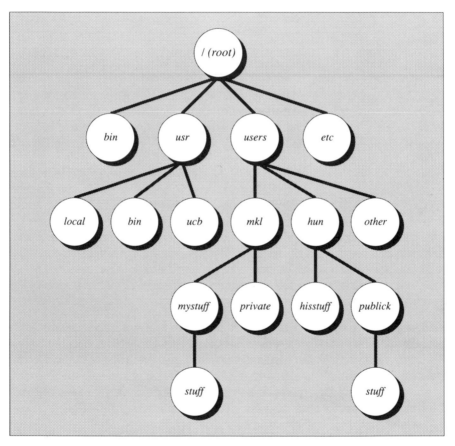

Figure 1-2. A UNIX file system tree

The tree structure allows many files within the file system to have the same name. They will be completely different, distinct files as long as they are in different directories; remember that the file's complete name is a full path, beginning with *root*. For example, the files *lusers/mkl/private/stuff* and *lusers/hun/publick/stuff* are completely different files. If your working directory is */users/mkl/private*, the name *stuff* refers to the file */users/mkl/private/stuff*. Similarly, if your working directory is */users/hun/publick*, the name *stuff* refers to */users/hun/publick/stuff*.

You almost never have to use a full pathname, starting with the root, to refer to a file. Instead of a full pathname, you can use a *relative pathname*. We have already seen that you can use a simple filename to refer to files in your current directory. In this case, the filename is technically a relative pathname: it is relative to your working directory. To refer to files in a subdirectory of your current directory, the relative path is just the subdirectory's name followed by a slash followed by the filename. For example, when the current directory is */users/hun*, you can refer to *stuff* as *public/stuff*. To refer to files that are further down the directory tree, add as many levels of subdirectories as you need. To refer to other locations in the filesystem, use the abbreviations . (dot) and .. (dot dot).

The ~ (tilde) is another abbreviation to help you use short filenames. A ~ means your home directory; likewise, the abbreviation ~*name* means the home directory of the user *name*. For example, if your home directory is */users/mkl*, then ~*/private* means the same as */users/mkl/private*.

At this point, you may be wondering how UNIX finds commands. As we said previously, a command is nothing more than a filename. In most cases, you do not have to enter a complete pathname for the command. UNIX maintains a list of directories, called a **PATH**, in which it looks for files whenever you enter a command. This **PATH** is part of your UNIX *environment*. To find out what the current **PATH** is, enter:

```
% printenv PATH
.:~/bin:/usr/ucb:/bin:/usr/bin
```

This reply means that when you enter a command, UNIX looks through the current directory (.), a directory called *bin* within your home directory, and the directories */usr/ucb*, */bin*, and */usr/bin*. This is an example of a typical **PATH**. If you need to modify it, read the sections describing the C shell (**csh**), environment variables, and the **setenv** command in the *UNIX Programmer's Reference Manual*.

CAUTION

If you set the **PATH** variable incorrectly, UNIX will not be able to recognize any commands without a complete pathname.

Simple Commands for Working with Files

So far, we have given little information about the commands used to work with the files and the file system. This section discusses some simple UNIX tools for working with files and directories.

To display one or more short files on your terminal, use the command **cat**, followed by a filename. For example:

```
% cat foo1
Lutes, lobsters, and limousines
%
```

cat is short for "con*cat*enate," which is what the command does: it concatenates a group of files and sends the output to the terminal. If, instead, you want to place the result in a file, *redirect* the output with a > (right angle bracket):

```
% cat foo1 foo2 > result
% cat result
Lutes, lobsters, and limousines
Make Jack a dull boy.
%
```

This gives us a simple way to create a new file. If you don't enter it any arguments, **cat** will take its input directly from the terminal. Remember that **> result** does not count as an argument. CTRL-D (end of file) terminates your input:

```
% cat > newfile
Twas brillig and the slithy toves
Did gyre and gimble in the wabe
          - Lewis Carroll
CTRL-D
%
```

This creates a completely new file, destroying the contents of *newfile* if it already exists. Using >> instead of > (e.g., **>> oldfile**) adds the input to the end of the file, if it already exists.

Now that we can create a simple file, we can manipulate it. We can copy the file, creating another new file using the copy command:

```
% cp foo1 other
%
```

This creates a file called *other* that is identical to *foo1*. We can also rename the file with the move command, **mv**:

```
% mv other movedfile
```

After this command, the file *other* no longer exists; a new file, *movedfile*, exists whose contents are identical to *other*.

We can now list the contents of all the files in this directory using the list command, **ls**:

```
% ls
foo1          movedfile          result
foo2          newfile
%
```

ls can have a number of arguments. The most useful argument is the **-l** option, which produces a long listing. This lists each file's protection status (who can read, write, or execute the file), its owner, length in bytes, and its creation date, in addition to showing the filenames:

```
% ls -l
-rw-r--r--  1 loukides    31 Jun  5 13:38 foo1
-rw-r--r--  1 loukides    20 Jun  5 13:38 foo2
%
```

The letters on the left side of the report show the file's protection status; we will discuss this topic in the section "File Access Permission" later in this chapter. **ls** can also be given the name of a directory or the names of a group of files within a directory. For example, to list the files in your home directory, you can enter the command **ls ˜**, where the ˜ (tilde) is a UNIX abbreviation for your home directory.

If you no longer need a file, delete it by using the remove command, **rm**. For example, to delete the file *foo1*, enter the command:

```
% rm foo1
% ls
foo2          newfile
movedfile     result
%
```

The **ls** command verifies that *foo1* has disappeared from the current directory.

Remember that all the commands discussed here can have any kind of filename as an argument: complete pathnames, files in the current directory, relative pathnames, and abbreviated pathnames. If you try to do something illegal (e.g., if you try to **cat** a file you are not allowed to read), UNIX will print an error message. But be forewarned: UNIX will let you do many destructive or unpleasant things, such as **cat** to an important data file, without any warning.

If you want to be safe, use the commands **rm -i** and **mv -i**. **rm -i** will ask for permission before deleting each file, giving you one last chance to change your mind. **mv -i** will ask you for permission if renaming a file requires destroying a file that already exists. In either case, typing **y** says "go ahead," while **n** means "STOP".

Simple Commands for Working with Directories

To create a new directory, use the make-directory command, **mkdir**, followed by the directory name:

```
% mkdir newdirectory
% ls
foo2            newdirectory        result
movedfile       newfile
% ls newdirectory
%
```

When you list the contents of *newdirectory*, you find out that UNIX always creates empty directories (i.e., directories without any files in them). If you try to create a directory that already exists, UNIX will complain by printing the message "mkdir: *name*: File exists."

If you finish with a directory and want to delete it, use **rm** to delete all the files within the directory, then use the remove directory command, **rmdir**, to delete the directory itself:

```
% rmdir newdirectory
%
```

If there are some files remaining in the directory, UNIX will complain "Directory not empty". If the name you give does not refer to a directory, UNIX will complain "Not a directory" or "No such file or directory". You can also use **rm -r** to delete the directory. This automatically deletes all files and directories with it. You won't get unwanted complaints, but you also won't get any warnings either.

The **ls** command does not normally list files whose names begin with a period (e.g., *.login*). Several UNIX customization files have names of this form, along with some scratch files created by UNIX programs. Therefore, a directory may appear empty and still have some files in it. To list all files, enter the command **ls -a**. Another useful variation is **ls -F**. This appends a / (slash) to all directory names and an * (asterisk) to all executables. It lets you easily distinguish between files and directories.

To move from one directory to another, use the change-directory command, **cd**. In most cases, you will follow this command with the name of the directory you wish to enter. If you do not enter any arguments, **cd** will move you to your home directory. The following commands use **cd** to move between directories:

```
% mkdir newdir
% cd newdir
% ls
% pwd
/usr/name/newdir
% cd
```

```
% pwd
/usr/name
%
```

Remember that you can use abbreviations like .. (dot dot) to mean the parent of the current directory and ~ (tilde) to mean your home directory.

Wildcards

You will often wish to refer to a group of files, and from time to time, you will also want to abbreviate long filenames. To do this, UNIX allows you to use *wildcards* in filenames. The UNIX wildcards are:

*   The asterisk matches zero or more characters (including numbers and special characters).

?   The question mark matches any single character (including numbers and special characters).

[]   The sequence [*selection*] matches any character appearing in *selection*. A group of consecutive letters or numbers can be expressed with a - (dash); for example, [a-z] means all English lower-case letters.

The name * means "absolutely everything" (except files beginning with . (dot), which are a special case). Remember that UNIX doesn't consider extensions separate; you don't need to say *.* . The name *myfile.** means "all filenames beginning with *myfile.*", the name *myfile.?* means "all filenames beginning with *myfile.* and followed by exactly one character", and the name *myfile.[Fo]* means "*myfile.F*, *myfile.o*, or both". You can use as many wildcards as you need in a filename. For example, the filename *.? is perfectly legal and means "all filenames that end with a period followed by one character."

It is legal to use a wildcarded filename in a command that requires a single argument, provided that the filename only matches a single file. If it matches several files, UNIX will print the error message "filename: Ambiguous".

File Access Permission

The letters on the left side of an **ls -l** report show the file's protection status, more commonly known as the *access mode* or *mode bits*. Here is a sample report:

```
% ls -lg
total 11
-rw-r-----  1 mikel staff  344 Jun 14 14:45 complex.txt
-rw-rw-rw-  1 mikel staff 1715 Jun 14 14:45 datarep.txt
-rwxrwxrwx  1 mikel staff 2345 Jun 14 14:45 program
drwx------  1 mikel staff 3522 Jun 19 10:33 mail
```

The far-left character shows whether the entry represents a file or a directory. A -
(dash) indicates a file; the **d** indicates a directory. In the listing above, *mail* is a
directory. The other entries show regular files. You may occasionally see **b**, **c**, or
s in this field. These letters stand for *b*lock devices, *c*haracter devices, and *s*ockets,
all of which are beyond the scope of this book.

The remaining nine letters are one-bit flags that control file access. A - indicates
that the flag is not set, while any other letter indicates it is. To make the display
more readable, UNIX uses an **r** to show that a bit controlling read access is set, a
w to show that a bit controlling write access is set, and an **x** to show that a bit
controlling execution access (i.e., permission to execute a program) is set. You
may also see **s** or **S** in fields where you expect an **x**. These encode some high-
order bits (e.g., the "setuid," "setgid," and "sticky" bits), which are also beyond
the scope of this book.

These flags are divided into three sets. One set controls access for the file's
owner (the three bits to the immediate right of the directory bit). Thus, the
sample report above shows that the owner has read and write access to all three
files. The owner only has permission to execute the file named *program*. The
other two files look like simple text files, which we wouldn't want to execute anyway. The access bits have slightly different meanings for directories, which we'll
discuss later.

The next three bits control access for members of the file's group. Each file
belongs to a group, as does each user. When a file is created, it belongs to the
same group as its creator, although you can change a file's group membership
with the **chgrp** command. All the files in the previous report belong to the group
staff. Thus, in our sample report, *complex.txt* can be read (but not written) by
staff members, *datarep.txt* can be read or written by members of the group, and
program can be read, written, or executed.

The rightmost three bits control access for all others. Only the owner and group
members can read *complex.txt*; others have no access to it. Others have both read
and write access to *datarep.txt* and are also allowed to execute *program*.

Earlier we mentioned that directories had special interpretations for these bits.
You can understand the read and write bits by realizing that the directory is also a
file. Listing the contents of a directory means reading the directory and requires
"read" access. Writing a directory means adding or deleting a file from the directory and requires "write" access. You can modify a file in a directory without

write access because modifying a file doesn't require any changes to the directory itself. The execute bits mean something completely different. For directories, execute access means permission to "search" a directory for a file. In other words, execute access means you are allowed to look up and access files within the directory. If you do not have execute access to a directory, you can't do anything to it. On the other hand, if you have only execute access, you can do quite a lot. You can't list the files in the directory (so you can't do anything with a file unless you already know its name); you can't add or delete files, but if you already know the name of a file, you can read, modify, or execute it.

The change-mode command, **chmod**, lets you change file-access permissions. It is used like this:

```
% chmod who op perm
```

where:

who   Indicates whose access you want to change and is optional but usually present. The **u** indicates the file's owner (user), **g** indicates the file's group, **o** indicates others, and **a** indicates all (i.e., user, group, and others). If *who* is omitted, it defaults to **a**.

op   Is either + (plus) to allow access or - (minus) to restrict access.

perm Indicates which permission you want to change. The **r** indicates read access, **w** indicates write access, and **x** indicates execute access.

For example, the command:

```
% chmod g+w complex.txt
```

allows group write access for the file *complex.txt*. Formerly group members were not allowed to write the file.

Standard Input and Output

On occasion, we have mentioned redirecting input and output. Now it's time to expand on what this means. Most UNIX commands read their data from *standard input*, write any data they produce to *standard output*, and send error reports to *standard error*. By default, standard input is taken from your terminal's keyboard and standard output and standard error are both sent to your terminal's screen. You can redirect any of these three to read input from a file, write output to a file, or send data directly from the output of one program to the input of another.

To send the output of a program to a file, use the > (right angle bracket):

```
% cat foo > outputfile
```

This is similar to entering **cp foo outputfile**. To redirect standard output and standard error to a file, use the command sequence:

```
% cat foop >& errfile
% cat errfile
cat: foop: no such file or directory
```

In this example, we redirected the error message "No such file or directory" to the file *errfile*. Therefore, no error message appears on the terminal until we list the contents of *errfile*. To redirect standard output and standard error to different files, enter the command:

```
% ( cat foop > outputfile ) >& errfile
```

Both the command and the standard output directive must be placed within () (parentheses). The standard error directive appears outside of parentheses.

If a file already exists, using > and >& to redirect output will destroy the data that are already there. To redirect output to the end of a file without touching anything you have put there already, use the sequences >> and >>&.

If you use the Bourne shell, the directive 2> redirects standard error. In addition, you do not need to enclose a command within parentheses to redirect standard error successfully. For example, the Bourne shell command:

```
$ cat foop > outputfile 2> errfile
```

is equivalent to the previous C shell command.

To take the input of a program from a file, use the < (left angle bracket):

```
% dc < script.dc
```

dc is a desk calculator program that normally takes its input directly from the terminal. However, you can place a series of **dc** commands in a file and then send the file to **dc** through standard input. The ability to read standard input from a file, rather than from the keyboard, lets you use **dc** and many other UNIX utilities as simple programming languages.

You may often wish to redirect both standard input and standard output. For example, consider the **spell** program, which produces a list of misspelled words. To check the spelling in a file named *text*, we can invoke **spell**:

```
% spell < text > spelling
```

This is particularly convenient if your editor allows you to look at several files simultaneously: you can edit both *text* and *spelling*, viewing both your work and the spelling errors at once.

Pipes

The UNIX standard I/O facility lets you connect one program's output directly to the input of another. This is called a *pipe* and is represented by a | (vertical bar). For example, if we wanted to find out whether the user **johnson** is logged in, we could use the command **who** to list all current users and pipe these data to the **grep** program, which reads standard input and outputs a list of all lines containing some pattern:

```
% who | grep johnson
johnson tty2 Jun 3 09:21
%
```

The **troff** typesetting system presents a more notable use of pipes. **troff** has several preprocessors for producing pictures, equations, and tables. These three programs, **pic**, **tbl**, and **eqn**, all read from standard input and write to standard output. They must all process the input file before **troff** gets it. Therefore, to send the text file *typeset.ms* through this chain, enter the command:

```
% pic < typeset.ms | eqn | tbl | troff -ms > typeset.out
```

pic reads *typeset.ms* as its standard input, sends its output to **eqn**, which sends its output to **tbl**, etc. Finally, this command redirects **troff**'s standard output to *typeset.out*, a printable file which can be sent to a typesetter.

Programs of this type are called *filters*. UNIX programmers typically use many filters, which are small programs that can be debugged independently but combined through pipes and other mechanisms to perform larger tasks. For example, imagine four signal analysis programs that gather data from some input device, read a file of data to produce a Fourier transform, strip the high-frequency components from a Fourier transform, and produce a graphical representation of a waveform from a Fourier transform. In most cases, writing these four smaller programs independently would be simpler than writing and debugging one large program that performed all four tasks together. When the smaller programs are working correctly, they can be connected through pipes to perform the larger task simply:

```
% sample | fourier | filter | plotfourier > output.plot
```

Controlling Execution

At the beginning of this chapter, we described how to use a UNIX command to run a program. This section describes some additional tools you have to control a program.

Stopping Programs

To stop a program, press CTRL-C. Under most circumstances, this will force the program to terminate. If it doesn't, any of a number of things may have happened. For example, the program may have sent a strange sequence of special characters to your terminal that managed to confuse it. In these cases, do the following:

1. Log in at another terminal.
2. Enter the command **ps -x**. This displays a list of the programs you are running, in the following form:

```
% ps -x
PID       TTY       STAT     TIME     COMMAND
163       i26       I        0:41     -csh (csh)
8532      i26       TW       2:17     vi ts.ms
22202     i26       S        12:50    vi UNIXintro.ms
8963      pb        R        0:00     ps -x
24077     pb        S        0:05     -bin/csh (csh)
%
```

3. Search through this list to find the command that has backfired. Note the process identification (PID) number for this command.
4. Enter the command **kill** *PID*, where *PID* is the identification number from the previous step.
5. If the UNIX shell percent prompt (%) has appeared at your terminal, things are back to normal. If it hasn't, find the shell associated with your terminal (identified by a tty number) and **kill** it. The command name for the C shell is **csh**. For the Bourne shell, it is **sh**. In most cases, this will destroy any other commands running from your terminal. Be sure to **kill** the shell on your own terminal, not the terminal you borrowed to enter these commands.
6. Check **ps** to ensure your shell has died. If it is still there, take more drastic action with the command **kill -KILL** *PID*.

7. At this point, you should be able to log in again from your own terminal.

The **ps** command, which lists all the programs you are running, also gives you useful information about the status of each program and the amount of CPU time it has consumed. Note that **ps** lists all the programs you are running, including many programs you may not know about (e.g., programs that other programs execute automatically). For more information, see the entry for **ps** in Section 1 of the *UNIX Programmer's Reference Manual*.

Foreground and Background

UNIX distinguishes between background and foreground programs. This feature allows you to run several programs simultaneously from your terminal. When a program is running in the foreground, anything you type at the keyboard is sent to the program's standard input unless you have redirected it. As a result, you can't do anything until the program finishes. When you run a program in the background, it is disconnected from the keyboard. Anything you type reaches the UNIX shell and is interpreted as a command. Therefore, you can run many programs simultaneously in the background. You can only run one program at a time in the foreground.

To run a program in the background, type an & (ampersand) at the end of the command line. For example:

```
% f77 program.F &
[1] 9145
%
```

This runs a FORTRAN compilation in the background, letting you continue other work while the compilation proceeds. UNIX responds by printing a job number in [ ] (brackets), followed by the process identification (PID) number for the command. It then prompts you for a new command. Entering the command **jobs** produces a short report describing all the programs you are executing in the background. For example:

```
% f77 program.F &
[1] 9145
% jobs
[1]  + Running f77 program.F
%
```

To bring a program from the background into the foreground, use the foreground command, **fg**. If you have more than one background job, follow **fg** with a job identifier: a % (percent sign) followed by the job number.

```
% jobs
[1]   + Running   f77 program.F
[2]   -           vi sinus.F
% fg %1
```

The + (plus) in the report from **jobs** indicates which job will return to the foreground by default.

To suspend a job running in the foreground, press CTRL-Z. This stops the program but does *not* terminate it. Entering the background command, **bg**, lets this program continue execution in the background. The foreground command, **fg**, restores this program to execution in the foreground. For example:

```
% f77 -o program program.F
CTRL-Z
Stopped
% bg
[1]   + Running f77 -o program program.F
%
```

There is no prompt after the **f77** command because the compiler is running in the foreground. After you press CTRL-Z, UNIX prints the word "Stopped" to indicate that it has stopped execution. At this point, you can enter any command; the **bg** command lets the job continue executing in the background. This feature is useful if you forget to type an & at the end of the command line.

To terminate a background job, you can use the command's job number rather than its process identification (PID) number, as follows:

```
% kill %1
```

Remember to include the % (percent sign) before the job number! If you omit it, UNIX interprets the job number as a process number. This will probably be the process number of some operating system function. UNIX will not let you make such a mistake unless you are superuser (a specially privileged user). If you are superuser, the command is fatal. You may be superuser from time to time and therefore should not develop sloppy habits.

A program running in the background cannot read input from a terminal. If a background job needs terminal input, it will stop; the **jobs** command will print the message "Stopped (tty input)". Before the program can continue, you must bring it into the foreground with the **fg** command and type the required input. You can save yourself this trouble by redirecting the program's input so that it reads all its data from a file. You may also want to redirect standard output and standard error. If you don't, any output the program produces will appear on your terminal. Since you will probably be using other commands, having miscellaneous data and other messages flying across your terminal may be confusing.

NOTE

The Bourne shell's job control features are more limited. An & (ampersand) will start a command in the background. It is impossible to move a job from the foreground to the background or vice versa. The **ps** command is the only tool available for determining what background jobs you have running.

Running a Job at a Later Time

To run a job at a later time (e.g., at night), use the command **at**, followed by a list of commands, as follows:

```
% at time
Command 1 and arguments
Command 2 and arguments
. . .
CTRL-D
%
```

time specifies the time at which you wish to execute the following *commands*. It can be one, two, three, or four digits. If it is one or two digits, UNIX will interpret it as a time in hours; if it is three or four digits, UNIX will interpret it as hours and minutes. *time* can also be followed by the letters **am** or **pm**, specifying whether the time is before noon or after noon; two other modifiers, **n** and **m**, specify whether the time 1200 refers to noon or midnight. **a** and **p** are legal abbreviations for a.m. and p.m. If no modifiers are present, **at** interprets the time in terms of a 24-hour clock (e.g., 2300 is the same as 1100pm and 0000 is the same as 1200m). The list of commands can be as long as you want. A CTRL-D, which must appear on a separate line, terminates this list.

Alternatively, you can place the commands you want to execute in a file and invoke **at** as follows:

```
% at time filename
%
```

Like programs running in the background, programs run through **at** cannot read any data from a terminal. If these programs read standard input, you must take standard input from a file. If they write data to standard output, you must redirect standard output to a file. If you do not redirect standard output, any data the program produces will be lost. Note that the command:

```
% at 9am commands <inputfile > outputfile
```

does not redirect standard input or standard output successfully. It redirects standard input and output for the **at** command itself, not for the commands you wish to run at 9 a.m.

A few UNIX systems also support batch job submission. The most common batch system is NQS, the *Network Queueing System*. If your system has this software, you can submit jobs to batch queues for later execution.

Shell Programs

The UNIX shell can be used as an interpretive programming language. Within the shell, you can create variables, read arguments, loop, branch, do I/O, etc. Shell programming allows you to break large programming tasks into many smaller tasks, write a group of small programs in many different languages to accomplish these subtasks, and connect these tasks in very flexible ways through a *shell script*. This kind of modularity makes large development projects much simpler, since each portion of the task can be developed and debugged separately. Furthermore, careful design may leave you with a whole that is more useful than the sum of its parts. Some of the subprograms in this larger project may come in handy for another development project later. This section discusses how to write simple shell scripts using the Bourne shell. Programming for the C shell is significantly different; for information, see the description of the C shell (**csh**) in Section 1 of the *UNIX Programmer's Reference Manual*.

By default, UNIX uses the Bourne shell to execute shell scripts. UNIX always uses the Bourne shell to execute shell scripts that begin with the line:

```
#!/bin/sh
```

If you begin the script with the line:

```
#!/bin/sh -x
```

UNIX will print each line in the shell script as it executes it. This is useful for debugging. The line:

```
#!/bin/csh
```

forces the script to run with the C shell.

The simplest shell script is nothing more than an executable file listing one or more commands. For example, consider the following task: We want to format two versions of a file called *shoplist*, one version for a line printer and another for a laser printer. To write a shell script for this task, place the commands needed to create these two versions in a file with a convenient name (e.g., *format*):

```
# use nroff and troff to format shoplist
troff < shoplist > shoplist.tr
nroff < shoplist > shoplist.nr
```

The first line is a comment, since the shell interprets lines beginning with a # (pound sign) as comment lines and ignores them (lines beginning with #! are an exception). The second line uses the UNIX program **troff** to format *shoplist* and produce an output file named *shoplist.tr*. The third line uses **nroff**, a similar program for formatting line printer documents, to produce the output file *shoplist.nr*.

Before using this script, you must make it executable: you must tell UNIX that you intend to use the filename *format* as a command). To do this, use the **chmod** command:

```
% chmod +x format
```

The **chmod** command changes a file's protection mode and, with the **+x** option, makes a file executable. You must also enter the command **rehash** to tell the shell to rebuild its table of command locations.

After making the file executable with the **chmod** command, typing the filename executes the commands listed in the file. That is, the command:

```
% format
```

executes the commands in the file *format*—in this case, producing the two formatted versions of *shoplist*. If you have *not* made the shell script executable with the **chmod** command, UNIX will print the error message "Permission denied" when you try to run your shell program. Note that there is no difference between invoking a shell script (such as *format*) and invoking a compiled binary program (such as **troff**). UNIX knows the difference between shell scripts and binary executables and acts appropriately.

Command Line Arguments

The previous simple shell script is not particularly useful. Unless it is modified, it can only process a single source file named *shoplist*. To make this program more useful, we shall modify it so that it can read the name of a file from the command line, then process this file to produce two appropriately named output files.

To read arguments from the command line, a shell program uses special symbols of the form **$n**, where *n* is an integer number. **$0** refers to the command itself, **$1** refers to the first argument on the command line, **$2** refers to the second, etc. We can use these symbols to rewrite the commands in *format* so that they take their arguments from the UNIX command line:

```
# format:   a shell script to format a file with
#           troff and nroff
troff < $1 > $1.tr
nroff < $1 > $1.nr
```

The second line tells **troff** to process the first name appearing after the command *format*. To generate a name for the output file, it adds the extension *.tr* to the name of the input file. The third line works similarly. For example, consider the command:

```
% format shoplist
```

During execution, the value of **$1** is *shoplist*. Therefore, using this command reads the source file *shoplist* and produces the output files *shoplist.tr* and *shoplist.nr*.

Shell Variables

Within a shell script, you can use *shell variables* to hold values. Following is a shell assignment statement:

```
name=value
```

This assigns *value*, which is interpreted as a character string to the variable *name*. Do not insert a space before or after the = (equal sign). To use the variable *name* in a statement, precede it with a $ (dollar sign), as follows: *$name*. For example, we might know that all shopping lists would be in the directory */usr/lib/shoplist*. To save the user the trouble of typing the entire pathname as an argument, we could write the script as follows:

```
name=/usr/lib/shoplist
troff < $name/$1 > $name/$1.tr
```

It is often useful to set a shell variable equal to the output from a UNIX command. To do this, enclose the command within ' ' (left single quotation marks), as follows:

```
name='ls'
```

When the command **ls** is executed, the shell assigns its output to the variable **name**. After doing this, the value of **name** will be a list of filenames.

Loops

What if we want to format a large group of files? The shell has a loop facility that lets you iterate through a group of arguments. The general form of a loop is:

```
for i in list
do
...Loop commands...
done
```

where *i* is a shell variable, like *name* in the previous example; it can have any string value. The shell executes the loop once for each value in *list*. On each iteration, it assigns the next value in *list* to the iteration variable *i*. If **in** *list* is omitted, the shell forms a default *list* from the command line arguments. For example, let's write a shell script to format a series of texts. We can do that by adding a loop:

```
# a simple do loop to pass several files through
# the formatter
for i
do
     troff < $i > $i.tr
     nroff < $i > $i.nr
done
```

With this modification, the command **format list1 list2 list3** will produce the files *list1.tr, list1.nr, list2.tr, list2.nr*, etc. Note that the variable **i** appears within commands as **$i**. This tells shell to substitute the value of **i** when it executes this line.

The shell expands any wildcards in *list*; the statement **for i in *** sets **$i**, in succession, to the name of each file in the current directory. Consequently, the command:

```
% format *
```

will format each file in the current directory, producing a large series of *.tr* and *.nr* files.

Conditionals

The shell has several kinds of conditional statements. We will describe the shell's **if** statement here, for it is one of the most useful. For information about the **case** statement and other control structures, refer to the discussions of the C shell (**csh**) and the Bourne shell (**sh**) in Section 1 of the *UNIX Programmer's Reference Manual*.

Many UNIX commands return a value to the shell upon completion. During normal interactive operation, this value disappears: as a user, you never see it. However, an **if** statement in a shell script can test this returned value and take action accordingly. A shell **if** statement has the following form:

```
if command
then
        Commands to execute if command returns true
else
        Commands to execute if command returns false
fi
```

command can be any valid UNIX command or command sequence. If the return value from *command* is 0 (or true), the shell will execute the commands following the **then** statement. If the return value is nonzero (or false), the shell will execute the commands following the **else** statement. The **fi** statement terminates the **if** structure and must always appear on a separate line.

For most UNIX commands, the returned value will be true if the command executes without incurring any system errors and false otherwise. Some commands use the returned value to encode the result of execution; for example, the compare command, **cmp**, which compares two files, returns true if the files are identical and false if they are not. The entry describing the command in Section 1 of the *UNIX Programmer's Reference Manual* will tell you whenever any particular command uses the returned value in any significant way. Finally, FORTRAN programs can return any value they wish by calling the subroutine EXIT(N), which terminates the program and returns the value N to the shell.

For example, consider a matrix diagonalization program, **diag**. This program calls **EXIT** to return a nonzero value if the matrix is singular. Imagine that we have some program, **fix**, that handles this situation in some way, and imagine that we have another program that finishes the job by doing some other processing after the matrix has been inverted. Finally, imagine that we have many such matrices to process. We can connect these programs with the following shell script called *work*:

```
for i
do
# diagonalize; finish if nonsingular
    if diag < $i > $i.diag
    then
            finish < $i.diag > $i.res
    else
            echo $i "is singular; fixing it"
            rm $i.diag
            fix < $i > $i.fix
```

```
        fi
done
# print out the files in the directory
ls
```

With this shell script in place, the command **work mat1 mat2** will process two
files called *mat1* and *mat2* accordingly:

```
% work mat1 mat2
mat2 is singular
mat1        mat1.diag mat1.res   mat2 mat2.fix
%
```

Note that neither *matrix2.diag* nor *matrix2.res* exists after the command has finished executing. The **if** statement prevented *work* from producing these files.

The **test** command is one of the most useful features for shell programmers. It
provides an easy way to write conditionals for **if** statements. It evaluates a conditional expression and returns 0 (true) or 1 (false) accordingly. To make programming easier, **test** can be abbreviated [*args*]. Note that you must have a space
before and after the arguments. In an **if** statement using **test** looks like this:

```
if [ args ]
then
        ...Commands...
else
        ...Commands...
fi
```

where *args* is an expression. Here are the basic building blocks for expressions:

str1 = str2	True if	*str1* equals *str2*
str1 != str2	True if	*str1* does not equal *str2*
-r *file*	True if	*file* exists and is readable
-w *file*	True if	*file* exists and is writable
-d *file*	True if	*file* exists and is a directory
-f *file*	True if	*file* exists and is not a directory
-s *file*	True if	*file* exists and has nonzero length
expr1 **-a** *expr2*	True if	Both *expr1* and *expr2* are true
expr1 **-o** *expr2*	True if	Either *expr1* or *expr2* is true

Here are some examples showing how basic *test* expressions can be combined:

```
if [ "$1"="foo" ]               # if the first argument
                                # matches the string "foo"
if [ -r file.txt ]              # if "file.txt" is readable
if [ "$1"="foo" -a -r file.txt ] # if both are true
```

You might want to use the **-r** or **-s** option to find out whether the input file for a
program exists; if it doesn't, you can print an error message or take some default
action. You can use the string comparison tests to handle command arguments.

Remember that this is a very basic introduction to shell programming. The shell allows more complicated control structures, including a **case** statement that is useful for testing command line flags, an **else if** structure, a **while** statement, and many other features. The article "An Introduction to the UNIX Shell" in the UNIX *User's Supplementary Documents* and the articles on the C shell (**csh**) and the Bourne shell (**sh**) in Part I of the *UNIX Programmer's Reference Manual* give much more complete information. (See the section "Standard UNIX Documentation" earlier in this chapter for a description of these books.)

Shell Customization

Both UNIX shells allow you to customize them: you can define your own abbreviations for commands (aliases) and set a number of variables (shell and environment variables) that control the shell's behavior. In this section, we will discuss customization for the C shell (**csh**).

Two files are used for C shell customization: *.cshrc*, executed whenever UNIX starts a new shell, and *.login*, which is executed once, when you log in to the system. When you first log in, *.cshrc* is executed first, then *.login*. See your system administrator or the UNIX manuals for details. Your system administrator should put default versions of *.cshrc* and *.login* in your home directory when it is created. On most systems, the default versions of these files are satisfactory. However, don't be afraid to edit these files to your own satisfaction.

The *.login* file normally contains commands relevant to your entire terminal session, such as terminal initialization commands and environment variable definitions (which are inherited by other C shells you start). The *.cshrc* file usually contains commands that have to be repeated whenever you start a new shell, like aliases and shell variable definitions.

Environment Variables

To define an environment variable, use the command:

```
% setenv VARNAME value
```

where *VARNAME* is the name of the new environment variable and *value* is the definition you want to give it. If you omit *value*, the variable is set but not given a value. By convention, environment variable names are uppercase. To see the defined environment variables at any time, enter the command **printenv**:

```
% printenv
HOME=/home/los/mikel
SHELL=/bin/csh
TERM=sun
USER=mikel
PATH=.:~/bin:/usr/local/bin:/usr/ucb:/bin:/usr/bin
LOGNAME=mikel
PWD=/home/los/mikel/sunview
PRINTER=ps
EDITOR=/usr/local/bin/emacs
```

To delete an environment variable, enter the command:

```
% unsetenv VARNAME
```

You can give environment variables any name you want. However, the shell and other programs recognize some special environment variables and use them to control their behavior. These variables are:

PATH   Determines the search path for commands (i.e., it specifies where **csh** looks to find the commands you execute). Its value is a list of directory names separated by colons. For example, the previous **PATH** variable displayed says "to find commands, look first in the current directory, then in the user's *bin* directory, then in */usr/local/bin*, and so on." Nonexistent directories along the path are ignored.

     Whenever you change the path or add a new command to any directory on the path, use the command **rehash**. This command rebuilds the hash tables the C shell uses to look up new commands. The C shell automatically executes a **rehash** at startup, so you don't need to add it to your customization files.

     Be careful about changing your path. If you make a mistake, the shell may not be able to find any commands. You will have to add a complete path name for every command you type until you get a correctly defined path.

TERM   Tells the shell what type of terminal you are using. Terminal types are defined in a database named */etc/termcap*. Here is a typical entry:

```
ye|w50|wyse50|wyse-50|Wyse 50 in Wyse mode:\
        :al-\EE:am:bs:bt=\EI:cd=\EY:ce=\ET:\
        :cl=^Z:cm=\E=%+ %+ :co#80:\
        :da:db:dc=\EW:dl=\ER:ei=\Er:\
        :im=\Eq:is=\E` 72200\EC\EDF\E'\E(:\
        :kd=^J:kl=^H:kr=^L:ku=^K:li#24:nd=^L:\
        :up=^K:us=\EG8:ue=\EG0:\
        :so=\EG4:se=\EG0:sg#1:sr=\Ej:ho=^^:ug#1:\
        :if=/usr/share/lib/tabset/stdcrt:
```

The first line of this entry—the only one you care about now—defines a number of different names for this terminal type. You can use any of these names, except for the last, to define the **TERM** variable. For example, the command **setenv TERM wyse50** tells the shell to use this entry for information about your terminal. If you need to define your own termcap entry, refer to the Nutshell Handbook *termcap & terminfo*.

Setting the **TERM** variable by itself has no effect. In your *.login* file, you should follow the **setenv** command with a **tset** command. **tset** forces the shell to read the **termcap** entry for your terminal, telling the shell what features the terminal has and how to use them.

Many UNIX users use a bit of additional code to detect whether they are using a remote login, dialing in through a modem, or directly connected. Once they figure this out, they set **TERM** appropriately for their situation. We won't discuss this here; if you look at a few *.login* files at your site, you should easily see how to do this.

EDITOR   Defines a default editor. Its value should simply be the name of your favorite editor. Several programs that ask you to edit files read this variable to decide which editor to invoke. If you don't set it, you get the standard editor, **vi** (discussed in Chapter 2, *Creating a FORTRAN Program with vi*).

PRINTER   Defines a default printer. Its value should be the name the system administrator has assigned to the printer you use most often. The UNIX print spooler, **lpr**, reads this variable and uses this printer unless you specify something different.

There are a number of other environment variables, some automatically defined, that have special purposes. For more information, see the entry for the C shell (**csh**) in the *UNIX Programmer's Reference Manual*.

Here is a typical piece of a *.login* file, showing how to set environment variables:

```
setenv PATH .:~/bin:/bin:/usr/local/bin:/usr/ucb:/usr/bin
eval `tset -s -Q 'dialup:vt100'`  # set terminal type from
                                  # ttytype (if direct) or
                                  # to vt100 (if dialup)
setenv EDITOR emacs               # my favorite editor:
                                  # an emacs-family editor
setenv PRINTER ps                 # a common name for
                                  # PostScript printers
```

The only magic here is the *tset* incantation. This sets the terminal type based on the *etc/ttytype* (or */etc/ttys*) file, which your system administrator should maintain. If you are dialed in over a modem, it will assume you are using a VT100 terminal. In these days of newtorked systems, this may not be adequate. You can make this part of the script as complex as you like, checking baud rates, hostnames, system architectures, or anything you wish to get setting. For a thorough discussion of *tset*, see the Nutshell Handbook *termcap & terminfo*.

Shell Variables

To define a shell variable, enter the command:

```
% set VARNAME=value
```

where *VARNAME* is the name of the variable and *value* is the value assigned to it. By convention, shell variable names are lowercase. If you omit *=value*, the variable is set but not assigned a value. The command **set** by itself displays all currently defined shell variables.

Unlike environment variables, shell variables are not inherited by subshells. Every time you start a new shell, you start with a clean slate. There are many (two dozen or so) significant shell variables. The most important of these are:

ignoreeof If set, pressing CTRL-D will not terminate the shell (possibly logging you off of the system). You have to enter the **logout** or **exit** command explicitly. This is a safeguard if you happen to press CTRL-D accidentally.

noclobber If set, standard output redirection is not allowed to destroy existing files by accident. For example, if **noclobber** is set, the command **ls > foo** will fail if the file *foo* already exists.

history The number of commands is saved in the shell's history list. For example, the command **set history=10** tells the shell to remember the most recent ten commands. You can retrieve and execute these commands with the notation **!***n*, where *n* is the number of a command, and you can display the history list with the command **history**. There are many more complicated ways to invoke the history feature; see the entry for the C shell (**csh**) in the *UNIX Programmer's Reference Manual* for more information.

A portion of a *.cshrc* file setting these shell variables might look like this:

```
set noclobber    # don't let standard output destroy files
set ignoreeof    # don't let CTRL-D terminate the shell
set history=28   # remember the last 28 commands
```

Aliases

Aliases let you define your own commands and abbreviations for commands. Alias definitions are commonly placed in *.cshrc* because they are not inherited by new shells. If you start a new shell, you must redefine your aliases. Placing the definitions in *.cshrc* automatically redefines the aliases.

To define an alias, enter the command:

```
% alias newname command
```

where *newname* is the name of the command you are defining and *command* is what you want *newname* to do. If the *command* contains any spaces, enclose the entire *command* string within quotation marks.

For example, assume that you want to define the command **clean** to delete all core dumps and all filenames beginning with the # (pound sign) in the current directory. Enter the command:

```
% alias clean "rm core #*"
```

After executing this command, entering **clean** is the same as entering the more complicated **rm** command.

One common use of the alias feature is to redefine commands that you commonly mistype. For example, if you find you often type **mroe** when you mean **more**, adding the line:

```
alias mroe more
```

to your *.cshrc* will take care of the problem. This isn't a good practice, but we admit to doing it.

Another common use of aliases is to make UNIX look like some other operating system. For example, if you are accustomed to typing **dir** to find out the contents of the directory, add the line:

```
alias dir ls
```

to your *.cshrc*. We aren't sympathetic to this usage. You are using UNIX and will be better off in the long run if you don't pretend that it is DOS, VAX/VMS, TOPS-20, or some other operating system.

One final important usage of command aliasing is to make commonly used commands safe. Earlier we mentioned that **rm** will gladly destroy all of your files, no questions asked, but that **rm -i** will ask for permission before deleting anything. To ensure that you never make any mistakes, add the line:

```
alias rm "rm -i"
```

to your *.cshrc*. You have now redefined the pure **rm** command as **rm -i**, meaning that you will always have to give confirmation before deleting a file. You may find this annoying, but at least it's safe.

It is not uncommon to see UNIX with several dozen aliases defined in the *.cshrc* file. Virtually every command given is an alias of one sort or another. You can work this way if you want, but it does cause a problem: the longer the *.cshrc* file is, the longer it will take to start a new shell. It is preferable to use a few aliases for the most commonly used commands and misspellings.

Other Basic Tools

The UNIX system has more than 300 standard programs covering an extremely wide range of applications. It would be impossible to discuss more than a few of them in this book. Here are a few of the tools that will be most useful to you in developing FORTRAN software. For more information about any of them, see Section 1 of the *UNIX Programmer's Reference Manual*.

grep   Finds all occurrences of a pattern within a file or a group of files. This facility can be used to generate cross-reference tables and lists while you are programming. For example, to find all occurrences of the variable name **FSMULT** in the program *test.f*, enter the command:

```
% grep FSMULT test.f
```

This lists all occurrences of the string "FSMULT" in the file *test.f* on your terminal (standard output). **grep** can look through many files with a single command. For example:

```
% grep FSMULT *.f
```

searches all FORTRAN files in the current directory. In this case, **grep** will report both the file and the line in which it finds "FSMULT". The pattern for which **grep** searches may contain wildcards, although these wildcards differ from the shell wildcards discussed in this chapter. **egrep** and **fgrep** are two important variations of **grep**. **egrep** has an extended wildcard mechanism that lets you make very general searches. It is also faster than **grep**. **fgrep** is allegedly the fastest but, in practice, is much slower than its relatives. For more information, see the entry for **grep** in Section 1 of the *UNIX Programmer's Reference Manual*.

more   Allows you to view a large file in read-only mode. It lets you search for strings and page through the file in a manner similar to the **vi** editor.

cmp   Takes two files as arguments. It reports the first location at which the two files differ. For example, the command:

```
% cmp foo1 foo2
foo1 foo2 differ: char 5, line 4
%
```

tells you that the files *foo1* and *foo2* are identical until the fifth character in the fourth line.

diff   Goes several steps farther than **cmp**. It produces a list of differences between two files. There are many circumstances in which this is useful. For example, you may have forgotten which is the most recent version of a file or you may need to integrate two different versions of a program that have branched from a common development tree.

spell   Reads a file and produces a list of misspelled words from the file. Its dictionary is built in to UNIX.

fsplit   Takes a FORTRAN file and splits it up into many separate files, with one routine per file. This makes it easier to work with large programs.

In this section, we have only included relatively simple tools that will not be discussed elsewhere in this book. We have devoted chapters to the more complex and more important tools, like **make** and RCS. Let us know if you find other tools that are important to your work, and we'll consider discussing them in a later edition.

Standard UNIX Documentation

The standard UNIX documentation is a multivolume set of manuals describing many aspects of the UNIX operating system. It is essentially a collection of command and procedure descriptions, papers, tutorials, and UNIX lore. For Berkeley UNIX Version 4.3, this manual has been split as follows:

- *UNIX Programmer's Reference Manual*. Reference pages describing individual commands, library routines, and file formats.

- *User's Supplementary Documents*. Supplementary papers including an introduction to UNIX, descriptions of editors, descriptions of the document production system, and other material of general interest.

- *Programmer's Supplementary Documents*. Supplementary papers describing languages, programmer's tools, and various aspects of system programming.

The *UNIX Programmer's Reference Manual* is further subdivided into the following eight parts:

- Commands and utilities, giving a summary of each command and all its optional flags.

- System calls, giving a summary of every operating system call.

- Library routines, summarizing every routine in libraries available to programs running under UNIX. Section 3F is of special interest to FORTRAN programmers; it describes versions of UNIX library routines that can be called directly from FORTRAN programs.

- Special files, which are the basis for low-level UNIX I/O.

- File formats, describing the formats of different UNIX files. This includes the formats of various system database files, different kinds of executable files, initialization files, etc.

- Games, describing game programs that are part of the UNIX system.

- Miscellaneous, describing the ASCII character set, typesetting macro packages, and other features that don't fit elsewhere.

- Special commands for system administration, describing how to perform tasks like accounting, file system management, disk quota management, etc.

Recently, Berkeley UNIX has rather unaccountably split these these eight sections into three volumes: a *User's Reference Manual* (Sections 1 and 6), a *Programmer's Reference Manual* (Sections 2, 3, 4, 5, and 7), and an *Administrator's Reference Manual* (Section 8). Rather than stick with this arbitrary and confusing division, we will refer to the entire set as the *UNIX Programmer's Reference Manual*.

The *User's Supplementary Documents* and the *Programmer's Supplementary Documents* are essentially technical papers written by the original authors of the tools they describe. They typically describe implementations of UNIX running on PDP-11 or VAX systems. Most manufacturers leave these documents untouched rather than rewriting them in terms of their particular product. If you are good at generalizing, you will find these papers useful.

On-line Help

The entire *UNIX Programmer's Reference Manual* is available on-line with the manual command, **man**. Use this command as follows:

```
% man part topic
```

where *part* is a number between 1 and 8 (including the combinations 3F, 3M, 3N, 3S, etc.) referring to a specific section of Volume I and *topic* is the name of some topic discussed in the manual (a command name or a filename). In most cases, you can omit *part*, and you can certainly omit *part* if you are interested in Part I of the manual.

The command **apropos** serves as an on-line index to the *UNIX Programmer's Reference Manual*. Typing **apropos** *keyphrase* produces a set of manual entries, section numbers, and summary descriptions that contain *keyphrase* in its entirety. For example, the following report will provide more information about the *sine* functions:

```
% apropos sin
awk (1-ucb)                    - pattern scanning and
                                 processing language
mailaddr (7-ucb)               - mail addressing description
moo (6-ucb)                    - guessing game
rcsintro (1-ucb)               - introduction to RCS commands
sin, cos, tan, asin, acos, atan, atan2 (3M-ucb)
                               - trigonometric functions
sinh, cosh, tanh (3M-ucb) - hyperbolic functions
%
```

Some of this material is extraneous; for example, the entry "moo" appears because the letters "sin" occur in the word "guessing". However, this report does have the information you want: the trigonometric and hyperbolic sine functions are discussed in Section 3M of the *UNIX Programmer's Reference Manual*. The commands **man 3m sin** and **man 3m sinh** will produce detailed descriptions of these functions.

The *UNIX Programmer's Reference Manual* begins with a permuted index that serves a similar function. If you look for the keyword "sin" in this index, you will again find entries for the trigonometric and hyperbolic sine functions, telling you to look up the entries for **sin** and **sinh** in Section 3M of the manual.

2

Creating a FORTRAN Program with vi

Invoking vi
Modes
Text Mode
Command Mode
Other Features

Many different editors are available under UNIX. You can use any of them to edit a FORTRAN program. Some of the editors available are:

- **vi**, the standard UNIX screen-oriented editor.

- **jove**, a version of the popular **emacs** editor that is distributed with Berkeley UNIX.

- Gnu-emacs, another version of the **emacs**, published by the Free Software Foundation.

Other versions of **emacs** and versions of various VAX/VMS editors may also be available commercially, depending on the computer or workstation you are using.

In this chapter, we give a general introduction to the **vi** editor. We have chosen to discuss this editor primarily because it is available on *all* UNIX systems, regardless of the vendor, it works on virtually all terminals, and it remains constant from user to user and from environment to environment (**emacs** users typically customize their editing environments, often changing the behavior of standard commands). This chapter does not give a complete discussion of **vi**'s features; it is intended to teach you how to edit a program's text as quickly as possible. For more detailed information about the **vi** editor, including discussions of its advanced features, see the Nutshell Handbook *Learning the vi Editor*.

Invoking vi

To begin editing a file with **vi**, type:

```
% vi filename
```

If the file exists, **vi** will display it on the screen. If it does not exist, **vi** will open a new file and print a message saying that you have started a new file. Each line on your terminal will begin with a ˜ (tilde), which is **vi**'s way of saying that these lines do not yet exist in your file, even though they appear on the screen. For example, **vi** looks like this when opening a new file:

```
This is the first and only line in this
file
~
~
~
"oldfile" 1 line, 45 characters
```

If you open a pre-existing file, **vi** will display the new file and, at the bottom of the screen, show the filename, the number of lines, and the number of characters in the file as follows:

```
~
~
~
~
"filename" [new file]
```

Again, the tildes at the beginning of the lines show that these lines do not exist; so far, *oldfile* is only one line long.

If you want to look at a file without changing it, you can invoke **vi** by typing:

```
% view filename
```

This starts **vi** in a read-only mode. You can't save the file unless you change its name or twist **view**'s arm by typing **:w!**. You can use all of **vi**'s features to move within the file. **view** is useful when you want to ensure that you don't inadvertently change something—for example, when you are reading someone else's code.

Retrieving Backup Versions

If the system crashes while you are editing, don't despair. When the system returns, **vi** can restore your file to within a few commands of the point you were at when the crash occurred. To restore a file after a crash, enter the command:

```
% vi -r filename
```

The **-r** flag tells **vi** to restore your file.

You can only retrieve files after a crash; it must be your first attempt to edit this file after a crash, and there must be no intervening crashes. You cannot enter the command **vi myfile**, decide you have made a mistake, then try to recover with **vi -r myfile**.

Modes

vi has two modes: one for adding text to a file, and another for inputting commands. In text mode, you can type text and do some limited editing (e.g., erase the character or word you just typed). In command mode, you can use commands to move from place to place within the file, delete text, etc., but you cannot type new text. When you are in text mode, pressing the ESCAPE key will take you from text mode to command mode. When you are in command mode, a number of commands (e.g., append text, insert text, substitute text) will place you in text mode. Pressing ESCAPE while in command mode rings the terminal's bell but has no other effect. Therefore, if you lose track of which mode you are in, press ESCAPE ; this will either place you in command mode, or if you are in command mode already, it will ring the bell. In either case, you are guaranteed to be in command mode.

Later in this chapter, we will give a more complete discussion of **vi** commands. At this point, we will highlight three commands that deserve special attention. To enter text mode in the simplest way, type **a** (for append) while you are in command mode. At this point, you can type text until you press ESCAPE . To exit **vi** and save the contents of the file you have been editing, enter **ZZ** when you are in command mode. The command **:q!** is an emergency exit that quits **vi** without saving the file. This is useful if you accidentally damage the file you are working on and don't want to (or can't remember how to) fix it.

In either mode, you are always located at a specific position in the file you are editing. On most terminals, **vi** shows the current position by displaying a blinking cursor. In text mode, this cursor shows the position at which you are typing. In command mode, this cursor shows the position at which any command will take effect. In this chapter, we will use the terms *current position* and *cursor* interchangeably.

Text Mode

In text mode, you can type text. Any characters, printing or nonprinting, can be included in this text. Lines may be up to 1023 characters long. **vi** wraps long lines around the end of the screen but doesn't break them. The TAB key (equivalent to CTRL-I) moves the current position right to the nearest column that is a multiple of eight. If you need to change the tabulation amount (the space between columns), see the section "Other Features" later in this chapter.

You can perform some editing while you are in text mode. Pressing CTRL-H (on many terminals, RUBOUT) deletes the last character you typed, pressing CTRL-W deletes the previous word, and pressing CTRL-U deletes everything you have typed on the current line. These commands *only* apply to text that you have typed in the current line since you entered text mode. For example, if you begin inserting text in the middle of a line, typing CTRL-U will only delete the text you have typed since you began inserting; it will not delete the entire line. Similarly, CTRL-W and CTRL-H only work until you reach the beginning of the current line. **vi** will ring the bell if you attempt to erase a character that is not from the current line and the current text mode. For more powerful editing facilities, you must use command mode.

In order to save time on slow terminals, **vi** does not erase any characters from the screen until you leave text mode and return to command mode. As you erase, **vi** will move the cursor backward, so that it is always in the correct position as you type. However, the characters you have erased will remain on the screen (although they are no longer in your file) until you leave text mode or until you type over them. At slow baud rates, **vi** will not insert a blank line when you press RETURN ; you will appear to be typing over text farther down in the file. In this case, you are not retyping or deleting anything; you are still inserting completely new text into the file. **vi** is trying to avoid spending time transmitting a lot of text. When you return to command mode, **vi** updates its display so that it shows the file's contents accurately. This may be confusing at first; you are better off experimenting with the editor than trying to understand on the basis of our description.

vi's text mode does *not* have any features for moving around within a file or within a line. To move from one place in the file to another, you must switch to command mode. Remember that pressing ESCAPE places you in command mode.

Command Mode

In command mode, you can use commands to move within the file, adding and deleting text, searching for text, and moving blocks of text. **vi**'s more advanced features include macros, an abbreviation facility, and tools to aid program indentation. This section describes **vi**'s basic commands; refer to *Learning the vi Editor* for more advanced commands.

There are two kinds of commands in **vi**. Most commands for adding text, deleting text, and moving to a specific position within a file have the form:

[*number*][*command*]

where *number* is an optional integer that *command* uses as an argument and *command* is a **vi** command (usually a single letter). In most cases, *number* means the number of times a command should be applied to some basic unit. For example, the command **3x** means "execute the command **x** (delete a character) three times," and **4dw** means "execute the command **dw** (delete a word) four times." However, *number* can have many other meanings (line numbers, etc.), depending on the command. If *number* is missing, **vi** defaults to 1. These commands are not followed by a RETURN; they take effect as soon as you type the complete command. They are not echoed on the screen. If you notice that a command of this form is incorrect while you are typing it, press ESCAPE to cancel the command and ring the bell.

vi commands can also have the form:

:[*command*] [RETURN]

where *command* is typically a single letter, often followed by a *filename* or some other information. These commands are echoed at the bottom of the screen as you type them. Commands of this sort are typically used for working with files (i.e., inserting files, editing new files, and saving the file you are editing). If you notice an error while typing commands of this form, press DELETE to rub out characters back to the error. When you rub out the : (colon) at the beginning of the command, the command will be canceled completely.

If you enter an illegal command of either type, **vi** will ring the bell and take no action. If you enter an incorrect command, the command **u** undoes the most recent command, if possible. Note that **u** can only undo the single most recent command and that some commands (e.g., saving a file) cannot be undone.

Moving Within a File

The basic cursor motion commands are **h, j, k, l, $, +,** and **-** . They have the following functions:

h　　　　Move the cursor one space to the left.

j　　　　Move the cursor one line down the screen.

k　　　　Move the cursor one line up the screen.

l　　　　Move the cursor one space to the right.

$　　　　Move the cursor to the end of the current line.

-　　　　Move the cursor to the beginning of the previous line.

+　　　　Move the cursor to the beginning of the next line.

RETURN　Move the cursor to the beginning of the next line (same as +).

vi will respond correctly to cursor motion keys for many terminals.

To move to a specific line within the file, enter the command *n***G**, where *n* is a line number. **vi** positions the cursor at the beginning of this line.

To scroll up within a file, press CTRL-U. To scroll down, press CTRL-D. These commands scroll a half-screen up and down, respectively. If possible, they avoid redrawing the entire screen. After scrolling, **vi** positions the cursor on the left edge of the screen, roughly in the middle.

To scroll up a single line, press CTRL-Y. To scroll down a single line, press CTRL-E. These commands do not change the position of the cursor within the file; they merely display an additional line at the bottom or top of your screen.

To move to the next full screen, press CTRL-F. To move to the previous screen, press CTRL-B. These commands leave two lines of context from the previous screen at the top or bottom of the new screen. These context lines make it slightly easier to orient yourself within the new display.

Marks

You can mark any position in the text with the command **m***mark*, where *mark* is any single letter. For example, the command **md** assigns the mark named **d** to the current position.

After placing a mark in the text, you can return to the mark at any time by typing `'mark`; for example, the command `'d` will move the current position to the location of mark **d**. A slightly different version of the command, `' mark`, moves you to the beginning of the line on which the mark is found.

You cannot delete marks; however, you can move marks to different places. For example, you can enter the command **ma** (place a mark named **a**) many times; each time, this command moves the mark to a new position.

Marks are never displayed on the screen and do not exist within the file itself; marks are only labels that **vi** manages within its own tables. All marks in a file disappear when you stop editing that file, either by exiting **vi** or by switching to another file via the command **:e**.

Adding and Deleting Text

vi's commands for adding text place you in text mode. These commands are:

i Insert text at the current position.

a Append text after the current position.

s Substitute text at the current position.

I Insert text at the beginning of the line, after any initial blanks.

A Insert text at the end of the line.

The insert command, **i**, and the append command, **a**, differ only in where they place the new text. When you enter the command **a**, the cursor will immediately move one space to the right. This reflects the difference between appending text after the current position and inserting text at the current position.

The substitution command, **s**, deletes one or more characters and lets you replace them with any text. The *count* preceding this command indicates the number of characters **vi** should replace; for example, entering **6s** replaces the next six characters with text. Replacements start at the current cursor position and extend to the right; **vi** marks the last character to be replaced with a $ (dollar sign). The replacement text need not be the same length as the original text; it may be longer or shorter and may even extend over several lines.

Here are the basic commands for deleting text:

x   Delete the character at the current position.

dw Delete the word to the right of the cursor.

db   Delete the word in back of the cursor.

dd   Delete the current line.

D   Delete everything to the right on the current line.

You may precede any of these deletion commands with a *count*, which tells **vi** to execute the command *count* times.

In addition to these, the command **d** ` *mark* deletes everything between the current cursor position and the location of the given *mark*. For example, **d** `**g** deletes everything between the current position and the mark named **g**. Similarly, the command **d**' *mark* deletes everything between the current line and the line on which *mark* appears. The difference between these two commands is slight but it is significant. **d** `**g** and **d**' **g** both delete regions of text. They differ in that **d** `**g** deletes partial lines, while **d**' **g** deletes entire lines on both ends of the region.

All of these commands place the deleted text in a buffer. This is called the *unnamed buffer* (as opposed to named buffers, which will be described later). The command **p** puts the current contents of this buffer *after* the current position of the cursor. Similarly, the command **P** puts the contents of this buffer *before* the current position of the cursor. Each successive deletion command destroys the old contents of the buffer (i.e., at any point the buffer contains only the most recently deleted text). In this respect, the command **4dd** differs from giving the **dd** command four times: after **4dd**, this buffer contains all four lines you deleted, while the the sequence of commands **dd dd dd dd** leaves the buffer containing a single line.

NOTE

With some terminals, **vi** will replace lines you delete with an @ ("at" sign) at the left margin. These marks show that these lines are nonexistent; they do not exist in your output. This saves **vi** from redrawing the screen on slow terminals, thus improving its performance.

Search Operations

Search operations provide another important way to move within a file. To search for any text string, use the command:

>   /*text-string*

where *text-string* is the string of characters you want to find, followed by a RETURN . If this string contains any backslash (\), dot (.), slash (/), caret (^), left bracket ([), right bracket (]), or asterisk (*) characters, it must be preceded by a backslash (\). For example:

/dir\/myfile\.txt

searches for the string *dir/myfile.txt*. These characters play a role in vi's pattern-matching facility. This is described in the section "Other Features" later in this chapter and also in *Learning the vi Editor*. **vi** will position you at the next occurrence of this string, or if it cannot find the string, it will display the message "Pattern not found."

To search for the next occurrence of this string, use the command **n** or the command / (slash), followed immediately by a ⃞RETURN⃞. You can also search for the *n*th occurrence of the string by preceding the search command with a *count*, as follows:

n/*string*

vi searches are generally case-sensitive (e.g., the strings "find THIS" and "find this" are different). The section "Other Features" explains how to do case-insensitive searches with **vi**.

vi searches loop around through the file; after searching forward from the current position to the end of a file, **vi** searches from the beginning until it returns to the search's starting point.

Moving Blocks of Text — Named Buffers

The simplest way to move a block of text is to delete a number of lines with a delete command (*n***dd**, etc.) and then restore that block somewhere else with a put command (**p** or **P**). Remember, though, that put only recalls the text that you deleted with the *most recent* deletion. It is too easy to delete some lines with the intention of moving them somewhere else and then inadvertently destroy the buffer by deleting something else along the way.

A more satisfactory way to move a block of text is to store it in a *named buffer* when you delete it. **vi** has 26 named buffers; their names are **"a** through **"z**. If you precede any deletion command with a named buffer, **vi** will store the text you delete in the buffer. For example, the command **"c6dd** deletes the next six lines and stores them in buffer **"c**. Similarly, preceding a put command with a named buffer retrieves the text stored in that buffer. Thus, the command **"cp** places the text stored in buffer **"c** in the position after the cursor. The contents of a named buffer remain stable until you explicitly store new data in it.

NOTE

When you move from one file to another, **vi** loses the contents of its unnamed buffer. However, it preserves the contents of the named buffers. Therefore, you must use named buffers to move data between files. (See the section "Editing and Inserting Other Files" later in this chapter.)

Moving text in a file is particularly convenient if you use the delete-to-mark commands, **d** `mark` and **d'** *mark*. However, be careful not to confuse marks, which have single-letter names, with the named buffers. A command of this form looks like:

> "*buffer***d** `mark`

or:

> "*buffer***d'** *mark*

These commands present many possibilities for confusion. However, they work just like the other previous commands: **d** ` and **d'** are different versions of delete-to-mark, and "*buffer* is a named buffer into which **vi** puts the deleted text. Note that there is no reason that the *mark* and the *buffer* cannot have the same name; these are completely distinct concepts. The command "**ad** `a` means "delete the text between the current position and the mark **a** and place it in named buffer **a**." The command may be confusing, but it is not ambiguous.

Saving and Exiting

There are many ways to save files and exit the **vi** editor. This section discusses the most common save and exit commands.

:w *filename*	Saves a file without exiting. If you omit *filename*, **vi** will save the file without changing its name.
:q	Exits **vi**. If you have not saved the latest changes to the file, **vi** will print the warning "No write since last change (:quit! overrides)" at the bottom of the screen. It will not quit unless you save the file first or use the emergency exit command **:q!**.
:q!	Exits **vi** without saving any changes to the file. This is useful if you inadvertently modify a file or make some other mistake.
:wq or **ZZ**	Saves a file without changing its name and then exits.
:e!	Restores the last saved version of the file you are editing. This command can revert only to the most recent version of the file you saved. Source management tools like RCS should be used for more comprehensive protection.

Editing and Inserting Other Files

To edit another file without exiting **vi**, use the command:

> **:e** *filename*

where *filename* is the name of the file you want to edit. As with the exit command, you must save any changes to the file on which you are currently working before **vi** will let you edit a new file. You can override this protection mechanism with the command **:e!** *filename*.

To insert another file into the file you are editing, enter the command:

> **:r** *filename*

vi will insert the file *filename* beginning on the line following the cursor.

Executing UNIX Commands from vi

To execute a UNIX command from within **vi**, use the command:

> **:!** *UNIX-command*

The editor will tell you whether you have saved the current version of the file and will execute the command. It will print any results at the bottom of the screen. When the command has finished executing, it will print the message "Type return to continue." After you press $\boxed{\text{RETURN}}$, **vi** will return to normal editing. The output generated by the command you execute does not change your file in any way.

You can also generate a new shell from within the **vi** editor by using the command:

> **:shell**

After this command, **vi** clears the screen and starts a new UNIX shell. You can do anything you wish within this shell, including starting other **vi** sessions. To return to **vi**, enter the UNIX command **exit** or press CTRL-D. **vi** will return to the file you were editing before you started the new shell.

There's no need to save your file before executing either of these commands.

Other Features

Options

vi has several internal options that control the way it behaves. In this discussion, we have only mentioned the option that sets the spacing between tab stops. By default, a tab stop occurs every eight spaces. To change this to some other value *n*, use the command:

:set ts=*n*

Learning the vi Editor discusses several other **vi** options that you can set in a similar way.

By default, all **vi** searches are case-sensitive (i.e., the characters "a" and "A" are distinct). This is often inconvenient, particularly if you are typing text: a search for "happiness" only finds the word if it does not occur at the beginning of a sentence. If you want case-insensitive searches, enter the command:

:set ignorecase

To restore case-sensitive searching, enter the command:

:set noic

set commands only last as long as the current editing session; all these options are forgotten when you exit **vi**. To set these options permanently (i.e., whenever you use the **vi** editor), create an environment variable called **EXINIT**. This variable can contain a string of **set** and other customization commands, each separated by a | (vertical bar). You will probably want to place a **setenv** command in your *.login* file to create this shell variable every time you login. This and other significant shell variables are described in the discussions of the C shell (**csh**) in Part I of the *UNIX Programmer's Reference Manual*.

Pattern Matching

vi's pattern-matching feature makes it easier to search for strings in the file. This feature is described fully in *Learning the vi Editor*. Here we will mention a few of the most useful pattern-matching tools.

When you are searching for a string, the . (dot) is a *wildcard*. This means that it is equivalent to any single character. For example, the search:

/ab.de

will find the strings "abade", "abbde", "abcde", etc. The two characters .* (dot asterisk) together represent any group of zero or more characters. For example, *m.** matches *ml, mel, mail, mabel, michael,* etc.

The ˆ (caret) allows you to search for a string that appears at the beginning of a line. For example, the search:

/ˆtext

finds the string "text" only if it is the first thing on the line.

Of course, this scheme has the limitation that the . (dot), the ˆ (caret), and others no longer behave normally when they appear in expressions. What happens if you want to search for the string "ab.de", where the period is really a period? To do this, you must escape the meaning of period by preceding it with a (backslash):

/ab\.de

Similarly, to find the string " ˆ is a caret", you must escape the ˆ :

/\ˆ is a caret

Other characters that must be escaped are the (backslash), . (dot), * (asterisk), [(left bracket), and] (right bracket).

3

Compiling and Linking FORTRAN Programs

FORTRAN Compilation
The Preprocessor
Assembling a FORTRAN Program
Linking FORTRAN Programs
Creating Libraries

Now that you can use **vi** to edit a program, you need to be able to compile it. The UNIX FORTRAN compiler is named **f77**. It does much more than just compile a program: by default, it compiles the source code, assembles the assembly language code this produces, and invokes the UNIX loader, **ld**, to produce an executable file. The compiler recognizes programs written in the EFL and RATFOR dialects of FORTRAN and invokes the appropriate preprocessor for these programs before compiling them. Finally, the compiler recognizes C language programs and invokes the **cc** compiler to process them. **f77** is a "window" into all the program development tools. It is the only command that you have to know. We'll discuss the assembler and linker for completeness, but keep in mind that you only need to be aware of these tools for very specific applications.

FORTRAN Compilation

The general form of the **f77** command is:

```
% f77 list-of-options list-of-files-and-libraries
```

Exactly how the compiler treats any file depends on the file's name. The compiler strips the initial part of the name, then determines how to process the file on the basis of the filename's extension. In each case, the compiler passes the file to the appropriate program for preprocessing, compilation, or assembly and links all resulting object modules together to produce an executable file. The following table shows how the compiler recognizes different file types:

Filename	Interpretation	Action
`file.f`	FORTRAN source	Compiled by **f77**.
`file.F`	FORTRAN source	Preprocessed by **cpp** and compiled by **f77**.
`file.r`	RATFOR source	Preprocessed by RATFOR and compiled by **f77**.
`file.e`	EFL source	Preprocessed by EFL and compiled by **f77**.
`file.c`	C source	Preprocessed by **cpp** and passed to **cc**.
`file.s`	Assembly language source	Assembled by **as**.
`file.o`	Compiled object module	Passed to **ld**.
`file.a`	Object module library	Passed to **ld**.

All other files, together with options that **f77** does not recognize, are passed to **ld**, the UNIX loader. As a result, almost all loader options are available directly through **f77**. For example, the command:

```
% f77 -o myexec file1.f file2.o file3.c
```

compiles *file1.f* with FORTRAN and compiles *file3.c* with C, then sends the resulting object modules, together with *file2.o*, to **ld** (the linker), producing an executable named *myexec*. You could also compile each file separately, linking the object modules with a separate command:

```
% f77 -c file1.f
% f77 -c file3.c
% f77 -o myexec file1.o file2.o file3.o
```

Using **f77** to invoke the linker is vastly preferable to using **ld** separately; **f77** ensures that the program is linked with the correct libraries and initialization routines.

This command also demonstrates how **f77** passes unrecognized commands and options through to the **ld** linker. Properly speaking, **f77** does not recognize the **-o** option, although it is traditionally listed as an **f77** option. Similarly, the argument to **-o**, the filename *myexec*, goes unrecognized. Both are passed to **ld**, where they serve to specify the name of the new executable file. Many linker options are commonly considered FORTRAN options. We'll describe these options twice: as part of **f77** (in keeping with the common usage) and as part of **ld** (where they belong).

Libraries

To specify an object code library on the command line, use an option of the form -l*name*. This causes the compiler to look for a library file named `libname.a`. To find this file, the compiler searches sequentially through any directories named with the **-L** option, the directory */lib*, and the directory */usr/lib*. The **-L** option lets you specify a private directory for libraries; it is described below. Again, note that these options are both (strictly speaking) loader options, rather than compiler options.

UNIX linkers search libraries in the order in which they occur on the command line and only resolve the references that are outstanding at the time when the library is searched. Therefore, the order of libraries and object modules on the command line can be critical. Consider the command:

```
% f77 -lmine file4.f
```

This command searches for the library file *libmine.a* to resolve any function references needed for linking. However, the linker has not yet processed the object module for *file4.o* (created by the **f77** command and normally deleted if compilation and linking are successful). Therefore, there are no outstanding function references, and the library search has no effect. If the program needs this library, the **f77** command will produce "Undefined" symbol messages during the loading phase, and the linker will not produce an executable file. To perform this compilation correctly, enter the command:

```
% f77 file4.f -lmine
```

Now the loader searches the library file after processing *file4.f* and will be able to resolve any references requiring this library. It is a good idea to list libraries last on the command line, unless you have a special reason for doing otherwise.

FORTRAN programs generally do not need to include any standard UNIX libraries explicitly. **f77** automatically searches the math library, system call library, I/O library, and run-time initialization routines. In FORTRAN, the **-l** option is used primarily to search user-supplied libraries.

Output Files

An **f77** compilation can produce four types of files: *.f* files (FORTRAN source, after preprocessing), *.s* files (assembly language source), *.o* files (object modules), and executable files (by default named *a.out*). Which of these files remain at the end of any compilation depends on how you invoked the compiler and which steps were executed.

UNIX FORTRAN compilers try to execute four steps, if possible:

- **Preprocessing.** The compiler does not run a preprocessor on source files whose names end with *.f*. It does run a preprocessor for files whose names end in *.F*, *.e* (EFL files), or *.r* (RATFOR files). The result is placed in a file whose name is the same as the original source file but with the extension changed to *.f*. For *.F* files, **f77** invokes the standard preprocessor, known as **cpp**; some of **cpp**'s more useful features are described later in this chapter. Any *.f* files created by preprocessing are normally deleted after compilation. (Of course, *.f* files that contain original FORTRAN source are never deleted.)

- **Compiling.** The compiler compiles the preprocessed source files (along with any other source files), generating assembly language files. The name of each file is the same as the name of the FORTRAN source file, with the extension changed to *.s*.

- **Assembling.** After compilation, the compiler invokes the assembler, **as**, on each *.s* file it has created, generating object modules. The names of these files are the same as the names of the assembly language file but with the extension changed to *.o*. After creating *.o* files, any *.s* files that were generated by the compiler (i.e., those that were not originally listed on the command line) are normally deleted.

- **Loading.** After assembly, the compiler invokes the loader, **ld**, on all the object modules it has created, and any other object modules named on the command line, plus any libraries specified on the command line, plus the default libraries and initialization routines. The name of the executable file defaults to executable *a.out*. After creating the *a.out* file, any *.o* files that were created by the assembler (i.e., those that were not originally named explicitly on the command line) are normally deleted.

For example, consider the compilation:

```
% f77 t1.F t2.f
```

If these two files contain a complete FORTRAN program which does not need to be linked to any additional files, then the previous command will produce an *a.out* file, but no others. The file *t1.f* will be created but deleted, together with the assembly files and object modules produced. If these files do *not* contain a complete program but must be linked with other files or object modules, the **f77**

previous command will produce an "Undefined:" error message. After compilation, the files *t1.o* and *t2.o* will remain. In this case, the **-c** option should have
been used. In short, this option means "leave object modules; don't run the
loader."

We have just finished a long discussion of the many kinds of input that the compiler takes and the different kinds of output that it can provide. Pictures are not
always worth a thousand words, particularly when it comes to summarizing a lot
of disparate information. But it may help you to remember this information if
you view the compiler as a kind of "machine" with different inputs and outputs,
as outlined in Figure 3-1 below.

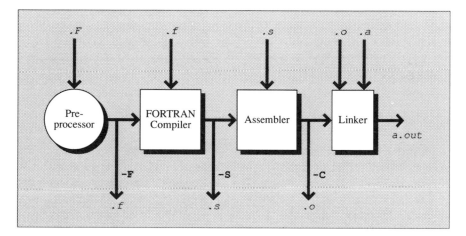

Figure 3-1. **f77** input and output

The input file's name determines where it goes into the machine. *.F* files go to the
preprocessor, *.f* files go straight to the compiler, and so on. Compilation options
determine which stage of the machine produces output (i.e., how many stages of
the machine you run). **-S** means that you stop after the assembler and the output
filename ends with *.s*. If you keep this picture in mind, the compiler's machina-
tions will not seem so strange; you will stop seeing preprocessing, compilation,
assembly, and linking as separate steps and come to see compilation as one big
assembly line for which **f77** is the production manager.

make and the Compiler

make is one of UNIX's most important tools and one that many FORTRAN programmers don't take advantage of. It is a program for automating compilations. Once you have created a *makefile* that describes how to build an executable, **make** automatically figures out which object files are out of date, recompiles those files from the most recent source code, and links together a new executable.

Because **make** is so important, we have devoted a separate chapter to it. You can do some simple experiments with **make** without reading that chapter or even without writing a makefile (a description of how to build your executable). For example, to compile the source file *ftn.f*, enter the command **make ftn.o**. **make** sees that *ftn.f* exists and enters the command **f77 -c ftn.f**. If *ftn.o* is newer than *ftn.f*, there is no reason to compile; in this case, **make** does nothing. **make** therefore can save a lot of compilation time. If you work on large FORTRAN applications, using **make** can save you hours. It can also save you many headaches, because you don't have to remember when you last compiled any object module.

Compilation Options

The following sections discuss the different options that are available with the standard UNIX FORTRAN compiler. The options in this list are applicable to virtually any UNIX FORTRAN compiler. The developers of your particular compiler may have added many implementation-specific options; these additional options may enable language compatibility features (e.g., VAX/VMS compatibility features), additional optimizations, vendor-specific debugging features, etc. For information about these additional options, consult your vendor's documentation.

Controlling Output from the Compiler

The options discussed in this section control what output files the compiler produces. They also control the degree of error reporting and other details about FORTRAN compilation.

-F   Apply the appropriate preprocessors to each FORTRAN source file but do not proceed with compilation. Leave each preprocessed source file with the suffix *f*. For example, the command:

```
% f77 -F p1.F p2.F
```

applies the preprocessor to *p1.F* and *p2.F* and leaves the results in the files *p1.f* and *p2.f*.

-S After compiling, do not proceed with assembly and linking. Leave each assembly language file with the suffix *.s*. Leave comments in the file specifying the source code line that corresponds to each assembly language instruction. For example, the command:

```
% f77 -S thing.F otherthing.F
```

compiles the programs *thing.F* and *otherthing.F*, creating two assembly language files called *thing.s* and *otherthing.s*. These may be assembled and linked later. You don't really need assembly listings unless you are going to use the **adb** debugger.

-c After assembling, do not proceed with linking. Leave each assembled object file with the suffix *.o*. For example, the command:

```
% f77 -c thing.F thing2.F
```

compiles and assembles *thing.F* and *thing2.F*, producing the object files *thing.o* and *thing2.o*, but does not try to link these two files to produce an executable (*a.out*) file. Common UNIX usage is to create object modules separately with the -c option, then to use **f77** with the -o option to create your executable. If you get into this habit, using **make** effectively will quickly become second nature.

-o *name* After loading, name the executable file *name* rather than *a.out*. There must be a space between the -o option and the argument *name*. For example, the command:

```
% f77 -o things thing.F otherthing.F
```

produces an executable file named *things* as a result of compiling and linking *thing.F* and *otherthing.F*. Without this option, the name of the executable file would have been *a.out*.

-w Suppress all warning messages.

-w66 Suppress all messages warning about possible incompatibilities with FORTRAN 66.

-v Verbose. Print the compiler's version number (and possibly other information).

FORTRAN Language Options

These options specify how the compiler should handle some details about the FORTRAN language.

-onetrip Compile so that the program will execute any **DO** loop it reaches at least once. The FORTRAN 77 standard specifies that, if the lower limit for a loop is greater than the upper limit (for example,

57

DO 10 I = 20, 10), the loop body must not be executed. The FORTRAN 66 standard left this behavior undefined; in practice, most FORTRAN 66 compilers executed the bodies of such loops exactly once. This option is provided so that programs written for such FORTRAN 66 compilers will run correctly.

-1   Same as the previous **-onetrip** command.

-u   Require explicit declarations for each variable by making the default type for all variables undefined. If this flag is present, it is an error to use a variable name without an explicit statement declaring the name's data type. This option can simplify debugging; most misspelled variable names will not correspond to any declaration and will therefore trigger "Undeclared variable" messages during compilation. Note that **IMPLICIT** statements within the program take priority over the **-u** option. Therefore, implicit typing as determined by **IMPLICIT** statements is always effective, regardless of the **-u** option.

For example, the compilation:

```
% f77 -u program.F mathstuff.F objects.o
```

requires that the FORTRAN source files *program.F* and *mathstuff.F* declare all the variables they use explicitly.

-U   Distinguish between upper- and lower-case letters. If this flag is present, the variable names "FOO", "Foo", and "foO" are different. In this case, all FORTRAN keywords are lowercase; for example, "dimension" is a valid keyword, rather than "DIMENSION". By default (i.e., if this flag is not present), FORTRAN does not distinguish between upper- and lower-case letters, *except* within character strings. Using this option is asking for portability problems. It also makes programs harder to debug. You wouldn't want two different variables named "FOo" and "Foo", would you?

-66   Restrict the FORTRAN language to features that were in FORTRAN 66. For example, specifying the **-66** option makes the "block IF" construct (**IF ... THEN ... ELSE**) illegal; this feature was added for FORTRAN 77. The **-66** option does *not* imply the **-onetrip** option.

-i2   By default, give **INTEGER** data the type **INTEGER*2** (16-bit integers). Only use 32-bit integers if the program explicitly requests the **INTEGER*4** data type. This option may make it easier to port very old FORTRAN code to UNIX. Older systems may assume that integers are 16 bits and may therefore assume that $65535 + 1 = 0$. Note that many modern systems are optimized for 32-bit data transfers. On such systems, using the **-i2** flag may make programs run slightly slower.

Preprocessor Options

The following set of options let you control the standard preprocessor, plus the RATFOR and **m4** preprocessors, from the command line. We describe the standard preprocessor later in this chapter. The RATFOR and **m4** preprocessors are defined in the *Programmer's Supplementary Documents*.

-D*name*   Define *name* to the standard preprocessor. There is no space between **-D** and *name*. By default, the preprocessor assigns this name the value 1. To give this name some other definition, use the statement -D*name=definition*, where *definition* can be any string of characters that does not include any spaces. Adding the option **-D**NAME=*definition* to the command line is equivalent to placing the statement:

```
#define NAME definition
```

at the beginning of the each file in the *list-of-files*. This option is typically used to define preprocessor variables governing conditional compilation. Each occurrence of **-D** defines a single name; the **-D** option can appear many times on a command line. For example, the command:

```
% f77 -DDEBUG1 -DDEBUG2 program.F utils.F
```

compiles the files *program.F* and *utils.F* with the preprocessor names *DEBUG1* and *DEBUG2* defined in both files.

-I*dir*   Look for files named in the standard preprocessor's **#include** statements in the directory given by *dir* after searching the current directory and before searching */usr/include*. For example, the command:

```
% f77 -I/usr/local/ftn_include program.F
```

tells the preprocessor to look in the directory */usr/local/ftn_include* for any files named in **#include** statements, before searching any of the "standard" places in which it usually looks. (For details, see the discussion of the preprocessor later in this chapter.)

-m   Apply the **m4** preprocessor to each file with the extension *.r before* using the RATFOR preprocessor (this may be **-m4** for some implementations).

-R*string*   Specify *string* as an option when using RATFOR to preprocess *.r* files.

Options to Specify Libraries

These two option request linking with nonstandard libraries. They are passed to the linker, **ld**. Your compiler may have other options for specifying libraries, particularly if your UNIX system supports "shared libraries."

-l*name*   Link the program to the library `libname.a`. This option was discussed previously.

-L*dir*   Search for libraries in the directory *dir* before searching in the standard library directories */lib* and */usr/lib*. This option lets you substitute your own libraries for the standard libraries.

Debugging and Profiling Options

These options request the compiler to create additional code and an expanded symbol table for the various profilers and debuggers (**dbx**, **prof**, **gprof**, and the branch count profiler). They are extremely helpful for debugging and tuning code under development but should not be used for production programs.

-C   Generate additional code for run-time array bounds checking. When the program is executing, the program will print a warning message on the terminal if a reference to an array element occurs that falls outside of the the array's declared boundaries. Many **f77** compilers do not implement this option.

-p   Link the program for profiling with **prof**. When you execute a program compiled with this option, it produces a file named *mon.out* that contains program execution statistics. The profiler **prof** will read this file and produce a table describing your program's execution. This option does not affect compilation; it alters the way the linker is invoked. To profile a program, you need only relink it by invoking **f77** with this option and a list of object files (for example, **f77 -p file1.o file2.o**).

-pg   Link the program for profiling with **gprof**. Executing a program compiled with this option produces a file named *gmon.out* that includes execution statistics. The profiler **gprof** will read this file and produce very detailed information about your program's execution. Note that this option does not affect compilation; it alters the way the linker is invoked. To profile a program, you need only relink it by invoking **f77** with this option and a list of object files.

-g   Generate an expanded symbol table for the debugger **dbx**.

For example, the following command compiles the file *program.f* generating code for profiling with **gprof**:

```
% f77 -pg program.f
```

Optimization

The compiler's ability to optimize a program and the options that control the optimization process vary from compiler to compiler. The traditional UNIX FORTRAN compiler only recognizes a single optimization option.

-O   Perform all applicable optimizations.

Many modern FORTRAN compilers recognize several optimization levels, each requesting different types or styles of optimization. Some compilers turn on optimization by default; this is common practice outside of the UNIX world but is nonstandard for a UNIX system. For more information, consult the manuals provided with your system.

Expanding Compiler Tables

This set of options determines the size of the compiler's internal tables. By default, most programs should compile correctly. If one of these tables overflows during compilation, the compiler will print a message informing you which table is causing the problem. Most of these limits apply on a "per-subprogram" (i.e., function or subroutine) basis and not to programs or files as a whole. For example, any program may have more than 150 equivalence classes. However, any subprogram within the program may define at most 150 equivalence classes (groups of variable names that refer to the same storage, as defined by **EQUIVALENCE** statements). The limit imposed on external names (subprogram names, common block names) is an exception to this rule; it applies on a "per-file" basis.

-Nq*n*   Set the number of equivalence classes allowed per subprogram to *n*. By default, **f77** allows 150 equivalence classes per subprogram. Note that this limit applies to the number of equivalence classes (or equivalence sets), not to the number of equivalenced variables or **EQUIVALENCE** statements. For example, the statement:

```
EQUIVALENCE (A, B, C)
```

defines a single equivalence class. To allow 1000 equivalence classes per subprogram, enter a compilation command like the following:

```
% f77 -o program -Nq1000 program.F
```

-Nx*n*   Set the number of external names allowed per file to *n*. External names are common block names, subroutine names, and function names. By default, f77 allows 200 external names per file. In this context, "file" means a file that appears on the command line, including within it any code inserted by the preprocessor or FORTRAN's **INCLUDE** statement. For example, the following compilation allows 800 external names per file:

```
% f77 -o program -Nx800 pr1.F pr2.F
```

-Ns*n*   Set the number of statement labels allowed per subprogram to *n*. By default, f77 allows 401 statement labels per subprogram. For example, the compilation below expands the statement label table to allow 1000 labels per subprogram:

```
% f77 -o program -Ns1000 pr1.F pr2.F
```

-Nc*n*   Set the maximum level of control statement nesting per subprogram to *n*. This includes nesting of loops, **IF** statements, and **ELSE IF** statements. By default, f77 allows the maximum nesting depth be 20. The following compilation allows a maximum nesting depth of 120:

```
% f77 -o program -Nc120 pr1.F pr2.F
```

-Nn*n*   Set the maximum number of identifiers (including variable names and external names) per subprogram to *n*. By default, f77 allows 1009 identifiers per subprogram. The following compilation allows 3000 identifiers per subprogram:

```
% f77 -o program -Nn3000 pr1.F pr2.F
```

The Preprocessor

If a FORTRAN source file ends with the extension *.F*, the FORTRAN compiler invokes the standard UNIX preprocessor, **cpp**. This preprocessor allows file inclusion, simple substitutions, and conditional compilation. The output of this pre-processor is a modified version of the original FORTRAN program, stripped of all preprocessor statements.

Although the preprocessor modifies the FORTRAN source significantly by insert-ing files, adding and deleting lines, etc., the FORTRAN compiler will still report diagnostic messages according to the line numbers and filenames of the original source. That is, when the compiler reports an error reported on line 55 of the file *source.F*, it is actually responding to an error that occurred on this line in this file, regardless of the preprocessor's work.

NOTE

In modifying the source code, the preprocessor implicitly changes line lengths and column positions. It is therefore dangerous to use pre-processor features (other than conditional compilation and file inclusion) if the program uses column-formatted lines. Tab-formatted lines (lines that use a $\boxed{\text{TAB}}$ to separate the statement label from the statement rather than the column position.

If you use the preprocessor, you are committing yourself to UNIX. You will have trouble porting your code to non-UNIX systems.

Preprocessor Statements

All preprocessor statements begin with a # (pound sign) in column 1, followed by a keyword. Preprocessor statements can be any length. The (continuation char-acter or backslash) allows a statement to be spread over several lines. If it is used, this must be the last character on the line; in particular, no blanks may fol-low it. For example:

```
#keyword        Text of the preprocessor statement followed \
                by more text continuing the statement
```

File Inclusion

The preprocessor replaces the line:

```
#include "filename"
```

with the file called *filename*. To find this file, it searches through */usr/include*, the current directory, and other directories specified on the command line with the **-I** option. The concept of a "search path" distinguishes **#include** from FORTRAN's INCLUDE statement. Similarly, the preprocessor replaces the line:

```
#include <filename>
```

with the file called *filename*, for which it searches in the */usr/include* and any other directories specified on the command line. It does not search the current directory. Note that */usr/include* is typically reserved for standard C language header files. FORTRAN programmers should not use this directory as a repository for locally developed FORTRAN include files; files placed here may be deleted during software upgrades. Your system administrator should designate a special place for standard FORTRAN headers, which should be listed on the command line with the **-I** option.

For example, the preprocessor replaces the statements:

```
#include "moresource.F"
```

and:

```
#include <moresource.F>
```

with the file *moresource.F*. In the former case, it looks for this file in the current directory, then in any directories specified with **-I**, and finally in */usr/include*. In the latter case, it looks for *moresource.F* in any directories specified with **-I** and in */usr/include*, but not in the current directory.

An included file may contain further **#include** statements.

Specifying Search Directories on the Command Line

The **-I** compiler option lets you specify additional directories in which to search on the FORTRAN command line. The statement:

```
% f77 -I/usr/local/fortran source.F
```

tells the FORTRAN compiler to search the directory */usr/local/fortran* (in addition to the current directory and */usr/include*) when it looks for a file named in an **#include** statement. The preprocessor will search this directory for *either* form of the **#include** statement.

The line:

```
#define name value
```

tells the preprocessor to replace every occurrence of *name* in a file with the string *value*. For example, the preprocessor will replace:

```
#define ARRAYSIZE 100000
#define FLOATSIZE 4
      DIMENSION BIGARRAY(ARRAYSIZE)
      IBYTES = ARRAYSIZE*FLOATSIZE + HEADERSIZE
```

with the statements:

```
      DIM BIGARRAY(100000)
      IBYTES = 100000*4 + HEADERSIZE
```

This is purely a textual substitution. The names **ARRAYSIZE** and **FLOATSIZE** never reach the FORTRAN compiler itself; the preprocessor strips all occurrences of these names from the file, replacing them with the character strings given in their **#define** statements. In this respect, **#define** differs substantially from FORTRAN's **PARAMETER** statement, which defines a symbolic constant that obeys the same implicit type rules as a FORTRAN variable. Superficially, the following **PARAMETER** statements appear equivalent to the previous **#define** statements:

```
      PARAMETER(ARRAYSIZE = 100000)
      PARAMETER(FLOATSIZE = 4)
      DIMENSION BIGARRAY(ARRAYSIZE)
      IBYTES = ARRAYSIZE*FLOATSIZE + HEADERSIZE
```

However, compiling these statements produces an error message, because **ARRAYSIZE** obeys FORTRAN's implicit type rules and, unless defined otherwise, will have type **REAL**. As a **REAL** number, it cannot be used to dimension **BIGARRAY**.

In FORTRAN, you don't really need substitutions. The **PARAMETER** statement can do everything you need. However, one special case is important. The statement:

```
#define name
```

without any *value* defines *name* to be 1. This is useful for conditional compilation which we will discuss below.

Normally, preprocessor definitions are effective from the point where the definition appears to the end of the file. Preprocessor definitions are not effective across files; for example, the statement **#define MULTI** in one file does not define the name "MULTI" in other files. You can force the preprocessor to "forget" a definition at any point by using the **#undef** statement:

```
#undef name
```

This immediately eliminates any definition currently in effect for *name*. For example:

```
#undef MYTHING
```

tells the preprocessor to discard any definition it may have for the name **MYTHING**.

Remember that **#define** statements do *not* use an = (equal sign); an equal sign within a **#define** statement becomes part of the definition. That is, the statement **#define ME = 6** defines "ME" to be the string "= 6". This is almost certainly incorrect.

The simple substitution facility is really only a subset of **cpp**'s general macro facility. However, macros don't fit neatly into the FORTRAN language because of FORTRAN's inhibitions about statement format. Therefore, macros are of limited use for FORTRAN programmers; we will not describe them here.

Conditional Compilation

For conditional compilation, the preprocessor "selects" portions of the program that it sends to the compiler, and it deletes other portions. This feature is extremely useful in many development situations, because it allows you to maintain several versions of a program in a single file, minimizing the degree to which these versions diverge. For example, consider adding extra statements to a program for debugging. Conditional compilation can be used to strip debugging statements from production compilations while keeping them in the source files for reference, future debugging, and development. By setting the appropriate compile-time switches, you can determine whether the preprocessor will pass the debugging statements to the compiler.

To compile a block of code conditionally, place an **#ifdef** statement before it and an **#endif** statement after it:

```
#ifdef name
      Statement 1 : Statements for conditional compilation
      Statement 2 : They will be compiled if name is defined
#endif
```

The statements between the **#ifdef/#endif** pair will be compiled if *name* is "defined." If *name* has not been defined, the preprocessor will delete these statements. To define *name*, use a **#define** statement or the **-D***name* compiler option.

An **#ifdef** block can have an **#else** statement within it, as in the following example:

```
#ifdef LARGE_MATRICES
        Statement 1
        Statement 2
#else
        Statement 3
        Statement 4
#endif
```

If **LARGE_MATRICES** has been defined, the preprocessor will pass statements 1 and 2 to the FORTRAN compiler and will delete statements 3 and 4. If it has not been defined, the preprocessor will pass statements 3 and 4 to the compiler and will delete statements 1 and 2.

An **#ifndef** statement is similar to **#ifdef**, except that it allows compilation if *name* has not been defined. For example, the following code fragment has the same effect as the previous example:

```
#ifndef LARGE_MATRICES
        Statement 3
        Statement 4
#else
        Statement 1
        Statement 2
#endif
```

Nesting Within Conditionals

All preprocessor statements (including more conditional statements) can occur within conditionals. Whether or not the preprocessor executes them depends on the conditional statement. For example, consider the code:

```
#ifndef NON_STANDARD
#include "standards.F"
#define STANDARD
#endif
```

If **NON_STANDARD** is undefined, the preprocessor will insert the file *standards.F* and define the name **STANDARD** (which will probably be used within later conditional compilation statements). Here is an example showing what happens when conditionals are nested:

```
#ifdef A
        Statement 1
#ifdef B
        Statement 2
#else
        Statement 3
```

```
#endif
#else
        Statement 4
#endif
```

If **A** is undefined, only statement 4 will be sent to the compiler, regardless of **B**. If **A** is defined and **B** is undefined, statements 1 and 3 will be sent to the compiler. If both **A** and **B** are defined, statements 1 and 2 will be sent to the compiler. Note that each **#ifdef** (and **#ifndef**) statement must have its own **#endif** statement.

Remember that preprocessor names are *not* FORTRAN variables. You cannot use a FORTRAN variable within an **#ifdef** statement. For example, consider the code:

```
        INTEGER A
        A = 1
#ifdef A
        Conditional code
#endif
```

The FORTRAN statement **A = 1** has nothing to do with the preprocessor conditional **#ifdef A**. The behavior of this compilation depends completely on the preprocessor's definition for **A**. If **A** is defined, the preprocessor will substitute its definition in the statements **INTEGER A** and **A = 1**. In most cases, this substitution will produce incorrect code in one of the two locations. Therefore, the compilation will probably fail when the compiler reaches this point. If **A** is undefined, the statement **A = 1** will compile correctly. The *conditional code* will not be compiled, because the preprocessor doesn't know anything about the FORTRAN statement **A = 1**.

The -D Option

The **-D** option to the FORTRAN compiler is particularly useful for conditional compilation. The option **-D***name* is equivalent to preceding each file being compiled with the preprocessor statement:

```
#define name 1
```

For example, the command:

```
% f77 -DNON_STANDARD source.F mixture.F
```

will compile the FORTRAN files *source.F* and *mixture.F* with the preprocessor name **NON_STANDARD** defined. Depending on the program's **#ifdef** and **#ifndef** preprocessor statements, this may cause certain files and certain FORTRAN statements to be included or omitted. Compiling the same program with the command:

```
% f77 -DSTANDARD source.F
```

will produce a significantly different object file because the preprocessor will present a different program to the compiler. By using conditional compilation properly, a single file may contain several different versions of the same program; compile-time options distinguish which version of the program reaches the compiler. This makes it much easier to maintain these versions simultaneously.

Conditional compilation with the **-D** option is particularly helpful when you need to port a program from one UNIX system to another. It allows you to add and delete code in a way that lets you compile the program correctly for both systems. Note that many vendors automatically define some preprocessor names to identify the computer on which you are working.

Comments

The preprocessor always replaces comments of the form:

```
/*text of comment*/
```

with a single space. Therefore, /* and */ can be used to delimit comments within FORTRAN programs. Unlike standard FORTRAN comments, preprocessor comments can occur anywhere within a line. For example, the statement:

```
A = FUNCTION(X,/*COMMENT*/Y)
```

is equivalent to:

```
A = FUNCTION(X, Y)
```

Comments of this type may be extended across several lines.

Summary of Preprocessor Statements

The following table summarizes the statements available through the standard preprocessor.

#define *name*	Define *name* for the preprocessor.
#else	Compile the following code if the *name* tested by the previous **#ifdef** statement was undefined or if the *name* tested by the previous **#ifndef** statement was defined.
#endif	End a conditional compilation block.

#ifdef *name*   Compile the following code if *name* is defined.

#ifndef *name*   Compile the following code if *name* is undefined.

#include *file*   Include the contents of *file* at this point in the program.

For an excellent discussion of the preprocessor's facilities, see *C, A Reference Manual* by S. P. Harbison and G. L. Steele (Prentice Hall), pp. 26-48.

Assembling a FORTRAN Program

Normally the FORTRAN compiler invokes the UNIX assembler automatically. You can ignore its existence unless your program requires some special treatment. Most compilers don't understand all of the assembler's special purpose options. In rare cases when you need these options, you will need to run the assembler as a separate program. This section does not describe the assembly language itself. To understand assembly language, read your computer's assembly language reference manual.

The assembler takes a program written in an assembly language and produces an object module. By convention, assembly language programs have the extension *.s*. If no errors occur during assembly and if this object module contains no references to external (imported) symbols, the assembler will make the file executable and name it *a.out*. If this object module includes references to external symbols, *a.out* will not be executable. The linker (described below) will be able to link this object module with other modules to produce an executable program.

Invoking the Assembler

To invoke the assembler, enter the command:

```
% as list-of-options source-file
```

where *list-of-options* is a series of assembly options and *source-file* is a single assembly language file. Note that the assembler only works with one file at a time. To assemble a group of files, **f77** invokes the assembler several times.

Assembler options are *not* standardized in any way; they depend on the computer's manufacturer, the processor and assembly language that it uses, and other factors. You can expect the assembler to have options that specify the exact processor you are using. Your FORTRAN compiler probably has a similar set of options because it needs to know what instructions it can generate. For example, an assembler for a 68000-based workstation would have options to differentiate between the 68000/68010 assembly language and the 68020/68030 assembly language (which is a superset). You would expect the workstation's compiler to have a similar group of options. There may also be options to specify whether the assembler should accept instructions for a floating-point coprocessor. By default, assemblers always accept the full instruction set for the processor you are using. You would only need to request the 68000 instruction set explicitly if you are compiling on a 68020-based computer but want to generate code that will run on a 68000.

It is also common for assemblers to have options that control the alignment (i.e., the base address) for the different segments of the object module. Object modules are divided into three segments:

- The *text segment* contains the executable code (i.e., machine language instructions) itself. It is normally read-only. A read-only text segment allows several processes running the same program to "share" the same text segment while they are running, conserving memory. This is called *shared text*.

- The *data segment* is used for all static data. In FORTRAN static data include **COMMON** blocks and variables named in **SAVE** statements. Depending on your compiler, argument lists may also be considered static data.

- The *bss segment* is used for uninitialized data.

Linking FORTRAN Programs

The linker combines several object modules and libraries into a single executable file. It resolves references to external variables, external procedures, and libraries, creating a complete, self-sufficient program. You never need to invoke **ld** explicitly. In most cases, it is simpler to use the **f77** command to link files, even if you do not have any source files to compile. **f77** guarantees that several libraries will be present in the proper order even if they are not listed on the command line. If you use **ld** as a linker, you will need to mention these libraries explicitly.

This section does not provide a complete description of all the linker's facilities. For more information, see the entry for **ld** in Section 1 of the *UNIX Programmer's Reference Manual*.

Invoking ld

The rules for invoking **ld**, if you must do so, are the same as for **f77**. The basic **ld** command is:

```
% ld list-of-options list-of-files-and-libraries
```

where *list-of-files-and-libraries* is a series of filenames and library specifications. To include a library in this list, use the notation -l*name*, where the name of the library file is either /lib/lib*name*.a or /usr/lib/lib*name*.a. The linker processes the *list-of-files-and-libraries* in order. When it reaches a library, it only extracts those programs from the library that it currently needs to resolve external references. Consequently, the position in which libraries appear in this list is important. For example, the command:

```
% ld prog1.o -lm prog2.o
```

will result in an "Undefined symbol" message if *prog2.o* refers to any programs in the library */usr/lib/libm.a*—unless you happen to be lucky and *prog2.o* only uses routines that the linker extracted for the sake of *prog1.o*. Note that libraries may refer to other libraries; thus, the command:

```
% ld prog1.o -lat -lfo
```

will lead to "Undefined symbol" messages if the *fo* library requires any routines from **at**. This situation will be more complex for user-generated libraries unless they are processed with the **ranlib** command.

If you want to create an executable file, the beginning of the first file in the *list-of-files* must be the program's entry point. This is *not* the same as the apparent entry point to your FORTRAN source program. Before your program begins executing, the computer must execute a standard run-time initialization routine. To ensure that this is in place, */lib/crt0.o* must be the first file in the *list-of-files*. This ensures that this initialization routine will be linked to your program.

Alternatively, you can "link" by using the **f77** command without any FORTRAN source files. When **f77** and **cc** invoke the linker, they automatically add this object file and many other libraries in the proper place. For example, the command **f77 -O exp.F** might generate the following **ld** command:

```
% ld -X -u _MAIN_ -z /lib/crt0.o exp.o -o a.out \
     /usr/lib/libF77.a   /usr/lib/libI77.a \
     /usr/lib/libU77.a   /lib/libc.a   /usr/lib/libm.a
```

In this command, the run-time initialization module */lib/crt0.o* appears explicitly, in addition to requests to resolve references to the *F77, I77,* and *U77* libraries and to the general run-time and math libraries (*libc.a* and *libm.a*). On your system, the exact details of the command may differ.

Linker Options

The **f77** compiler passes any options it does not recognize to the linker. Many options traditionally considered compiler options (such as -o) are really linker options. The most important options can therefore be placed directly on the **f77** command line. These options are:

-o *name*   Instead of naming the executable output file *a.out*, name it *name*.

-l*name*   Link the program to the library named `libname.a`. The linker looks in the directories */lib* and */usr/lib* to find this library.

-L*dir*   To find any libraries, look in the directory *dir* before looking in the standard library directories */lib* and */usr/lib*.

-s   Remove the symbol table from the executable output file. This makes the output file significantly smaller but makes debugging almost impossible. Therefore, this option should not be used until the program works successfully. Note that using the program **strip** has the same effect.

-x   Remove local symbols from the output file. Global symbols (subprograms and common block names) remain in the output file. This reduces the object file's size.

-X   Save local symbols in the output file, but not symbols generated purely by the compiler for internal record keeping. All such compiler-generated symbols begin with **L**. The **f77** compiler specifies this option by default when it calls **ld**.

-n   Align the program's text and data segments on page boundaries; allow all users executing this program simultaneously to use the same copy of the text segment (shared text). This allows more efficient use of the system's memory and reduces the need to load commonly used programs from disk repeatedly. On most UNIX systems, this option is in effect by default.

-z   Align the program's text and data segments on page boundaries; allow all users executing this program simultaneously to use the same copy of the text segment; allow demand paging" (i.e., identical to **-n**, with the addition of demand paging). On most UNIX systems, this option is in effect by default.

-r   Create an object file that can be included in further linking runs (i.e., further passes through **ld**). Among other things, this inhibits "Undefined symbol" messages (because these symbols may be defined in a later **ld** pass) and prevents **ld** from creating common storage immediately. If you wish to create common storage at this time, use the **-d** option in addition.

-e*name*   Use the symbol *name* as the entry point to the executable program. By default, the entry point is the beginning of the first object module. The FORTRAN and C compilers automatically link your object files with a run-time initialization module (*/lib/crt0.o*) that starts your program and provides its initial entry point. If you run the linker separately, you must do this yourself.

For example, the command:

```
% ld -r -o bigofile.o prog1.o prog2.o -lmylib
```

links the files *prog1.o* and *prog2.o* and the library file */usr/lib/libmylib.a*. The resulting file is named *bigofile.o*; it can be linked further and may still contain unresolved references.

Recent developments have greatly complicated the picture. "Shared libraries" have introduced many new **ld** options, all of which are system-dependent. To make matters worse, these new options sometimes conflict with **f77** options. If you want to generate your own shared libraries, check your system's documentation.

Error Messages

It is fairly common to get a linker error when compiling. This can be confusing to new UNIX programmers, since the linker's error messages are not as clear as one might like and are not documented anywhere. Here is a basic list of linker errors; keep in mind that your system may have different messages, depending on your vendor's creativity.

-flag: **arg missing**
-flag: **too small**
      These messages mean that you invoked **ld** or **f77** with the linker option *-flag*; this option requires an argument that was either missing or incorrect.

bad flag
      You invoked **ld** or **f77** with an option flag that the linker did not recognize.

file: **Bad magic number**
      A magic number is a part of a file's header that identifies its type. A bad magic number indicates that the file did not have the correct type; in this case, it indicates that the named file is not a valid object module. For example, you will get this message if you try to link a program to an ASCII text file.

symbol: **multiply defined**

> This indicates that the given symbol was defined more than once in the files that you were linking. Linking two routines with the same name will cause this message. You may have inadvertently listed an object module twice on the command line or accidentally given the same name to two routines.

Premature EOF

> This message means that one of the object modules ended without a proper end-of-file. This usually means that the file was damaged in some way (e.g., the system crashed while generating it).

Read failed (gulpfile)

> One of the files you are linking has length zero.

Undefined: *name*

> When linking the files you specified, **ld** did not find any definition for the symbol *name*. Find out which object file or library you are missing and relink.

User attempt to redefine loader-defined symbol

> One of the files being linked tried to redefine the symbols **_end**, **_etext**, **_edata**, or **_ejump**. These symbols are reserved for the loader's use and cannot be used by a program. FORTRAN symbol names do not have this form; this message can only occur while linking C programs.

Creating Libraries

Two UNIX commands, **ar** and **ranlib**, create libraries (or archives). Normally, you create libraries from object modules, but there is no reason you couldn't create text libraries or source code libraries. **ar** takes a group of files and creates a single library file from them, and **ranlib** takes this library file and adds a "directory," allowing the linker to access the library efficiently. It also orders the files in the library so that dependencies between different programs in the library will be resolved correctly. This section gives a brief description of how to use these commands. For more information about these commands, see the entries discussing them in Section 1 of the *UNIX Programmer's Reference Manual*.

NOTE

ar and **ranlib** do not manage shared libraries. Consult your system's documentation to find out whether it supports shared libraries and, if so, how to manage them.

To create a new library, use the **ar** command, as follows:

```
% ar r lib-name list-of-files
```

The option **r** indicates that the command **ar** should add the files named in the *list-of-files* to the library named *lib-name*, creating a new library if necessary. If a file is mentioned twice in the *list-of-files*, **ar** will include it in the archive twice.

To update a library, use the command:

```
% ar ru lib-name list-of-files
```

This compares the dates of any listed files with the version of the file in the library. If the file in *list-of-files* is more recent than the version contained in the library, **ar** will substitute the newer version for the older version.

To delete one or more files from a library, use the command:

```
% ar d lib-name list-of-files
```

This deletes all the files found in *list-of-files*.

To extract one or more files from a library, use the command:

```
% ar x lib-name list-of-files
```

This does not modify the library file itself. It extracts the files named in the *list-of-files* from the library, regenerating them in the current directory with their original names. Normally, the timestamp of the extracted files will be the time at which **ar** recreated them. If you use the option **xo** instead of **x**, **ar** will set the timestamp of the extracted files to the time recorded in the archive.

ar creates an ordered library, rather than a random-access library. An ordered library is like a tape: it is a list of data that must be searched sequentially. Because **ld** only makes one pass through a library, routines only call library routines that follow it. You have to plan the order of the library carefully to avoid this problem; use a random-access library. *Random-access libraries* begin with a *directory* that lets **ld** look up the function it wants and extract it without a detailed search. After reading the directory, **ld** knows what is in the library and doesn't care about the order of routines within the library. To create a random-access library from an "ordered" library, use the **ranlib** command:

```
% ranlib lib-name
```

This converts the library *lib-name* to an random-access library by adding a symbol directory as the first element in the library. The name of this directory is _.SYMDEF; in order for the linker to work correctly, this name must not be used as a symbol within your program.

For example, let's create a random-access library called *libgraph.a* from the object modules *square.o*, *line.o*, *ellipse.o*, and *toplevel.o*:

```
% ar r libgraph.a square.o line.o ellipse.o toplevel.o
% ranlib libgraph.a
% mv libgraph.a /usr/lib/ftnlib/libgraph.a
```

We are assuming that */usr/lib/ftnlib* is a special directory that your system administrator has created to hold site-specific FORTRAN libraries. Now we can link this library to an application, *drawit.f*, with the command:

```
% f77 -o drawit drawit.f -L/usr/lib/ftnlib -lgraph
```

This compilation finds the library named *graph* in the directory *usr/lib/ftnlib*, extracts any routines needed by *drawit.f*, and builds a complete executable named *drawit*.

FORTRAN Working Environment
FORTRAN I/O
UNIX System Calls and Functions
Installing Local Programs

This chapter discusses the environment in which FORTRAN programs run. It discusses the relationship between FORTRAN programs and the UNIX operating system: how to run programs correctly, how to initialize I/O properly for FORTRAN programs, how to use UNIX system calls to get command line arguments, and other topics of interest.

FORTRAN I/O

UNIX defines three standard data streams, called *standard input*, *standard output*, and *standard error*. By default, standard input is preconnected to logical unit 5, standard output is connected to logical unit 6, and standard error is connected to logical unit 0. Therefore, you can read unit 5 and write units 0 and 6 without first opening them. By default, standard output and standard error send output to the terminal and standard input normally reads from the terminal. You can redirect any of these streams by using the following command qualifiers:

< *file*	Read on unit 5 from *file*.
> *file*	Write on unit 6 to *file*.
>> *file*	Append from unit 6 to *file*.
>& *file*	Write units 0 and 6 to *file* (**csh**).
2> *file*	Write from unit 0 to *file* (**sh**).

If you don't want to use the standard data streams, you can redefine them by using the **OPEN** statement. You may also close standard input or output, although it is not necessary to do so. It is always an error to close standard error (logical unit 0).

Default Filenames

If a program writes to a logical unit without first assigning a filename to the unit, the program will write to the file named `fort.nn`, where *nn* is the logical unit's number. It will create the file if it does not already exist. Likewise, if a program reads from a logical unit without first assigning a filename, the program will read from the file named `fort.nn`, if that file exists.

For example, the short program below writes to the file named *fort.21*; this is the default filename for logical unit 21:

```
OPEN (UNIT=21)
WRITE (UNIT=21,*) "hi there"
END
```

FORTRAN I/O Initialization

Many FORTRAN programs assume some kind of external I/O initialization; that is, they assume that some system utility has previously opened files and connected them to certain logical units. The **IOINIT** system call lets you handle these situations with minimal modifications to the program.

The function **IOINIT** changes the default FORTRAN I/O initialization. By default, FORTRAN I/O:

• Does not recognize carriage control on any logical unit.

• Ignores leading and trailing blanks in input data fields.

- Positions files opened for sequential access at the beginning.

- Associates unit *nn* with file `fort.fInn` unless a filename is given explicitly.

IOINIT lets you change all of these defaults. The changes apply globally (i.e., they apply to all FORTRAN I/O operations that take place after the call to **IOINIT**).

Call **IOINIT** as follows:

```
LOGICAL IORESULT
LOGICAL CARRIAGE, ZERO, APPEND, VERBOSE
CHARACTER*(any) PREFIX
IORESULT=IOINIT(CARRIAGE, ZERO, APPEND, PREFIX, VERBOSE)
```

The arguments **CARRIAGE, ZERO, APPEND, PREFIX**, and **VERBOSE** mean:

CARRIAGE	If **CARRIAGE** is **.TRUE.**, the FORTRAN I/O system will recognize carriage control for all logical units except logical unit 0, which UNIX reserves for diagnostic output. If it is **.FALSE.**, the I/O system will ignore all carriage control (the default).
ZERO	If **ZERO** is **.TRUE.**, FORTRAN will treat leading and trailing blanks in input data fields as zero. If **ZERO** is **.FALSE.**, FORTRAN will ignore leading and trailing blanks (the default).
APPEND	If **APPEND** is **.TRUE.**, FORTRAN will position itself at the end of files upon opening them, rather than at the beginning. This allows you to append data to the end of a file, rather than writing at the beginning of the file. If **APPEND** is **.FALSE.**, FORTRAN will position itself at the beginning of any files it opens (the default).
PREFIX	The character string **PREFIX** lets you associate logical devices with files through the **setenv** command. For example, if the value of **PREFIX** is BASE, FORTRAN will associate each logical unit *nn* with the environment variable named BASE*nn*, where *nn* is a two-digit logical unit number (e.g., 00, 01). After making this association, any operation on logical unit *nn* refers to the file named by the environment variable BASE*nn*.
VERBOSE	If **VERBOSE** is **.TRUE.**, **IOINIT** will send messages to standard error describing its activity; otherwise, it will act silently (the default).

IOINIT lets you use the **setenv** command to associate logical units and files at run-time. For example, if the statement:

```
IORES=IOINIT(.FALSE., .FALSE., .FALSE., 'PROG', .FALSE.)
```

occurs in the program **work**, then this sequence of UNIX commands:

```
% setenv PROG02 input.asc
% setenv PROG03 output.asc
% work
```

automatically opens the file *input.asc* as logical unit 2 and the file *output.asc* as logical unit 3. Depending on how they are used in the program, these files will be opened for sequential formatted reading or sequential formatted writing. By using **IOINIT** in conjunction with environment variables, you can eliminate the need for explicit **OPEN** statements. It will help you to port older programs that expect to find files preconnected to logical units. This is often the behavior of programs that run under older operating systems with a separate job control language. Under these systems, a JCL card would open the file and connect it to a logical unit. The FORTRAN program would not open the file but would expect to find the file preconnected.

IOINIT returns .**TRUE.** if it executed successfully and .**FALSE.** if it fails. It can be used at any time during the program and affects all subsequent I/O operations.

Simple Character I/O

In addition to the standard FORTRAN I/O statements, a program can use many UNIX I/O facilities. For some applications, these facilities might be more convenient. To perform simple character I/O, you can use the **PUTC** and **GETC** functions to read and write standard input and standard output. It may be easier to use these statements if you do a lot of character I/O. Use the **PUTC** and **GETC** functions as follows:

```
CHARACTER C
I=GETC(C)
I=PUTC(C)
```

GETC reads a character from standard input and writes it into the **CHARACTER** variable **C** (unit 5). PUTC takes the **CHARACTER** variable **C** and writes it on standard output (unit 6). The return value **I** will be 0 if everything had proceeded normally; nonzero otherwise. GETC will return the value -1 if it reads an end-of-file (CTRL-D) from standard input. If either function returns a positive nonzero value, an error has occurred. In these cases, the returned value is a UNIX error code. You can use the routine **PERROR** to print an error message; **PERROR** is discussed in the section "Error Handling" later in this chapter.

The functions **FPUTC** and **FGETC** provide a more general way to do character I/O. These two functions read and write from any FORTRAN logical unit. Use them as follows:

```
INTEGER UNITNO
CHARACTER C
I=FPUTC(UNITNO, C)
I=FGETC(UNITNO, C)
```

where **UNITNO** is a logical unit number. **FPUTC** writes a single character C to a logical unit. **FGETC** reads a single character from a logical unit and stores that character in **C**. Both return values as previously described for **PUTC** and **GETC**. Zero indicates that the operation took place successfully, -1 indicates that **FGETC** has reached an end-of-file character, and positive nonzero indicates a system error.

Do not mix **GETC**, **PUTC**, **FGETC**, or **FPUTC** with the FORTRAN **READ**, **WRITE**, or **PRINT** statements. On any unit, I/O must be performed exclusively by FORTRAN I/O statements or by these UNIX character I/O statements. This applies, in particular, to standard input (unit 5) and standard output (unit 6).

These four routines provide a simple way to do character I/O. However, heavy use of these operations is very inefficient and leads to poor performance. The FORTRAN **READ**, **WRITE**, and **PRINT** statements provide much greater efficiency, particularly if you use unformatted I/O. I/O operations are most efficient when you read and write arrays and character strings as a whole, rather than reading and writing individual array elements. For example, consider these two code fragments:

```
C Less efficient (one        C More efficient (entire
C element at a time)         C array in one operation)
      DIMENSION A(10000)            DIMENSION A (1000)
      DO 10 I = 1,1000
      WRITE (UNIT=8)A(I)            WRITE (UNIT=8,FMT=100)A
10    CONTINUE               100    FORMAT (10000F)
```

The code on the right is much more efficient; the difference may be a factor of 20 or 30 in some cases, depending on how you structure the **FORMAT** statements. You will never find the loop on the left to be more efficient than the loop on the right.

File System Information

The FORTRAN **INQUIRE** statement provides a lot of general information about files and file types; it is particularly good at finding out which FORTRAN I/O parameters are in effect for any file. However, there are times when you need system-specific information that **INQUIRE** cannot supply. To get at this information, use the **FSTAT**, **LSTAT**, and **STAT** functions. They provide information about the properties of any file or file system. These properties include user and group ownership, access information, access times, file size, and the file system block size. **FSTAT** provides information about the file that is connected to a FORTRAN logical unit, **STAT** provides information about any file whether or not it is connected, and **LSTAT** provides information about symbolic links (the other two provide information about the actual file, or the target of a link).

These functions are called as follows:

```
CHARACTER*n FILENAME
INTEGER*4 LOGICALUNIT, IRETURN
INTEGER*4 STATS(13)

IRETURN=FSTAT(LOGICALUNIT,STATS)
IRETURN=STAT(FILENAME,STATS)
IRETURN=LSTAT(FILENAME,STATS)
```

where **FILENAME** is a valid UNIX pathname, **LOGICALUNIT** is the FORTRAN logical unit number assigned to an open file, and **STATS** is a buffer of 13 32-bit words in which the function writes statistics pertaining to the file. All of these functions return the value 0 if they execute successfully; they return a positive error code if they fail.

The **STATS** buffer is defined as follows:

STATS(1) The number of the *UNIX device* on which the file resides. Bits 15:8 of this number are the major device number, identifying a particular device type, and bits 7:0 are the minor device number, indicating a particular device and device partition. Bits 31:16 are unused. The command **ls -l /dev/*** shows the major and minor numbers for I/O devices.

STATS(2) The *inode number* (file number) assigned to the file. Each file has a unique inode number within its file system.

STATS(3) The UNIX *file access mode* assigned to the file. Bits 8:6 describe access for the file's owner (read, write, execute), bits 5:3 describe access for members of the owner's group, and bits 2:0 describe access for all others. Bit 15 is set for regular files, and bit 14 is set for directories. We describe access modes in Chapter 1, *Introduction to the UNIX Operating System.*

STATS(4) The number of *hard links* to the file. Hard links are created by the command **ln**. Soft links created by **ln -s** are not counted.

STATS(5) The *user identification (uid) number* of the file's owner. The uid numbers are assigned in the *passwd* group.

STATS(6) The *group identification (gid) number* of the file's owner. The gid numbers are assigned in the *group* database.

STATS(7)   When accessing a special file (i.e., when accessing a device directly), this field reports the device's major and minor numbers. When accessing any other file this field is undefined.

STATS(8)   The file's *length*, in bytes.

STATS(9)   The file's *last accessed time*. The last accessed time is reset whenever any program reads, writes, or creates the file. It is also reset whenever any program modifies changes the file's timestamp.

STATS(10)   The file's *last modified time*. It is reset whenever any program writes or creates the file. It is also reset whenever any program modifies the file's timestamp.

STATS(11)   The file's *last status change time*. This field reflects changes to the file's inode (a data structure used by the UNIX file system). It is reset whenever any program reads, writes, creates, or renames the file. It is reset whenever a hard link to the file is created or deleted. It is also reset whenever the file's ownership or access is changed.

STATS(12)   The *block size* of the file system on which the file resides, in bytes. For the best I/O performance, always transfer a multiple of this block size.

STATS(13)   Currently unused.

UNIX reports system times in terms of the number of seconds since midnight, January 1, 1970, GMT. To convert system times to more reasonable times, use the functions **CTIME** and **LTIME**, described in Section 3 of the *UNIX Programmer's Reference Manual*.

Tape I/O

To read and write files on magnetic tape, use the tape I/O functions described in Section 3F of the *UNIX Programmer's Reference Manual*. The tape I/O functions are **TOPEN, TCLOSE, TREAD, TWRITE, TREWIN, TSKIPF,** and **TSTAT**. The standard FORTRAN I/O statements (**OPEN, READ, WRITE,** etc.) should only be used for disk-based I/O.

UNIX System Calls and Functions

This section describes how to write FORTRAN programs that take advantage of the UNIX operating system's features. For the most part, it discusses the system calls listed in Section 3F of the *UNIX Programmer's Reference Manual*. No special libraries are needed to use these routines.

The most important features discussed here are:

- How a FORTRAN program reads arguments from a program's command line.
- How a FORTRAN program accesses shell and environment variables.
- How a FORTRAN program handles errors.

Command Line Arguments

Two routines let FORTRAN programs read arguments from the command line. These are **GETARG** and **IARGC**. The former is a subroutine that copies any command line argument into a **CHARACTER** variable; the latter is a function that returns the total number of command line arguments.

Call the subroutine **GETARG** as follows:

```
CHARACTER*8 ARG
CALL GETARG(I, ARG)
```

This sets **ARG** equal to the Ith command line argument. **ARG** must have type **CHARACTER**; **I** must have type **INTEGER**. Argument 0 is the command name itself; argument 1 is the first argument, etc. The variable **ARG** should be long enough to accommodate the longest argument you expect. If an argument is longer than **ARG**, **GETARG** discards characters from the right-hand side of the argument until it fits. **GETARG** does not distinguish between different argument types; it treats all arguments as strings of characters, and your program must perform any necessary interpretation and conversion.

Use the **IARGC** function:

```
INTEGER I
I=IARGC()
```

IARGC has no argument; it returns an index to the last argument for this program on the command line (i.e., the total number of arguments passed to this program). For example, the FORTRAN statement:

```
CHARACTER*8 C
CALL GETARG(IARGC(),C)
```

sets **C** equal to the first eight characters of the last argument on the command line.

The qualifiers for redirecting standard input and standard output are not command line arguments; they are interpreted by the shell. In the command:

```
% command 346 > file
```

346 is argument 1; the redirection > *file* is not an argument and does not change the argument count. A call to **IARGC** would reveal that this command has only one argument.

Similarly, **GETARG** and **IARGC** only count arguments intended for the program in which they occur. Consider the following UNIX command line, which has several pipes:

```
% com1 a 32.6 in.txt <infile | com2 list.txt 3e5 | \
com3 -n -a >outfile
```

A call to **IARGC** in **com1** will return the value 3, counting the arguments **a**, **32.6**, and **in.txt**. Likewise, **com2** has two arguments (**list.txt** and **3e5**), as does **com3**.

The previous example illustrates another important fact about UNIX command line arguments. Command line options are no different from any other argument. Therefore, **-n** is argument 1 to **com3**, and -a is argument 2. For another example, consider the FORTRAN compiler. The compilation command:

```
% f77 -o tangle tangle.F
```

has three arguments. In order, they are the option **-o** and the filenames *tangle* and *tangle.F*. The FORTRAN compiler reads these arguments as strings and interprets them accordingly.

Accessing the Environment

A number of UNIX system calls give FORTRAN programs access to the UNIX environment. These calls report the login name, group identification number and user identification number of the person running the program, the values of environment variables, and other environment information.

The function **GETCWD** copies the complete pathname of the current working directory into its argument, which must be a **CHARACTER** variable. It returns 0 if it is successful and an error code if it fails. Use it as follows:

```
CHARACTER *60 WORK
I = GETCWD( WORK )
```

This function call writes the current working directory into the **CHARACTER** variable **WORK**. If the pathname is longer than **WORK**, GETCWD will only copy the beginning of the pathname.

The function **GETLOG** copies the user's login name into its argument, which must be a character variable. This login name will be the null string if the program calling **GETLOG** is disconnected from a terminal. If **GETLOG** succeeds, it returns zero; if it fails, it returns a positive error code. For example:

```
CHARACTER*15 NAME
I=GETLOG(NAME)
```

copies the user's name into the variable **NAME**. Again, it only copies the first part of the name if the variable **NAME** isn't long enough.

The function **GETPID** returns the identification number of the process in which the program is running. For example:

```
INTEGER PID
PID=GETPID()
```

sets the variable **PID** equal to the process identification (PID) number. Note that this function is particularly useful when you need to construct a name for a temporary file. Building a temporary filename from a PID number virtually guarantees that the filename will be unique.

The subroutine **GETENV** reads the value of any environment variable. The call:

```
CHARACTER*20 VARNAME, VALUE
CALL GETENV(VARNAME, VALUE)
```

reads the environment variable named **VARNAME**. It copies the value of this variable into **VALUE**. If there is no variable named **VARNAME**, **GETENV** will fill **VALUE** with blanks. Again, **VARNAME** and **VALUE** can have any length. If the value of **VARNAME** is longer than **VALUE**, GETENV will only copy the beginning of **VARNAME**. For example, the statement:

```
CALL GETENV("TERM", VALUE)
```

copies the initial portion of the **TERM** variable into **VALUE**.

Timing

Two functions, **ETIME** and **DTIME**, let FORTRAN programs measure time. This is useful for performance tuning. They are used as follows:

```
REAL TIMEARRAY(2)
REAL ELAPSE
REAL DELAPSE
ELAPSE=ETIME(TIMEARRAY)
DELAPSE=DTIME(TIMEARRAY)
```

ETIME returns a real number which is the total CPU time used for this process since it began executing. **DTIME** returns a real number which is the running time for this process since the last call to **DTIME**. Both procedures use **TIMEARRAY** to return the user time and system time separately; **TIMEARRAY(1)** reports the user time, and **TIMEARRAY(2)** supports the system time. For example, the statements:

```
REAL DELAPSE, TIMEARRAY(2), X
INTEGER I
X=1
DELAPSE=DTIME(TIMEARRAY)
DO 10 I=1, 100000
X=X+1/X
10    CONTINUE
DELAPSE=DTIME(TIMEARRAY)
```

set **DELAPSE** to the time required to compute the loop **DO 10 I=1,100000**.

IDATE and **ITIME** are subroutines that report the current date and time in numerical form. They are used as follows:

```
INTEGER DMY(3)
INTEGER HMS(3)
CALL IDATE(DMY)
CALL ITIME(HMS)
```

IDATE fills **DMY(1)** with the current day of the month, **DMY(2)** with the current month of the year (as an integer between 1 and 12), and **DMY(3)** the current year (as a number greater than 1969). **ITIME** fills **HMS(1)** with current hour of the day on a 24-hour clock, **HMS(2)** with the current minute within the hour, and **HMS(3)** with the current second within the minute. You can use these subroutines to compute elapsed ("wall-clock") time.

Mathematical Routines

RAND, **DRAND**, and **IRAND** are UNIX functions that return random numbers. **RAND** and **DRAND** return single- and double-precision random numbers between 0 and 1. **IRAND** returns a positive integer between 0 and 2147483647 (2**31-1). They are used as follows:

```
INTEGER FLAG, IRANDOM
REAL RANDOM
DOUBLE DRANDOM
IRANDOM=IRAND(FLAG)
RANDOM=RAND(FLAG)
DRANDOM=DRAND(FLAG)
```

where **FLAG** is an integer that determines the seed for the random number generator. If **FLAG** is 0, these functions return the next random number generated by the current seed. If **FLAG** is 1, these functions return the first random number generated by the current seed (i.e., they return to the beginning of the random number sequence). If **FLAG** has some other positive value, that value is used as a new seed for the random number generator.

UNIX provides a complete set of intrinsic functions. In Berkeley Version 4.3, these functions are exemplary in their accuracy but have been justly criticized for their speed. This has forced vendors for whom performance is critical to develop their own intrinsics, combining improved speed with the accuracy of the standard set. In addition to the intrinsic functions, the math library also provides Bessel functions.

Executing UNIX Commands

The function **SYSTEM** lets a FORTRAN program execute any UNIX command. Its argument is a character variable; it executes the character variable as a command and returns the command's exit code, which is defined in the next section. For example:

```
CHARACTER*14 CMD
CMD='diff a b > c'
I=SYSTEM(CMD)
```

executes the UNIX command **diff a b > c** in the current directory. The returned variable **I** is the exit code returned by **diff**. In this case, the exit code contains some information about the differences between files *a* and *b*, although **diff** is something of an exception; most UNIX commands return 0 to indicate success and 1 to indicate some kind of error.

Note that the **SYSTEM** call starts a new UNIX shell to execute its argument. This means that the program it executes (for example, the previous **diff** command) can use standard input and standard output without interacting with any I/O your program does.

System Error Handling

UNIX programs have three different methods for handling errors:

- **Exit codes.** Every program you run has a *return value*. By convention, this value is 0 if the program finishes correctly and nonzero otherwise. You can use nonzero return values to provide information about what kind of error occurred.

- **Standard system errors.** If an error occurs while a program is executing a system call, UNIX sets the **errno** variable. The function that fails will return some value indicating that it was unsuccessful. Programs can then inspect the **errno** variable to find out more about what happened. In some cases, the failing function may simply terminate the program, as this is often the case with I/O errors.

- **Signals.** Signals are used to handle severe errors. When the operating system detects a severe error (e.g., an attempt to reference a memory address that does not belong to the program), it sends the program a signal. While programs have some freedom about how they handle signals, by default most signals cause the program to terminate immediately.

Returning an Exit Code

Whether they are FORTRAN programs, C programs, or standard utilities, UNIX programs always return an exit code. Exit codes usually go unnoticed but are always present. Exit codes are most often used by shell scripts and by **make**, which may take some alternative action if the program doesn't finish correctly.

By convention, most programs return an exit code of zero to indicate normal completion. Nonzero exit codes usually mean that an error has occurred. There are some notable violations to this convention (e.g., **cmp** and **diff**), but we recommend you obey it. FORTRAN programs always return a 0 exit code unless you use EXIT to do otherwise:

```
INTEGER CODE
CALL EXIT(CODE)
```

The argument **CODE** must have a value between 0 and 255.

C shell users can print exit codes by entering the command:

```
% echo $status
```

If you use the Bourne shell (**sh**), after running a program, you can print the exit code with the command:

```
$ echo $?
```

Standard System Errors

The UNIX standard system errors, commonly referred to as *errnos*, provide a way of codifying the errors that occur during system calls. Whenever an error occurs during a system call, UNIX stores an *error number* in a global variable called **errno**. This number identifies what kind of error took place. UNIX then terminates the system call, returning a value that indicates something has gone wrong. By convention, a returned value of positive or zero indicates success, while negative values indicate that an error has occurred. However, there are exceptions to these rules, particularly among the FORTRAN functions. Before interpreting the returned value of a system call, make sure that you check its description in the *UNIX Programmer's Reference Manual*. System calls that you can make directly from FORTRAN are discussed in Section 3F. A complete list of error numbers and their meanings can be found in Appendix D, *UNIX Error Numbers and Signals*. Right now we will discuss techniques to access the **errno** variable in FORTRAN.

FORTRAN I/O statements give you direct access to the error number. If you use an **IOSTAT=** specifier in an I/O statement, your error variable will be set to the error number if the I/O statement fails. If you do not use an **IOSTAT=** or an **ERR=** specifier, the program will print an error message, showing the error number and the explanatory string associated with it, and terminate.

Aside from I/O, FORTRAN programs cannot usually access error numbers directly. As we have said, all system routines have some way of telling you whether an error occurred, but there is no general rule for how this is done. Three system calls are provided to help you: **IERRNO**, **PERROR**, and **GERROR**. **IERRNO** simply returns the most recent error code by reading the **errno** variable. The program can then interpret the error code on its own and take corrective action, if possible. **IERRNO** has no arguments and returns an **INTEGER**.

PERROR provides a convenient way to report error information to the user. It is used as follows:

```
CHARACTER*any ERRSTRING
CALL PERROR(ERRSTRING)
```

PERROR reads the **errno** variable and translates it into a standardized error message. It then prints **ERRSTRING** followed by the standardized message on logical unit 0. For example, consider the call:

```
CALL PERROR("I/O processing")
```

If this call to **PERROR** takes place after system error 2 has occurred, the message "I/O processing: no such file or directory" will be sent to logical unit 0. "No such file or directory" is the standard message that is associated with system error 2. Again, we'll discuss the standard system error codes later in this chapter.

GERROR simply copies the standard message associated with the most recent error into a string and lets the program format the string on its own:

```
CHARACTER*128 ERRSTRING
ERRSTRING=GERROR()
```

The error message will be at most as long as **ERRSTRING**. If it is longer than **ERRSTRING, GERROR** will omit the end of the message.

Signals

The UNIX operating system sends signals to programs to indicate program faults, user-requested interrupts, and other situations. Many signals are purely informative; others cause the program to change its state in some way. For example, when you enter CTRL-C at the keyboard, you are sending the program signal 2 (SIGINT), which tells the program to terminate. When you press CTRL-Z, you are sending signal 18 (SIGTSTP), which tells the program to stop. The commands **fg** and **bg** send signal 19 (SIGCONT), allowing a stopped program to continue. Other signals represent illegal instructions, segmentation violations, etc. A complete list of UNIX signals can be found in Appendix D, *UNIX Error Numbers and Signals*.

At the most basic level, a signal is simply an interprocess communication mechanism. Programs are allowed to use the standard UNIX signals to send certain predefined messages. Even the most extreme signals are nothing more than interprocess messages between the kernel and the application. After deciding that an error has occurred, the kernel sends the application a message telling it to quit as soon as possible.

By default, a program takes one of five actions when it receives a signal:

Ignore   Ignore the signal, and keep running as if nothing happened. This is the default action for most signals that are purely informative (e.g., if the status of a child process changed). You must install a signal handler for these signals if you want to take notice of them.

Terminate   Quit; it is impossible to restart the program. This is the default action for most signals that are not informational (e.g., the hang-up signal).

Core dump   Quit; it is impossible to restart the program. Leave a copy of the program's image in the file *core* subject to size limitations imposed by the UNIX shell. This is the default for signals reporting a serious error (e.g., a memory access violation).

Stop   Stop running in a way that allows the program to be restarted.

Continue   Resume running, given that the program is currently stopped.

The system function **SIGNAL** lets you change the default action for any signal. It is used as follows:

```
EXTERNAL HANDLER
INTEGER SIGNUM, ACTION
IRESULT=SIGNAL(SIGNUM, HANDLER, ACTION)
```

The argument **SIGNUM** is a signal number; signal numbers are integers from 1 to 31. The argument **ACTION** sets the new default action for the signal and can have the following values:

-1   When the given **SIGNAL** is sent to the program, call the signal handler **HANDLER**. The signal number is passed to the handler as an argument.

0   Restore the signal's default action. The **HANDLER** argument is ignored.

+1   When the given **SIGNAL** is sent to the program, ignore it completely. The **HANDLER** argument is ignored.

The returned value, **IRESULT**, shows you whether the call to **SIGNAL** succeeded. It also tells you what the previous action was for the signal. In many cases, this is important; you may want to restore the previous action or the default action at some later time. The following list shows how to interpret **IRESULT**:

negative   The call failed; **IRESULT** is the negative of an error number.

0   The call succeeded; the signal's default action was changed.

+1   The call succeeded; prior to this call, the signal was ignored.

positive, greater than one
    The call succeeded; **IRESULT** is the address of the old signal handler (i.e., the handler that would have been called prior to this call).

For example, to make a program ignore a signal, make the following system call:

```
IRETURN=SIGNAL(NUMBER, ANYTHING, +1)
```

This call means "ignore the signal specified by **NUMBER**." The argument **ANYTHING** is ignored; by convention, it should be an integer. After this call to **SIGNAL**, the program will continue running uninterrupted upon receiving the signal **NUMBER**. You cannot ignore signals 9 or 17; if **NUMBER** has either of these values, this call to **SIGNAL** has no effect. For example, if you want a program to ignore the hang-up signal, add the statement:

```
IRETURN=SIGNAL(1, 0, +1)
```

With this line of code, the program will continue running even if your terminal is disconnected from it.

After having changed the program's behavior for some signal, you can restore the default behavior with the following call to **SIGNAL**:

```
IRETURN=SIGNAL(NUMBER, ANYTHING, 0)
```

Again, **ANYTHING** is ignored.

Rather than ignoring a signal, you may want to install your own signal handler. This handler is a subroutine that you have written; it may do anything you want. To install a signal handler, call **SIGNAL** as follows:

```
EXTERNAL HANDLER
...
IRETURN=SIGNAL(NUMBER, HANDLER, -1)
```

This call means "call the subroutine **HANDLER** upon receiving the signal **NUMBER**." **HANDLER** is called with **NUMBER** as an argument. You may not install your own handler for signals 9 and 17; if **NUMBER** has either of these values, the call to **SIGNAL** has no effect.

For example, consider a signal handler for signal 18, which is generated by entering CTRL-Z at the terminal. This signal normally stops the program; you can resume execution at a later time. We want to write a handler that will disable this feature and print a warning message on standard error. The following subroutine achieves this:

```
SUBROUTINE MYHANDLER(ISIGNUM)
PRINT (UNIT=0, FMT=*) "SIGNAL:  NUMBER", ISIGNUM
PRINT (UNIT=0, FMT=*) "CAN'T PAUSE THIS WAY"
RETURN
END
```

To install this handler (i.e., to tell UNIX to call **MYHANDLER** when signal 18 occurs), add the following code to the program's **MAIN** routine:

```
EXTERNAL MYHANDLER
IRETURN=SIGNAL(18, MYHANDLER, -1)
```

You must declare **MYHANDLER** as an external function, even though it may appear within the same file.

SIGNAL returns an integer value. If this value is negative, the call to **SIGNAL** failed; it was probably called incorrectly. If this value is zero, the call to **SIGNAL** succeeded in changing the default action. If the returned value is 1, then the call succeeded in restoring some signal handling action when the signal was previously ignored. If the returned value is greater than 1, the call to **SIGNAL** succeeded and the returned value is the address of the old program-defined signal handler (i.e., the signal handler that is being replaced by this call).

NOTE

SIGNAL does not warn about attempts to change the default behavior of signals 9 and 17. In these cases, **SIGNAL** returns 0, as if everything had proceeded normally.

Installing Local Programs

After you have developed and debugged a program for use at your site, you may want to install it so that all users of your system have access to it. A directory named */usr/local/bin* is reserved for locally developed programs. This directory should be on the **PATH** of all users of your system.

Before installing a program, make sure that its name is unique (i.e., that its name does not conflict with the name of any other public program). To do this, use the command **whereis** *name* or **which** *name*, both of which tell you whether a command called *name* exists.

- Use the **strip** command to strip the symbol table from the program by entering the command:

      % **strip** *progname*

  where *progname* is the name of the program you are installing. This reduces the program's size but makes it difficult to use the **adb** and **dbx** debuggers.

- Move the program's executable binary to */usr/local/bin* with the command:

      % **mv** *progname* /usr/local/bin

- Use **chmod** to change the program's access mode to 755 with the command:

      % **chmod 755** *progname*

  This lets all users execute the program.

- Use **chgrp** to make the program's group *bin* (the group for most public programs) with the command:

    ```
    % chgrp bin progname
    ```

- Make sure that the program can access any files it needs in its new location.
- Send mail to all users telling them to give the command **rehash**.

NOTE

You will need to be logged in as superuser to change the file's owner and group. See your system administrator for the superuser password, or have the administrator install your program.

At your site, the system administrator may have decided to rename this directory. If */usr/local/bin* does not exist or is not in use, ask your system administrator where to put a released program. Note that program libraries should be placed in the directory */usr/local/lib*, or the equivalent thereof.

After installing a program, you should also write a reference page entry to provide on-line documentation for the program. We won't describe how to use **troff** or **nroff** to format this entry properly; rather, copy a file from the directory */usr/man/man1* and use that as a base for your reference page. Before doing this, it will be helpful to read the introduction to **troff** in the *User's Supplementary Documents*. The best way to learn this macro package is to copy and experiment with the descriptions already in the on-line manual.

When you have developed a new reference page, install it in the directory */usr/man/man1* with the filename *progname.l* using the procedure previously described (where *l* is the letter "l", not the digit "1"). This directory is reserved for documenting programs developed at your local site; it is initially empty. After installing your **man** page, enter the command **catman** -w. This rebuilds the database that **apropos** uses. When you are finished, other users will be able to use **apropos** and **man** to read your documentation.

5

Debugging FORTRAN Programs

Source-level Debugging with dbx
Debugging at the Assembly Level
with adb

This chapter describes the tools available for debugging FORTRAN programs. Two general purpose debugging tools are available: the **dbx** source-level symbolic debugger and the **adb** machine language debugger. The **dbx** debugger lets you work with your program on the source-code level: you can refer to variables by name and you can work in terms of program line numbers (rather than memory addresses). The **adb** debugger is extremely powerful but difficult to use. If you know the assembly language of your system, you can do almost anything with it; if you really need (or want) to dig into the bits, you need **adb**. Even if you don't know assembly language, you can still gather some important information. We will not discuss the **sdb** debugger, which is the System V equivalent to **dbx**.

Debugging code produced by any optimizing compiler is difficult since, by nature, optimization changes the program itself. The changes introduced by optimization will cause the program image to diverge from a strict interpretation of the source code. Your life will be easier if you debug new programs as thoroughly as possible before trying to optimize them. It is also easiest to debug code that conforms strictly to the FORTRAN standard. Programs that play fast and loose with the standard can be hard to debug. On some systems, optimizing such code may reveal bugs that were not previously apparent.

Source-level Debugging with dbx

dbx is a source-level symbolic debugging tool. It can be used with programs written in FORTRAN, C, and several other languages. It lets you run a program, stop execution within the program, examine and change variables during execution, call subroutines, and trace how the program executes. This section proceeds by describing **dbx**'s basic features and commands in their simplest terms. At first, we'll make the examples as simple as possible. We will address more difficult issues later.

The **dbx** debugger represents some very good ideas, coupled with some significant problems. As you start learning **dbx**, be aware of its biggest problems. You will end up less frustrated and able to appreciate how useful the tool is, despite its problems. The two most important limitations of **dbx** are:

- While **dbx** was intended to debug C, FORTRAN, PASCAL, and another language called Modula, it is definitely biased in favor of C. As a FORTRAN programmer, you will have to learn some C idioms. Fortunately, these are relatively minor; we will discuss the C features you need to know as the topics come up.

- Some of the breakpoint and execution trace options can make your program run extremely slowly—intolerably slowly, for any practical application. These tend to be the most interesting options. Don't despair. There are some workarounds that limit the flexibility of these options but still give a reasonable (if not stunning) performance. We will point out which debugging features lead to unacceptable debugging performance and how to work around them.

Compilation for dbx

Before you can use **dbx** to debug a program, compile your code with the **-g** option. This causes the compiler to generate an augmented symbol table. For example, the command:

```
% f77 -g file1.F file2.F file3.o
```

compiles the FORTRAN source files *file1.F* and *file2.F*, generating an expanded symbol table for use with **dbx**. These files are linked with *file3.o*, an object file that has already been compiled. **dbx** can be used to debug source code in *file1.F* and *file2.F*, but not code from *file3.F* unless the code was also compiled with the **-g** flag. On some systems, **-g** and **-O** are incompatible; **dbx** won't work on optimized code. It is more often the case that **dbx** will let you work with optimized code, but it won't be as useful.

Starting dbx

To debug a compiled program with **dbx**, use the command:

```
% dbx program core-dump
```

program is the filename of the executable file you want to debug. If you do not supply an executable, **dbx** will prompt you by printing the message:

```
enter object file name (default is 'a.out'):
```

If you press RETURN , **dbx** will read the object file *a.out* if it exists. If you type a filename, **dbx** will read the object file you request. If **dbx** cannot find a file with the appropriate name or if that file is not an object file, **dbx** will quit, printing the message:

```
dbx: fatal error: can't read filename
```

core-dump is optional; it is the name of a core dump file left from an earlier attempt to run your program. By examining the core dump with **dbx**, you can discover where the program failed and the reason for its failure. For example, the command:

```
% dbx exps core
```

tells **dbx** to read the executable file *exps* and the core dump *core*.

You do not have to give **dbx** the name of the source file corresponding to the object file you are debugging. It determines the names of the relevant source files from the executable's symbol table. When **dbx** has finished reading the symbol table and is ready for a command, it will print the prompt "(dbx)".

Options

You can request several options when you invoke **dbx**. The most useful are:

-r   Run immediately. **dbx** executes the program immediately. If execution terminates normally, **dbx** exits without giving you the chance to execute any debugging commands. If execution terminates prematurely, **dbx** reports the problem and enters its debugging mode, as shown below:

```
% dbx -r a.out
Type 'help' for help.
   TYPE X                  Output from the program a.out
345                        Input to the program
Entering debugger ...
reading symbolic information ...
 type 'help' for help

floating point exception in computeab at 0xf0
(dbx)
```

This shows that a floating-point exception occurred in the function or subroutine called **COMPUTEAB** at location 0xf0. (The prefix "0x" is a UNIX notation to indicate a hexadecimal number.) This may be a routine in your program or the name of a library routine that is otherwise unfamiliar to you. **dbx** prompts you for further commands, which can give you more information about where and why this exception occurred. The command **where** (discussed below) gives more information about where the failure occurred. After an exception, **where** is always useful.

-I *dir* Normally **dbx** looks for source files in the current directory and in the directory in which the object file is located. This option adds *dir* to the list of directories in which **dbx** will look. For example, consider a large program called **digest** located in the directory */work/bin* and with sources in the directories */work/phase1*, */work/phase2*, and */work/gastro*. To debug this program easily, use the command:

```
% dbx -I /work/phase1 -I /work/phase2 \
     -I /work/gastro digest
```

With these options, **dbx** will look in five directories to find source files for the executable program **digest**: */work/phase1*, */work/phase2*, */work/gastro*, */work/bin*, and your current directory. Sources for a large development effort will typically be organized with different sections of the program's source code located in different directories.

-c *file* Before accepting any commands, **dbx** will read and execute the commands in *file*. This is a good way to initialize **dbx**. You can also initialize **dbx** by placing start-up commands in file *.dbxinit* in your home directory.

Basic dbx Commands

The basic **dbx** commands are:

list   List the contents of the source file corresponding to the program being executed.

run   Execute the program.

stop   Set a breakpoint in the program.

cont   Continue execution from a breakpoint.

trace   Trace the execution of a variable, subroutine, or expression.

when   Execute **dbx** commands when the program reaches a certain line or subroutine.

status   Show all outstanding breakpoints and traces.

delete   Delete a trace or breakpoint.

print   Print the value of a variable or expression.

whatis   Print the type of a variable, subroutine, or function.

where   Print the current location within the program and a stack trace showing how the current location was reached.

assign   Assign a value to a variable.

next   Execute the next source line, executing a function or subroutine in its entirety.

step   Execute the next source line, stepping into a function or subroutine if necessary.

call   Execute a function or subroutine.

quit   Exit **dbx**.

exit   Exit **dbx**.

Listing a File

To see the contents of the source file from which the executable program was compiled, use the command **list**:

```
(dbx) list
    1              INTEGER I
    2              REAL EXPX, PWR, X
    3
    4   10         PRINT *, "TYPE X"
->  5              READ *,X
    6              EXPX = O
 . . .
```

The numbers on the left side are the line numbers of your source program; FORTRAN labels are shown to their right (e.g., line 4 of this file has the FORTRAN label 10). You will use **dbx**'s line numbers to issue debugging commands. **dbx** counts all lines, including comments and blank lines. On the left margin, as in line 5, **dbx** prints a – (hyphen) on each line for which a breakpoint or some other debugging command is in effect at this line. **dbx** prints a > (right angle bracket) at the line where it is stopped. You often see – and > together, as in the display above. **dbx** is is telling you that it is currently stopped at a breakpoint on line 5.

To print a group of lines from the file you are currently debugging, use a **list** command of the form:

```
(dbx) list line1,line2
```

To list the first 10 lines from a particular subroutine, use a **list** command of this form:

```
(dbx) list routine-name
```

If you repeat the **list** command without any arguments, **dbx** will list the next few lines and so on until it reaches the end of the file. By default, **dbx** lists 10 lines each time you enter the command. The section "Advanced Features" later in this chapter explains how to change this default setting.

dbx can't take into account changes to the code produced by conditional compilation (**#ifdef**) or file inclusion (**#include** or **INCLUDE** statements). You will see these statements in your listings *verbatim*; it is your responsibility to know what they did. You have to know how the program was compiled—in particular, what was included and what was omitted. However, **dbx** will always be able to find source code, regardless of how it is included.

If **dbx** cannot find the source file required to produce any listing, it will print the message:

```
Couldn't read filename
```

In this message, *filename* identifies a source file that **dbx** cannot access.

If **dbx** is asked to list a line that falls past the end of the file, it will print the message:

```
"filename" has only 14 lines
```

If **dbx** is asked to list (or otherwise work with) a subroutine that is not defined in the program, it will print the message:

```
"routine-name" is not defined
```

Executing a Program

To run the program you are debugging, use the **run** command. This may be followed by any arguments you want to pass to the program, including the standard input and output specifiers < and >. Arguments may not include the shell metacharacters for wildcards (*, ?, [,]) and history (!). For example, consider running the program **exp** through **dbx**. The following **dbx** command runs **exp** with the argument -b, taking the standard input to **exp** from *invalues* and redirecting standard output to the file *outtable*:

```
% dbx exp
reading symbolic information ...
Type 'help' for help
(dbx) run -b < invalues > outtable
```

That is, this command runs **exp -b < invalues > outtable**. If you have not set any breakpoints or used any other **dbx** debugging features, **exp** will run until it terminates, either correctly or incorrectly. When the program terminates, **dbx** prints the message:

```
execution completed, exit code is n
(dbx)
```

where *n* is the exit code returned by the program. FORTRAN programs can call the system routine **EXIT(***n***)** to return a nonzero value; if you do not call **EXIT**, the program will return zero by default. Upon termination, **dbx** prints the prompt ("dbx") to show that it is waiting for the next command. If you invoked **dbx** with the -r option and the program terminates without a fatal error, **dbx** returns to the UNIX shell.

When used without arguments, the **rerun** command will execute the program again with the same arguments it had the last time it was executed. When used with arguments, **rerun** is identical to **run**.

To terminate a program while it is running under **dbx** control, press CTRL-C. This returns control to **dbx**, which then prompts for a new command; it does not return directly to the shell. To exit **dbx**, enter either **quit** or **exit**:

```
(dbx) run
CTRL-C
interrupt in read at 0x92f8
(dbx) quit
```

quit and **exit** behave identically when used as keyboard commands. Their behavior differs when they appear in scripts. **exit** always terminates **dbx**, returning to the UNIX shell. **quit** only returns to the next higher command level (i.e., to whatever invoked the script in which the **quit** command appears). In most cases, this means **quit** returns to the **dbx** keyboard command level. If one script invokes another script and **quit** appears within the second script, the **quit** command returns control to the first script. This is similar to a subroutine **RETURN** statement.

If the program terminates abnormally, control returns to **dbx**. You can then use **dbx** commands to find out why the program terminated. The preceding example shows a program run that failed because of a floating-point exception during execution. The **where** command provides information about the routine and about the line that was executing when the exception occurred:

```
(dbx) run
Floating Exception
(dbx) where
fact(j = 35, factorial = 2.952326e+038), line 43
    in "adbplay2.f"
fmyexp(x = 0.0, j = 345), line
27 in "adbplay2.f"
main, line 14 in "adbplay2.f"
main at 0x63c4
(dbx)
```

where produces a list of all active procedures and the arguments with which they were called, starting with the most recent. This example shows that the routine **FACT** was executing line 43 when the exception occurred, **FACT** was called by **FMYEXP** at line 27, **FMYEXP** was called by the program's **MAIN** procedure at line 14, and the **MAIN** procedure was called by the FORTRAN run-time library's main procedure at location 0x63c4. **dbx** prints FORTRAN routine and variable names in lowercase because **f77** translates the FORTRAN program into lowercase by default.

You can inspect the variable values by using the **print** command:

```
(dbx) list 43
   43                   FACTORIAL = FACTORIAL*I
(dbx) print factorial
5.904652e+038
```

The **list** command shows the statement in which the exception occurred. Note that the number 43 is a **dbx** line number, not a FORTRAN statement label. The **print** command tells **dbx** to print the current value of the variable **FACTORIAL**. The current value of **FACTORIAL** appears on the next line. In this case, it is a good guess that the floating-point exception occurred because of a floating-point overflow when computing **FACTORIAL**.

Breakpoints

Breakpoints let you stop a program temporarily while it is executing. While the program is stopped at a breakpoint, you can examine or modify variables, execute subroutines and functions, or execute any other **dbx** command. This lets you examine the program's state to determine whether execution is proceeding correctly. You can then resume program execution at the point where it left off.

The **stop** command sets breakpoints in the program you are debugging. This command has the following four different forms:

stop at *line-number* Stop the program just before executing the given line.

stop in *routine-name* Stop the program just before entering the named routine.

stop if *condition* Stop the program if the following *condition* is true.

stop *variable* Stop the program when *variable* changes values.

The four breakpoint commands fall into two categories: *positional breakpoints* that occur at a particular location in the code (i.e., at the entrance to a subroutine or at a particular line) and *conditional breakpoints* that occur when any particular condition is met (e.g., when two variables are equal). The first two forms of the **stop** command set positional breakpoints, and the second two forms set conditional breakpoints. Positional breakpoints are absolutely basic to debugging. Conditional breakpoints look more useful than they actually are; setting a conditional breakpoint can make execution so slow that the debugger is next to useless. Fortunately, you can mitigate this effect by combining positional and conditional breakpoints. Asking **dbx** to stop when the variable **K** changes will have a disastrous effect on execution speed, but asking **dbx** to stop at line 25 if **K** has changed will work.

Now let's revisit the breakpoint commands in more detail. The command **stop in** *routine-name* sets a breakpoint at the entrance to the specified function or subroutine. When the program is executing, **dbx** will temporarily halt the program at the first executable line of the given function or subroutine. If the subroutine you name does not exist, **dbx** prints the message:

```
"function-name" is not defined
```

and ignores the command. For example, the **stop** command below sets a breakpoint at the entrance to the subroutine **FMYEXP**. The **run** command executes the program until it reaches the beginning of the routine **FMYEXP**. Execution stops at the first executable line within **FMYEXP**, which is a DO loop beginning on line 24 of the source file:

```
(dbx) stop in fmyexp
[11] stop in fmyexp
(dbx) run
[11] stopped in fmyexp at line 24
    23 C   mclaurin loop
->  24        DO 10 I = 1,J
    25        CALL FACT(I,FCT)
    25        F = F+POW(X,I)/FCT
(dbx)
```

When you set the breakpoint, **dbx** assigns an identification number (in this case, 11) and prints its internal description. Whenever it reaches a breakpoint, **dbx** prints the breakpoint's identification number, the description, and the current line number. If you have several breakpoints set in the program, the identification number tells you which one caused the program to stop. Note that the internal description may differ from your original breakpoint command. After describing the breakpoint, **dbx** lists a few lines from the program, showing the line at which you are stopped. The -> (right arrow) shows that a breakpoint has been set at line 24 (the first executable line of **FMYEXP**) and that you are currently stopped at this breakpoint. Remember that the – (hyphen) and the > (right angle bracket) are two separate symbols. The – shows the location of a positional breakpoint, and the > shows the line at which execution has stopped.

To stop execution when the program reaches a particular source line, use the **stop at** *line-number* command. In this command, *line-number* must be one of the line numbers assigned by **dbx**, not a FORTRAN label. Remember that **dbx** listings show line numbers in the left column. For example, the following **stop** command sets a breakpoint at line 25 of the program:

```
(dbx) stop at 25
[17] stop at 25
(dbx) run
[17] stopped in fmyexp at line 25
->  25    10    CALL FACT(I,FCT)
```

The **run** command executes the program, which halts before executing the statemnet on line 25. **dbx** prints out the number identifying this breakpoint, the name of the function, the line number, and the line at which the program is stopped. If the program is built from many source files, you set breakpoints in files other than the current source file like this:

```
(dbx) stop at "filename":line-number
```

Remember that the filename must be inside quotation marks. If you set a breakpoint at a line that is not an executable statement (e.g., a comment or a **DIMEN-SION** statement), **dbx** will print the message:

```
no executable code at line n
```

where *n* is the line number you requested for the breakpoint. A few **dbx** implementations consider **CONTINUE** statements nonexecutable. This is unfortunate; it is often very useful to set a breakpoint at the end of a loop body.

To set a conditional breakpoint, use the command **stop if** as follows:

```
(dbx) stop if expr
```

where *expr* is a legal **dbx** expression. Some implementations require *expr* to be a relational expression. **dbx** will stop the program when the value of *expr* is nonzero (or, in the case of a relational expression, true). For example, the command:

```
(dbx) stop if I > 10
[4] stop if module.routine.I >  10
```

will cause **dbx** to check the value of **I** after every instruction and halt the program when **I** is greater than 10. Unfortunately, you can't use FORTRAN expressions here; you have to use C-style comparisons taken from the following table:

Relationship	Sign	FORTRAN Equivalent
Greater than	>	.GT.
Less than	<	.LT.
Greater than or equal to	>=	.GE.
Less than or equal to	<=	.LE.
Equal to	==	.EQ.
Not equal to	!=	.NE.

In the previous example, the breakpoint will cause **dbx** to check the value of **I** after each instruction to determine whether **I** has changed values. This slows the program's execution speed considerably—by a factor of 100 or so. This is tolerable in short examples but unusable in practice. You can get reasonably fast execution by combining the **stop if** and **stop at** commands as follows:

```
(dbx) stop at 25 if I > 10
[7] if module.routine.I > 10 { stop } at 25
```

This command asks **dbx** to suspend execution if the value of **I** is greater than 10 when the program reaches line 25. It has a minimal effect on the program's execution speed because **dbx** only needs to check the value of **I** at line 25. Note that it evaluates the expression **I > 10** *before* executing line 10. This is a common source of confusion.

The **stop** *variable-name* command sets a conditional breakpoint that will stop execution whenever the variable *variable-name* changes value. It may be combined with another conditional breakpoint to stop execution if *variable-name* changes value and if some other expression is true; for example, the breakpoint:

```
(dbx) stop LIMIT if LIMIT > 10000
```

will halt execution if the value of **LIMIT** changes, provided that the new value is greater than 10000. Again, this leads to significantly slower program execution because the value of **LIMIT** must be tested after each instruction.

NOTE

When mixing the **stop if** command with other breakpoint commands, the **if** clause must follow an **at** clause, an **in** clause, or a simple variable name. For example:

```
stop if I > 10 at 25
```

is not legal; **dbx** will print the error message "Syntax error" and set a simple conditional breakpoint for the condition **I > 10**.

Continuing Execution from a Breakpoint

When stopped at a breakpoint, you can continue execution with the **cont** command:

```
[9] stopped in fmyexp at line 25
-> 25      CALL FACT(I,FCT)
(dbx) cont
```

Execution will continue until the program ends, you reach another breakpoint, or an error occurs.

If you use the **cont** command when there is no program running, **dbx** will print the message:

```
can't continue execution
```

You will see this message if you have not yet given the **run** command or if the program you are running has terminated, either normally or abnormally.

Deleting Breakpoints

To delete a breakpoint, you need to know about two commands: **status** and **delete**. The **status** command lists all the breakpoints you have created in the program. For example:

```
(dbx) status
[9] stop at 25
[11] stop if adbplay2.fmyexp.i > 2
[12] stop in fmyexp
```

This shows that three breakpoints are currently active, with identification numbers 9, 11, and 12. This list shows how each breakpoint is defined, using **dbx**'s internal representation. Remember that the internal representation is different from the command you gave when you entered the breakpoint.

Once you know the breakpoint's identification number, you can use the **delete** command to get rid of it. For example, the command **delete 9** deletes the breakpoint **stop at 25**. These two commands are also used to delete traces and patches, other **dbx** features that are similar to breakpoints.

Inspecting and Assigning to Variables

While a program is stopped at a breakpoint, you can investigate what has happened during execution. These five basic commands manipulate variables:

whatis   Identify the type of an array or variable.

whereis   Identify where any array, variable, or function name is defined.

print   Print the value of an expression.

assign   Assign a new value to any variable.

dump   List all active variables.

To find the type of any variable, use the command:

```
(dbx) whatis variable-name
```

where *variable-name* is the name of an active variable or array. For example:

```
(dbx) whatis factorial
 (dummy argument) real factorial
```

The **whatis** command shows that the variable FACTORIAL has the type **REAL** and is a dummy argument to a subprogram. Not all versions of **dbx** are as informative, but they will at least give you the FORTRAN data type of a variable.

NOTE

If the program has been optimized, it may not be possible to print the value of a variable or assign it a value. For example, a variable that is assigned to a register or eliminated from the code entirely will not be accessible to **dbx**. It is always possible to use **whatis** to determine a variable's type.

The **whereis** *name* command prints a report showing where *name* is defined within the program. If *name* is a variable, **whereis** will show the routines in which *name* is used. If *name* is a subroutine or function, **whereis** will show the files in which it occurs. For example, consider these two commands:

```
(dbx) whereis i
adbplay2.fact.i adbplay2.fmyexp.i adbplay2.main.i
(dbx) whereis subr
adbplay2.subr
```

The first command shows that three routines within the module **adbplay2** (compiled from **adbplay2.F**) use variables named **I**. This name appears in the routines **FACT** and **FMYEXP** and the program's **MAIN** routine. The second command shows that the routine **SUBR** is also located within the module **adbplay2**. Either it is part of **adbplay2.F** or it is contained within a file that has been included into **adbplay2.F**.

NOTE

The Sun implementation of **dbx** uses left single quotes instead of periods to separate fields in variable names. For example, the preceding report would be:

```
(dbx) whereis i
`adbplay2`fact`i  `adbplay2`fmyexp`i  `adbplay2`main`i
```

We don't know if other manufacturers have followed suit. We will use the traditional **dbx** format.

The **print** *expression* command prints the current value of any variable or expression. For example, the command:

```
(dbx) print A[I]
1.345E002
```

reports that the current value of the array element **A(I)** is 134.5. Note that **dbx** uses C-style array notation rather than FORTRAN notation. You can use **print** to print the value of **COMPLEX** or **DOUBLE COMPLEX** variables, although these may not enter into expressions:

```
(dbx) list 11
   11              Z = CMPLX(RES,X)
(dbx) print z
z = (1.0,0.0)
```

Use the command **assign** to modify or set any variable:

```
(dbx) assign variable = expression
```

where *variable* is the name of a currently active variable and *expression* is a valid
dbx expression. *expression* must match the type of the variable. If it doesn't,
dbx prints the message "Incompatible types." For example, consider the following **assign** commands:

```
(dbx) list 20
20              REAL FLOATV
(dbx) assign floatv = 4.3
(dbx) print floatv
4.3
(dbx) assign floatv = 4
incompatible types
```

The first **assign** gives **FLOATV** the value 4.3. The second **assign** is illegal
because **FLOATV** is a **REAL** variable and cannot be assigned an integer. For
information about **dbx** expressions and a discussion of the rules governing an
expression's type, see the section "dbx Expressions" later in this chapter.

The **dump** command prints the names and values of all the variables in one or
more active routines. It has the following three forms:

dump   With no arguments, the **dump** command prints all of the vari-
                 ables in the current function.

dump .   With the . (dot) argument, the **dump** command prints all of the
                 variables in all active functions and all global variables:
                 FORTRAN common block elements, FORTRAN variables with
                 SAVE status, and C global variables.

dump *function*   With a function or subroutine name as an argument, **dump**
                 prints the names and values of all the variables in the named
                 routine. This routine must be active when you use the **dump**
                 command. We will discuss active and inactive routines later in
                 this chapter.

Single-step Execution

dbx provides two forms of single-step execution. The **next** command executes
the next line of the source program, executing function and subroutine calls wher-
ever necessary. The **step** command executes the next line of the source program,
stepping into a subroutine or function if necessary. To understand the difference

between these two commands, look at their behavior in the context of debugging a simple program. Consider the following example:

```
(dbx) list 12
   12      RES = FMYEXP(I+X,LIM)
(dbx) step
stopped in fmyexp at line 25
 > 25      DO 10 I = 1,J
```

The **step** command executed statement 12 and stopped at the first statement in the function **FMYEXP**, which statement 12 invoked. It did not execute **FMYEXP** in its entirety; instead, it single-stepped into the function. Giving the **step** command repeatedly will execute **FMYEXP** one line at a time, eventually returning to line 13 of the original program.

In contrast, the following **next** command executes line 12 as a whole, including the call to **FMYEXP**:

```
[26] stopped in MAIN at line 12
(dbx) list 12
 > 12      RES = FMYEXP(I+X,LIM)
(dbx) next
stopped in MAIN at line 13
 > 13      PRINT *,RES
```

After the **next** command, **dbx** is ready to execute the next sequential line in the source program. It has executed line 12 entirely, including the call to **FMYEXP**.

The **step** command does not step into built-in functions or library functions. Both **step** and **next** work correctly if the program's source files are not present. **step** prints the warning message:

```
couldn't find "filename"
```

if it cannot find the source file for the routine it is stepping through. It still executes the routine one source line at a time.

Calling Functions

The **dbx** debugger lets you execute a single subroutine call. Three commands support work on individual functions:

whatis *name*   Print the declaration for the named function or subroutine.

call *name*   Call and execute a function or a subroutine.

return *name*   Continue execution until the named subroutine returns, then stop.

The **whatis** command shows how the given subroutine or function is declared, the type of the value it returns, if any, and the types of all its arguments. For example, the **whatis** command in the following example asks for information about the function **FMYEXP**:

```
(dbx) whatis fmyexp
 real function  fmyexp (x, j)
 (dummy argument) real x
 (dummy argument) integer j
```

This shows that **FMYEXP** is a function that returns a **REAL** value; it requires two arguments whose types are **REAL** and **INTEGER**, respectively.

The **call** command executes the named function or subroutine. It has the form:

```
(dbx) call function( arguments )
```

For example, the command:

```
(dbx) call fmyexp(2.0,3)
```

executes the routine **FMYEXP** with the arguments 2.0 and 3. Breakpoints, traces, and any other **dbx** features may be used within the routine. For example:

```
(dbx) call fact(4,factorial)
(dbx) print factorial
factorial = 24.0
```

We use the **call** command to call the subroutine **FACT**. This subroutine stores its result in the second argument. To save this argument, provide the name of a variable within the program, then use the **print** command to inspect the argument. To call a function and print its returned value automatically, use the **print** command directly:

```
(dbx) print fmyexp(1.0,13)
fmyexp(1, 13) = 14.496395111083984
```

dbx is very fussy about type checking for subroutine and function calls. It does not perform any type conversion; the actual arguments to a routine must exactly match the declared types for the dummy arguments. If the arguments do not match, **dbx** prints the message "Type mismatch" for *argument* in *routine-name*. For example, the command **call fmyexp(2,3)** is incorrect, because the first argument to **FMYEXP** has type **REAL**. **dbx** will not implicitly convert the integer 2 to a floating-point number.

If you are stopped at a breakpoint within a subroutine, the command **return** will continue execution until the current subroutine returns. The command:

```
(dbx) return name
```

will continue execution until the procedure *name* (not necessarily the current subroutine) returns.

Tracing Execution

The trace facility lets you watch the value of a variable as it changes or lets you watch the way a routine is called as the program executes. Traces do not stop execution; **dbx** prints reports as the program executes but does not suspend execution. Traces can be global, printing the value of a variable each time it changes, or they can be confined to a routine or to a particular line. **dbx** shows the location of many (but not all) trace commands on a program listing with a - (hyphen).

The **trace** command has several different forms:

trace   Unqualified trace; list every line as it executes.

trace *line-number*

> Print a report each time the program reaches the specified line. **dbx** marks *line-number* with a hyphen.

trace *expression* **at** *line-number*

> Print the value of *expression* each time the program reaches *line-number*. **dbx** marks *line-number* with a hyphen.

trace *variable* **in** *routine*

> Print the value of *variable* each time it changes while executing *routine*. The clause **in** *routine* is optional. **dbx** marks *routine* with a hyphen.

trace *routine1* **in** *routine2*

> Print a report each time *routine1* is called, showing its arguments and returned value, if any. The clause **in** *routine2* is optional. If present, it restricts **dbx** to print reports only when *routine2* is active. **dbx** marks *routine1* and *routine2* with a hyphen.

By itself, the **trace** command prints each line the program executes, noting every function and procedure call. This command produces the following reports:

```
trace:  line-number      fortran-source-line
entering function name
leaving function name
```

A global trace like this usually produces too much information and executes much too slowly to be useful; it prints at least one line for each line of source code that executes. More restricted **trace** commands will usually be more helpful in debugging a program.

The **trace** *variable-name* command will print a report every time *variable-name* changes value. For example:

```
(dbx) trace res
[1] trace res in main
(dbx) run
  X; ITERATIONS initially (at line 9):   res = -2.199219
0
4
after line 28: res = 1.708333
    1.70833
after line 28: res = 6.0
    6.00000
```

This report shows the initial value of **RES** at line 9; it continues by reporting the value of **RES** each time it is changed. This form of the **trace** command executes very slowly, unless qualified with an **at** *line-number* clause.

The **trace** *routine-name* command is one of **dbx**'s most useful debugging features. It doesn't slow execution speed and provides helpful information by showing where and how routines are called. It also works on almost all optimized code. The **trace** *routine* command prints a line whenever the program enters or exits the procedure *routine* during execution. This report shows the arguments with which *routine* is called and its returned value, if any. For example:

```
(dbx) trace fmyexp
```

tells **dbx** to report whenever the program enters or exits **FMYEXP**. The results look like this:

```
(dbx) run
calling fmyexp(x = 1.0, j = 4) from function main
returning 1.708333 from fmyexp
    1.70833
calling fmyexp(x = 2.0, j = 4) from function main
returning 6.0 from fmyexp
    6.00000
calling fmyexp(x = 3.0, j = 4) from function main
returning 15.375 from fmyexp
    15.3750
```

This report shows what happened during three successive calls to **FMYEXP**. By adding the clause **in** *calling-routine*, you can restrict **dbx** to print only calls to *routine* that are made when *calling-routine* is active. This includes calls made by *calling-routine* itself and calls made by any routine that is underneath *calling-routine*.

The command **trace** *expression* **at** *line-number* prints the value of *expression* every time the program reaches *line-number*. **dbx** computes the value of *expression* before executing the given line. Often, *expression* is a single variable, but it can be any expression allowed in **dbx**. For example, the command **trace RES+1 at line 15** prints the value of the expression **RES+1** just prior to executing line 15:

```
(dbx) trace res+1 at 15
[3] trace res+1 at 15
(dbx) run
at line 15: res+1 = 16667
   3.99168e+07
at line 15: res+1 = 16668
   3.99168e+07
at line 15: res+1 = 16669
   3.99168e+07
at line 15: res+1 = 16670
   3.99168e+07
(dbx) list 14,15
   14      RES = FMYEXP(I/10+X,LIM)
   15      CALL FOBA(11.3)
```

This example shows a typical trace report. It shows the value of **RES+1** just after executing line 14 and prior to executing line 15. This output is mixed with other output from the program. The **at** clause is required. If it is not present, **dbx** will print the message "Can't trace expressions." This facility is particularly useful because it does not significantly slow execution. It cannot be used with optimized code and may not be available on some versions of **dbx**.

It is also possible to combine **trace** commands with conditional clauses. For example:

```
(dbx) trace res if i > 10
```

prints the value of **RES** whenever it changes, but only if **I** is greater than 10. Execution speed severely limits the utility of such traces.

To delete a trace, use the **status** command to show the active traces and find the identification number for the trace you want to delete. Then use the **delete** *id-number* command.

Patches

Some versions of **dbx** have added a **when** command. While this feature is relatively rare, it can be extremely useful.* The **when** command lets you add patches

---

* "Added" is a bit euphemistic. The command is present in most versions of **dbx**, but it does not work and is not documented. A few manufacturers, Sun in particular, have gotten this code to work correctly.

to a program. This command determines when you have reached a given line or routine, executes a series of **dbx** commands automatically, then lets the program continue executing. As with breakpoints and traces, the **list** command prints a - (hyphen) before each line on which a **when** command is in effect.

when has two basic forms:

when at *line* { *c1*; *c2*; ...; }
>   Execute **dbx** commands c1, c2, etc., whenever the program encounters *line*.

when in *proc* { *c1*; *c2*; ...; }
>   Execute **dbx** commands *c1*, *c2*, etc., whenever the program enters the routine *proc*.

Each **dbx** command within { } (curly braces) must be followed by a ; (semicolon). Don't forget the semicolon after the last command.

For example, if we want to print the values of **I**, **LIM**, and **RES** at line 15, use the following command:

```
(dbx) when at 15 {print "at 15:", i, lim, res;}
[4] print 15, $adbplay2.main.i, lim, res at "adbplay2.F":15
(dbx) run
at 15: 1 2 1.2 These are values printed by the "when" statement
at 15: 2 2 1.2
at 15: 3 2 1.2
...
```

Whenever the program reaches line 15, it executes the **print** command to print a quoted string (the label **"at 15:"**) followed by the values of **I**, **LIM**, and **RES**. This is a convenient shorthand for a series of **trace** commands.

Now let's imagine you have determined certain variables are not being initialized upon entering the routine **FMYEXP**. Normally, you would have to change the source code and recompile in order to continue debugging. The **when** command lets you effectively add code to initialize these variables:

```
(dbx) when in fmyexp {assign f77t = 0.0; assign f = 0.0;}
[10] {   :=   f77t 0;   :=   f 0; } in fmyexp
(dbx) run
...
```

The two **assign** commands take care of initialization and ensure you enter **FMYEXP** correctly whenever it is called. With this under control, you can see whether there are any other problems. This lets you debug more efficiently because you do not need to recompile as often.

when commands are, in many respects, similar to breakpoints and traces. **dbx** assigns an identification number to each patch when you enter it. The **status**

command includes these identification numbers in its report, and the
delete *id-number* command deletes the patch.

Current File and Current Function

So far, this discussion of **dbx** has assumed that a single source file contains the
entire program. For most programs, this will not be the case. Two commands,
file and **func**, help you to work with programs contained in many different source
files. These commands change the current file and the current function, respectively.

Current file and current function are notions **dbx** uses to keep track of its position
within a program. The current file is the file containing the source lines with
which you are currently working. The current function is the subroutine on which
you are currently working.

By themselves, the commands **func** and **file** print the name of the current function
or the current file:

```
(dbx) file
f66compat.F
(dbx) func
initialio
```

With an argument, these commands change the current function or the current
file. For example, the following first command changes the current file to
f66compat.F; the second changes the current function to **IOINIT**:

```
(dbx) file f66compat.F
(dbx) func ioinit
```

Changing the current function implicitly changes the current file. For example,
after giving the **func** previous command, the current file will be the file containing the code for **ioinit**. Changing the current file does not change the current
function.

For example, the following commands change the current file to *file2.F*, list lines
3 through 7 in *file2.F*, then set a breakpoint at line 6:

```
(dbx) file
initialfile.F
(dbx) file file2.F
(dbx) list 3,7
```
Lines 3 through 7 of file2.F
```
...
(dbx) stop at 6
[3] stop at "file2.F":7
```

The **file** command changes the file that **dbx** uses to locate any given line number. Therefore, the **list** and **stop** commands refer to lines in *file2.F*, rather than to *initialfile.F*.

When **dbx** starts, the current function is the first routine in the executable file that was compiled with the **-g** (debugging) option, according to the order in which the program was linked. The current file is the source file containing this routine. Whenever the program stops at a breakpoint, the current function is initially the routine in which the program stopped. The current file contains this routine's source code.

For example, consider a program compiled and debugged with the following series of commands:

```
% f77 -g -c libsrc.F
% f77 -o program mainsrc.F libsrc.o
% dbx program
```

When **dbx** starts, the current function will be the first routine in *libsrc.F* and the current file will be *libsrc.F*. **dbx** has only limited ability to work with routines in *mainsrc.F*, because this module was not compiled with the debugging option.

As part of changing the current function, the **func** command changes the variables that are available for inspection. For example, consider a program with routines named **MAKEFA** and **BOZEA**. Both routines use local variables named **I**. As you debug, the name **I** always refers to the variable named **I** in the current function. Therefore, you can use the **func** command to guarantee that you are referring to the correct variable. For example, the command:

```
(dbx) func makefa
(dbx) print i
```

prints the value of **I** in **MAKEFA**. The following section shows another method for selecting a specific variable from many variables with the same name.

Definitions and Conventions

The next section describes the definitions and conventions that **dbx** uses to refer to variables, functions, and expressions. In most cases, you can use variable and function names directly, as the examples have up to this point. From time to time, however, **dbx** will not do what you expect: it will complain that a variable is "not active" or may refer to a variable with an unexpected name in a different function. The next section explains why these conflicts occur and how to resolve them.

Active and Inactive Variables

At any time, a variable is either *active* or *inactive*. When you are debugging, you may only refer to active variables. If you refer to an inactive variable (e.g., if you try to print the value of an inactive variable), **dbx** will respond with the message:

```
"variable-name" is not active
```

The following rules determine whether a variable is active.

- Global variables are always active, whether the program is running. Global variables are: FORTRAN variables with SAVE status, variables in FORTRAN COMMON blocks, and C global variables. To refer to these variables, you must enter the full variable name. For a discussion of full variable names, see the section "Variable Names" later in this chapter.

- If the program is not running, all nonglobal variables are inactive. A program is considered "running" after it has started and before it has terminated (e.g., when it is stopped at a breakpoint). A program is no longer running after it has terminated.

- A local variable within any routine is active whenever the routine, or any subroutine called by the routine, is running. For example, the variable **I** in the routine **G1** is active whenever **G1** is executing. It remains active while **G1** and any routines that **G1** calls are executing.

Examining a core dump file left by a program that terminated abnormally is a special case. When you are doing this, **dbx** allows you to examine any variable that was active when the program terminated. **dbx** does not allow you to change the value of the variables in a core file; this would be meaningless, since you may not continue execution after an abnormal termination.

Variable Names

A full variable name has the form:

```
$module.routine.name
```

where *name* is the name of the variable, *routine* is the name of the routine in which *name* is found, and *module* is the name of the module in which *routine* is found (i.e., the name of the object file, without the *.o* extension). For example, the full name of the variable **FOO** in a routine named **TRANS** that is found in the object file *objs.o* is **$objs.trans.foo**. The module name is always preceded by a $ (dollar sign). Note that Sun's implementation of **dbx** replaces the dollar sign and each dot with a left single quote (e.g., **'objs'trans'foo**).

You do not need to type the full name every time you refer to the variable **FOO**. First, the module name is superfluous for FORTRAN programs; it is occasionally needed for C programs and is included here for completeness. You do not need to specify the routine name if the variable name is unambiguous. For example, if there is only one variable named **FOG** in a program, you never need to name the routine in which **FOG** is used. You can omit the routine's name if you are referring to a variable in the current function. Finally, you can omit the routine name if you want to refer to the closest active variable to the current function. Suppose that the routine **F1** calls **F2**, which in turn calls **F3**. A variable named **VAR** exists in the routines **F1** and **F3**, but not in **F2**. If you are currently stopped at a breakpoint in **F2**, then the name **VAR** refers to the variable **VAR** in **F1** because there is no such variable in **F2**, and none of the variables in **F3** are active.

The previous rules are not sufficient to distinguish between a variable, a subroutine, and a module with the same name. For example, **dbx** may occasionally become confused if you refer to a common block variable named **BLKELMT** that occurs in a file named *blkelmt.o*. It is hard to predict when such confusion occurs.

dbx Expressions

dbx can evaluate and use expressions. Expressions may contain constants, variables, function calls, array elements, and operators. Valid operators include:

Operator	Function	FORTRAN Equivalent
+	Addition (integer or floating point)	+
−	Subtraction (integer or floating point)	-
*	Multiplication (integer or floating point)	*
/	Division (floating point)	/
div	Division (integer)	/
	Remainder, modulus (integer)	MOD intrinsic
<<	Left shift	LSHIFT intrinsic
>>	Right shift	RSHIFT intrinsic
&	Bitwise AND	AND intrinsic
|	Bitwise OR	OR intrinsic
~	Bitwise complement (inverse of each bit)	NOT intrinsic
<	Less than	.LT.
>	Greater than	.GT.
<=	Less than or equal to	.LE.
>=	Greater than or equal to	.GE.

Operator	Function	FORTRAN Equivalent
==	Equal to	.EQ.
!=	Not equal to	.NE.
!	Logical complement (not)	.NOT.
&&	Logical AND	.AND.
||	Logical OR	.OR.

Parentheses, (), may be used for grouping operations. If you know the C language, you will recognize that these are, for the most part, the standard C operators. If you don't know C, the operators at least make common sense. Your biggest problem will be remembering that the equality logical operation is == (rather than =). You may also have trouble remembering the difference between logical operators (&&, ||, and !) and bitwise operators (&, |, and ˜).

To refer to an array element, you must use a C-style array reference. In C, an array reference is written:

```
array-name[ i1 ][ i2 ][ ... ][ in ]
```

where *i1* through *in* are the array's indices. FORTRAN stores arrays in column-major order, in which the left-most subscript varies first. C and virtually all other languages store arrays in row-major order, in which the rightmost subscript varies first. Therefore, you must reverse the order of the array indices. For example, to print the array element **A(I, J)**, use the **dbx** command:

```
(dbx) print a[j][i]
```

There are several restrictions on **dbx** expressions:

- **dbx** does not accept character expressions.

- The exponentiation operation (**) may not appear within an expression.

- **COMPLEX** and **DOUBLE COMPLEX** variables and constants may not appear within expressions. (However, it is legal to print the value of a single **COMPLEX** or **DOUBLE COMPLEX** variable or array element.)

The C operator & means "the address of." It is useful for inspecting arguments passing between routines written in FORTRAN and C and for referring to addresses when using **dbx**'s machine language debugging features. (Note that this overlaps with a bitwise AND. The difference is that the "address of" operator is monadic—it only has one operand, while a "bitwise AND" has two operands.)

If an arithmetic expression is a mixed mode expression (i.e., if the expression combines two or more different data types), **dbx** performs type conversion implicitly while evaluating the expression. In general, consider the expression:

```
EXPR1 operation EXPR2
```

where *operation* is a valid operation and *EXPR1* and *EXPR2* are valid expressions. The type of the expression *EXPR1 operation EXPR2* is the higher of the types of *EXPR1* and *EXPR2*. "Higher" is interpreted according to the following hierarchy:

DOUBLE PRECISION   *Highest*
REAL
INTEGER
INTEGER*2
INTEGER*1   *Lowest* (if available on your system)

For example, if *EXPR1* has type **DOUBLE PRECISION** and *EXPR2* has type **INTEGER**, then *EXPR1+EXPR2* has type **DOUBLE PRECISION**.

As we've said, **dbx** is very fussy about type checking for assignments and subroutine calls. Some versions of **dbx** document operators for casting data (i.e., changing their type), which is a way of getting around the debugger's prudishness. We are not aware of any **dbx** implementations in which this works correctly.

Advanced Features

This section discusses more advanced **dbx** features. These features include tools for working with recursive procedure calls, tools for working with assembly language, and other features not generally needed for FORTRAN programming.

Moving Up and Down the Call Stack

The commands **up** and **down** move you up and down one level in the current call stack. The commands **up** *n* and **down** *n* move you up or down *n* levels in the stack. Down the stack means farther away from the program's **MAIN** procedure; up means closer to the **MAIN** procedure. For FORTRAN, which is not recursive,* this is equivalent to changing the current function. For C, which allows recursive

---

*Most UNIX FORTRAN compilers claim to support recursion as an extension to the language. Compilers for which recursion is implemented correctly are rare. Because recursion is not part of standard FORTRAN, this usually is not a problem.

procedure calls, the **up** and **down** commands allow you to distinguish between different recursive invocations of the same routine. In particular, it allows you to investigate the local variables and arguments for any recursive procedure call.

For example, consider a program in which procedure **B** calls **C**, which calls **D**. Imagine that the current function is C and you enter the **where** command. **dbx** prints a report like the following:

```
(dbx) where
    d( q = 23.3 ), line 23 in "aux.f"
>   c( intarg = 13 ), line 67 in "file.f"
    b( x = 1.1 ), line 45 in "file1.f"
    MAIN(), line 20 in "file.f"
```

After entering the **down** command, the **where** command prints the following report:

```
(dbx) where
>   d( q = 23.3 ), line 23 in "aux.f"
    c( intarg = 13 ), line 67 in "file.f"
    b( x = 1.1 ), line 45 in "file1.f"
    MAIN(), line 20 in "file.f"
```

This shows that the current function is now **D**, which is farther away from the program's **MAIN** procedure. References to variables, line numbers, etc. now refer to the function **D** by default. If you now enter the command **up**, the current function will be **D** once again.

If procedure **C** calls itself recursively and you are stopped in the third recursive invocation of **C**, then the command **up** will move you to the previous invocation of the procedure. You can now inspect this invocation's local variables and arguments. The command **down** returns you to the third recursive call to C.

Machine Language Facilities

dbx provides a few commands for working with machine language. They are useful for inspecting a few machine language instructions or performing some other low-level operations while doing source-level debugging. However, if you really want to work with your program at the machine level, use **adb**. We'll discuss **dbx**'s machine language facilities briefly but won't go into detail.

The commands **stepi** and **nexti** are equivalent to **next** and **step** but work on the level of machine language instructions rather than source statements. The **stepi** command executes the next machine language instruction; the **nexti** command executes the next instruction, unless that instruction calls a subroutine, in which case **nexti** executes the entire subroutine.

The command **stopi at** *address* sets a breakpoint at the entrance to a subroutine. *address* must be the address of a subroutine, in the following form:

```
(dbx) stopi at &routine-name
```

Like **stop, stopi** can be used with **at, in,** and **if** clauses. The meaning of these clauses is the same; again, using an **if** clause decreases execution speed significantly. Note that an **if** *condition* clause within a **stopi** command causes **dbx** to test the *condition* after every machine language instruction. Execution will be very slow.

Likewise, the **stopi** *address* command is analogous to **stop** *variable*. The **stopi** command will cause the program to stop at a breakpoint whenever the location given by *address* is modified. Again, this causes very slow execution.

The memory inspection command / prints the contents of memory. It can be used in two ways:

```
(dbx) addr1,addr2/ format
(dbx) addr1/count format
```

The first form prints the contents of memory between *addr1* and *addr2* according to *format*. The second form prints the *count* items, beginning at *addr1*, according to *format*. *count* and *format* are optional. If *count* is omitted, the value 1 is assumed. If *format* is omitted, **dbx** uses the same format as the last memory inspection command.

format is a single letter that determines how **dbx** will interpret and print the data in memory. The following list shows the different formats allowed:

i   Print assembly language instructions.

d   Print (decimal) the contents of memory as 16-bit halfwords.

D   Print (decimal) the contents of memory as 32-bit words.

o   Print (octal) the contents of memory as 16-bit halfwords.

O   Print (octal) the contents of memory as 32-bit halfwords.

x   Print (hexadecimal) the contents of memory as 16-bit halfwords.

X   Print (hexadecimal) the contents of memory as 32-bit halfwords.

b   Print (octal) the contents of memory as 8-bit bytes.

c   Print, as ASCII characters, the contents of memory as 8-bit bytes.

s   Print, as a null-terminated character string, the contents of memory as 8-bit bytes.

f   Print, as single-precision floating-point numbers, the contents of memory as 32-bit words.

g   Print, as double-precision floating-point numbers, the contents of memory as 64-bit word pairs.

A group of special **dbx** variables lets you inspect and modify the computer's general purpose registers. These are described in the section "dbx Variables" later in this chapter.

Signals

dbx normally traps most signals that are sent to it. By trapping signals, **dbx** gets to decide what to do with the process you are running. For example, pressing CTRL-C sends the interrupt signal to **dbx**, which would normally terminate it. But you probably don't want to interrupt **dbx**; you really want to interrupt the program that **dbx** is running. Therefore, **dbx** catches the signal and stops the program it is running; this lets you do some debugging.

The commands **catch, ignore,** and **cont** control signal handling:

catch *signal*   Trap the signal identified by *signal*. The signal is not sent to the process. *signal* may be either a signal name (e.g., **SIGCHILD**) or a signal number (e.g., 20). **dbx** suspends the program's execution. Execution can be resumed with the **cont** command.

ignore *signal*   Ignore the given signal entirely. This signal will not be passed to the process.

cont *signal*   This is the general form of the **cont** command discussed previously. Pass *signal*, which may be a signal name or a signal number, to the program being debugged and continue execution. If *signal* is omitted, the program continues as if it has not received any signal.

With no arguments, the **ignore** command prints a list of the signals **dbx** is currently ignoring. Similarly, **catch** with no arguments prints a list of signals **dbx** is currently catching.

For a complete list of signals used by UNIX, see Appendix D, *UNIX Error Numbers and Signals*. By default, **dbx** traps all signals except for **SIGALRM**, **SIGCHILD, SIGCONT, SIGKILL,** and **SIGSTOP**.

This feature is useful primarily for system programming. Applications programmers probably won't need to use this feature.

dbx Variables

The **dbx** debugger lets you define **dbx** variables. These variables may appear in expressions. A number of special variables control certain **dbx** features and let you read or write hardware registers.

A **dbx** variable may have any name, provided it obeys these rules:

- The name is composed of digits and letters, plus the characters _ (underscore) and $ (dollar sign).

- The name does not begin with a digit.

- The name does not match name in the source program being debugged.

dbx variable names are case-sensitive (e.g., the variable **naME** is distinct from the variable **NAme**).

The **set** command defines and assigns values to **dbx** variables. It is used as follows:

```
(dbx) set variable=expression
```

This command assigns the value *expression* to the named *variable*. If *=expression* is omitted, the variable is defined but not assigned any value. The command:

```
(dbx) unset variable
```

deletes *variable* and its definition.

The following special **dbx** variables control certain debugging features:

$hexin   If this variable is set, **dbx** interprets any numbers you type as input in hexadecimal.

$octin   If this variable is set, **dbx** interprets any numbers you type as input in octal.

$hexchars   If this variable is set, print the value of all **CHARACTER** variables in hexadecimal.

$hexints   If this variable is set, print the value of all **INTEGER** variables in hexadecimal.

$hexoffsets If this variable is set, print the value of all offsets from registers in hexadecimal.

$hexstrings If this variable is 1, print the value of pointers to **CHARACTER** variables in hexadecimal.

$listwindow Print **$listwindow** lines from the source program (by default, 10) whenever the **list** command is given without specific line numbers.

$stepwindow Print **$stepwindow** lines from the source program (by default, 10) whenever you use the **step** command.

$unsafecall Do not perform type checking for arguments to subroutine or functions when the **call** command is used.

$unsafeassign Do not perform type checking for **assign** commands.

These variable names must not conflict with variable names in the program being debugged.

A set of special **dbx** variables refers to the computer's hardware registers. These variables have the form:

```
$<register>
```

where *<register>* identifies a particular register, using whatever notation is appropriate for your system. For example, on a 68000-series system **$a4** refers to address register 4 and **$d6** refers to general data register 6. **$fp4** often refers to "floating-point register 4" if the system is equipped with a floating-point coprocessor.

In addition, there are special-purpose register names for the stack pointer, the program counter, and the processor status word:

$sp Stack pointer register. This register points to the start of the current subroutine's stack.

$pc Program counter register. This register points to the current instruction.

$ps Processor status word. This register contains information about the state of the processor.

The exact notation used to refer to hardware registers depends heavily on the type of processor you are using, whether a floating-point coprocessor is present, etc. Furthermore, your system may have other special registers in addition to those described here. In any case, the notation should be similar to what we have described. For example, on a system that does not distinguish between address and data registers, the notation **r***n* would usually refer to "general register *n*."

Working with Source Files

To aid in finding a particular line of source code, **dbx** provides a command for searching through source files. The command /*text* prints the next line in the current file that contains the string *text*; likewise, the command ?*text* prints the previous line containing *text*. The (slash) may appear in search commands beginning with a ? (question mark); the ? may appear in search commands beginning with /. More generally, *text* may be any UNIX regular expression. We won't discuss regular expressions here; they are covered in the Nutshell Handbook *Learning the vi*

Editor. For example, the command /CONTINUE searches for the file's next CON-TINUE statement; the command /SET.NO searches for the next string that begins with the letters "SET" and ends with the letters "NO", with any single character in the middle. In a regular expression, a . (dot) is a single-character wildcard.

The command **use** modifies the list of directories through which **dbx** searches. It has a similar function to the **-I** option. Normally, **dbx** looks for source code in the current directory and in the directory in which the executable file is located. If you enter the command:

The command **use** modifies the list of directories through which **dbx** searches. It has a similar function to the **-I** option. Normally, **dbx** looks for source code in the current directory and in the directory in which the executable file is located. If you enter the command:

```
(dbx) use list-of-directories
```

dbx will search through the directories in *list-of-directories* first, then look through the current directory and the executable file's directory. For example, after entering the command:

```
(dbx) use ../home ../othersrcs
```

dbx will look through the directories given by the paths *../home* and *../othersrcs*, prior to searching the current directory.

If given without any arguments, the **use** command lists the directories through which it currently searches. For example, the command:

```
(dbx) use
. tests
```

reports that **dbx** is looking for source files in the current directory and the directory *tests*.

NOTE

dbx does not check to determine whether the arguments to **use** are valid directory names.

Aliases, Customization, and Command Files

The **alias** command lets you create your own abbreviations or names for **dbx** commands. The **alias** *new old* command defines *new* to be a **dbx** command equivalent to typing *old*, which must itself be a valid **dbx** command. By itself, the **alias** command lists all the aliases that are currently defined. The **alias** *name* command prints the **dbx** command currently assigned to the abbreviation *name*. This command lets you create your own environment for working with **dbx**.

Whenever **dbx** begins execution, it looks for the file *.dbxinit* in your home directory. This file can contain a list of **dbx** commands which **dbx** will execute as it starts up. This file can be used to define aliases or abbreviations for commonly used commands or expressions. For example, if you want to use the letter "s" as an abbreviation for the **stop** command, include the following line in your *.dbxinit* file:

```
alias s stop
```

The **source** *file* command reads a file and executes the **dbx** commands contained in the file. For example, the command:

```
(dbx) source setbkpts.dbx
```

reads and executes the commands in the file *setbkpts.dbx*. This features lets you combine long or complicated sequences of commands in a file and execute them with a simple command. For example, *setbkpts.dbx* might contain commands to set a number of breakpoints in a particular program. Executing this file with the **source** command when you start debugging would be easier than giving this sequence of commands at the keyboard.

Interface to UNIX

The **sh** command starts a UNIX shell. When you exit this shell by typing CTRL-D, control returns to **dbx**.

The command **sh** *shell-command* executes the given shell command and returns control to **dbx** immediately. For example:

```
(dbx) sh date
Mon Apr  6 16:51:20 EST 1987
(dbx)
```

These commands let you execute one or more shell commands quickly without leaving the debugger.

By default, **dbx** will start a C shell. To change this default, use the **SHELL** environment variable to request a different shell. For example, the command:

```
% setenv SHELL /bin/sh
```

requests the Bourne shell (**sh**).

For more information about **dbx**, refer to Section 1 of the *UNIX Programmer's Reference Manual*. There is also an article describing **dbx** in Part I of the *Programmer's Supplementary Documents*; this contains a tutorial example but lacks a comprehensive discussion of **dbx**'s features.

Debugging at the Assembly Level with adb

adb is an assembly-level debugging utility. This section explains how to use this utility for debugging FORTRAN programs. It does not intend to be an **adb** reference manual or a complete **adb** tutorial. Rather, this chapter provides a supplement to the paper "A Tutorial Introduction to **adb**" in the *Programmer's Supplementary Documents*. This paper is oriented toward system programming, using the C language on the VAX. This standard paper is still useful and shows a much wider range of commands than are discussed here. This chapter provides a discussion of **adb** oriented toward FORTRAN programming on a 68000-series workstation; the concepts can be transferred to UNIX systems based on other processor families. Another important summary of **adb** can be found in the discussion of **adb** in Part I of the *UNIX Programmer's Reference Manual*.

To use **adb** effectively, you need at least a minimal knowledge of your computer's architecture and assembly language. Before proceeding, you should become familiar with your system's assembly language and architecture reference manuals.

Invoking adb

Begin a debugging session with **adb** with the command:

```
% adb object-file core-file
```

where *object-file* is the name of the compiled program you want to debug and *core-file* is the name of a core dump that may exist. Both of these arguments are optional. If you omit one of them, type a - (hyphen) as a place holder. By default, **adb** will look for an executable named *a.out* and a core dump called *core* in the current directory. If there is no core dump, you can still use **adb** to run the executable. If there is no executable, you can use **adb** to inspect a core dump.

If you want to modify the core dump or the executable, invoke **adb** with the **-w** option:

```
% adb -w object-file core-file
```

This lets you change data or instructions while you are debugging the program. These changes are permanent. When you modify the object file during an **adb** session, you are modifying the object file itself. Your changes will remain in the file when you exit **adb**.

adb does not prompt you for commands. To exit from **adb** and terminate a debugging session, enter CTRL-D or $q. Both return you to the UNIX operating system.

adb Commands

Once you have entered **adb**, you can use it many different commands or requests. In general, **adb** commands have the following form:

[*address*][*count*][*command*][*modifier*]

All of these fields are optional. *address* specifies the location at which a command should be executed, and *count* specifies the number of times the command should be executed. If *count* is not present, **adb** will execute the command once. If *count* is present, it must be preceded be a comma, even if you omit *address*. *command*, together with *modifier*, describes some action that the debugger should take.

Addresses, Expressions, and Symbols

The *address* field specifies a starting address for the command. This address may be in either the object file or the core file, depending on the command itself. If *address* is not present, **adb** uses the current address, abbreviated . (dot). The current address is generally the address following the address for the last command. Repeatedly entering the command **?ia** (decode and print machine language instructions) will march through the file by decoding sequential instructions, even though machine language instructions may have different lengths.

An address may be any legal **adb** expression. The discussion of **adb** in Section 1 of the *UNIX Programmer's Reference Manual* explains the elements from which you can form detailed expressions. Here is a summary of the most important features. Expressions may contain:

- *Symbols*, which are strings of letters, digits, and underscores beginning with a letter.

- A . (dot), which stands for the current address.

- *Integer constants*, which may be in any radix (determined by an **adb** command).

- The *arithmetic operators* + (integer addition), - (subtraction and monadic negation), and * (integer multiplication).

- The *logical operators* & (bitwise AND) and | (bitwise OR).

- A *register name* in the form *<register-name*, which stands for the current contents of the given register.

For example, the address **_find_lcd_+4** refers to the location 4 bytes after the symbol **_find_lcd_**. The address **.+4** refers to the location 4 bytes after the current location, and the address **_find_lcd_+(4*6)** refers to the address 24 bytes (i.e., six words) after the location **_find_lcd_**.

A **symbol name** can be any combination of underscores, upper- and lower-case letters, and digits, provided that it begins with a letter or an underscore. If you need to refer to a symbol in which other characters appear, precede each nonalphabetic, nonnumeric, and nonunderscore character with a \ (backslash). For example, to refer to the symbol "foo.bar?", type:

```
foo\.bar\?
```

The FORTRAN compiler forms symbol names from subroutine or function names by converting them to lowercase and adding underscores before and after. For example, the symbol **_find_lcd_** is the entry point for a FORTRAN routine named **FIND_LCD**. If you compiled your program with the case-sensitive option (**-U**), the compiler will *not* change subroutine names to lowercase. It will still add underscores before and after. The entry point to your program will be named **_MAIN_**, which will always be uppercase.

NOTE

adb supplies the initial underscore for you; you don't need to type it explicitly. **adb** always prints this underscore when it prints a symbol name. This manual shows the initial underscore so that **adb**'s input and output agree in appearance.

A register name can be any of the following:

a*n*   For any of the 68000-series processor's address registers.

d*n*   For any of the 68000-series processor's general-purpose data registers.

fp*n*   For any of the 68000-series floating-point coprocessor's data registers.

sp   For the stack pointer register; this register points to the start of the current subroutine's stack.

ps   For the processor status word register.

pc   For the program counter.

Thus, **<a2** uses the contents of address register 2 as an address, and **<pc** uses the contents of the program counter as an address. The actual mechanism used to specify a register may differ, depending on your processor's architecture, whether a floating-point coprocessor is present, and other factors.

Finally, a **number** can appear in any radix between binary and hexadecimal. By default, **adb** interprets numbers in hexadecimal. We will explain how to change the default radix later. Numbers beginning with the hexadecimal digits a through f must be preceded by a zero. This allows **adb** to distinguish between numbers and symbol names. For example, 0f equals 15 decimal; 10 equals 16 decimal; and f isn't a number but a symbol which may or may not be defined. To express a number in decimal, precede it with the prefix 0t; for example, 0t10 equals 10 decimal. To express a number in octal, use the prefix 0o (lower-case O); for example, 0o10 equals 8 decimal.

Counts

The *count* field of a command indicates that **adb** should execute the command *count* times. For example:

```
_MAIN_,10?ia
```

tells **adb** to execute the command **?ia** ten times, beginning at the address _MAIN_. If *count* is not present, **adb** will execute the command once. If it is present, it must always be preceded by a comma. For example, **,10?ia** means "execute the command **?ia** ten times beginning at the current address."

Like an address, a count can be any legal expression.

Basic Commands and Modifiers

The most basic **adb** commands are:

?	Print the contents of a location in the object file.
/	Print the contents of a location in the core-dump file.
=	Print the value of the *address* itself.
RETURN	Repeat the previous command, operating on the next address.
$	Print long reports, set the radix (depending on the modifier).
:	Manage program execution.

The latter two commands are collections of many miscellaneous features. The following most important features they provide will be discussed in a task-oriented way.

The command **?** (print values from the object file) is useful for inspecting any statically initialized data or FORTRAN argument blocks and for probing the machine code generated by the compiler. The command **/** (print values from the core image) is useful for inspecting the actual values of variables as a program is executing. Only use the **/** command if you are currently running a program (i.e., stopped a a breakpoint) or inspecting a core dump. Finally, the command **=** is useful for doing desktop calculations, to print the value of a symbol, or to perform base conversions. Each of these commands can be followed by a modifier that describes how to print the data. The most useful modifiers are:

i	Decode and print the next instruction in assembly language.
ia	Print the address with each instruction equivalent to **i**.
O	Print the next word in octal.
X	Print the next word in hexadecimal.
D	Print the next word in (signed) decimal.
U	Print the next word in (unsigned) decimal.
f	Print the next word as a single-precision floating-point number.
F	Print the next two words as a double-precision floating-point number.
c	Print the next byte as a character.

The commands in the following example display the contents of **_fact_** and the locations following it in many different formats. To distinguish between **adb**'s responses and your commands, we will display commands in boldface. Additional comments that cannot be typed as input to **adb** are displayed in italic.

```
% adb play -
_fact_ ,2?ia        Print out two instructions
_fact_ :
```

```
_fact_ :            linkw     a6,#0
_fact_+4:           addl  #-0x2c,a7
_fact_,2?D          Print out two words in decimal
_fact_ :            1314258944      -537067521
_fact_,2?X          Print out two words in hex
_fact_ :            4e560000  dffcffff
_fact_,2?O          Print out two words in octal
_fact_ :            011625400000    033777177777
_fact_,2?f          Print out two numbers in REAL
_fact_ :            +8.9758106e+08  -3.6461140e+19
_fact_,2?F          Print out two numbers in DOUBLE
_fact_ :            2.3724767464504184e+69
                    -5.6977132748354633e+307
```

Each of these commands reads the object file and displays the two entities following the symbol **_fact_**. Each command prints these data with a different format. Whether any particular format makes sense depends on what is stored in these locations. If you are trying to inspect a **REAL** quantity, the report that **_fact_** and **_fact_+4** contain the hex constants 80 and 0 is meaningless unless you are intimately familiar with floating-point representation. Furthermore, if **_fact_** and **_fact_+4** are **REAL** quantities, the **DOUBLE** values for **_fact_** and **_fact_+8** shown previously are nonsense. And finally, since **_fact_** looks suspiciously like the symbol name for an entry point to a routine, the only previous command that is useful is the first: print the two instructions following the program counter value **_fact_**. It is a trivial point but worth being careful about: specify a format appropriate to quantities you are looking at.

If you omit a modifier, **adb** will use the modifier from the previous command. Therefore, if you want to inspect several locations storing 32-bit decimal numbers, you only need to use the **D** modifier once.

Examining Registers

To print out the contents of any register, use the command:

    <*register-name*=

For example, the command:

    <d4=X

prints the contents of data register 4 in hexadecimal. The command:

    <d4=f

prints the contents of register 4 as a single-precision floating-point number. Because the abbreviation <*register-name* is an address, we can also use it to examine memory: the command <a3/X prints the contents of the location addressed by address register 3 in hexadecimal.

To display all the processor's registers, enter the command **$r**. This produces a long report showing the current value of each register in the system. Here is a typical report:

```
$r
d0      0x0
d1      0x4
d2      0x1
d3      0x0
d4      0x0
d5      0x0
d6      0x0
d7      0x0
a0      0x0
a1      0x0
a2      0x0
a3      0xefffec8
a4      0xefffed0
a5      0x0
a6      0x0
sp      0xefffec4
pc      0x2034      start+0x14
ps      0x0
        0x0
start+0x14:         pea   a4@
```

This report shows data register 1 holds the value 0x4 and address register 3 has the value 0xefffec8 (a hexadecimal number). The stack pointer (the base of the current subroutine's stack) is 0xefffec4, and the program counter (the current instruction, or the instruction at which the program is stopped) is 0x2034, which has the symbolic value **start+0x14**. The processor status longword has the value 0. The current instruction (at the address **start+0x14**) is **pea a4@**.

Controlling adb's Output

Initially, **adb** expects you to type all numbers in hexadecimal, unless you use a prefix like "0t" or "0o". You can change the default radix by using the command *new-radix***$d**. Here are some useful examples:

0t10$d	*New default radix is base 10*
0t8$d	*New default radix is base 8*
0t2$d	*New default radix is binary*

new-radix can specify any base between 2 and 16. Note that **adb** interprets the *new-radix* in terms of the current radix. Thus, the command **10$d** never changes the current radix. The previous commands work because they specify explicitly that the new radix is given in decimal.

Note that the default radix only affects the numbers you type. The numbers **adb** reports are controlled by the *format* characters shown previously.

Executing a Program Under adb

The **adb** commands and modifiers for executing a program are:

:r   Run the program under **adb**'s control.

:c   Continue program execution after it has stopped.

:k   Terminate a program running under **adb**.

:s   Execute the next instruction (single-step). If preceded by a *count*, execute the next *count* instructions.

None of these commands may be preceded by an address.

The command **:r** starts a program executing under the control of **adb**. The program will continue until it reaches a breakpoint, terminates normally or abnormally, or until you press CTRL-C. Note that CTRL-C terminates the program running within **adb**, not **adb** itself. You may follow the **:r** command with standard I/O qualifiers. The command:

```
:r <input.test >output.test
```

runs the program under **adb**'s control, letting it read standard input from the file *input.test* and letting it write through standard output to the file *output.test*. Spacing must be exactly as shown in the example. That is, there must be no space between < and the name of the input file or between > and the name of the output file. There must be at least one space between the end of the standard input specification and the beginning of the standard output specification.

The command **:c** lets a program halted at a breakpoint continue running. The command **:k** cleans up after a program that is halted, preventing you from continuing it. Finally, the command **:s** lets you single step through the program. If you enter the command a *count*, the command **:s** will execute the next *count* instructions before halting. When the program stops (after an instruction or a group of instructions), **adb** will print the location at which it stopped and the instruction it is about to execute. For example:

```
:s
stopped    at    start+0x18:          movl d2,sp@-
```

executes the next instruction and halts. After stopping, the next instruction is at location **start+0x18** and is a "move long" instruction. Entering the **:s** command again will execute this instruction and stop at location **start+0x1a**.

Some implementations support the **:S** command. The meaning of this command depends on the system. On some, it continues execution until the next assembly language branch instruction. On others (Sun workstations in particular), it continues execution until the beginning of the next source code line. This command may cause confusion because it is easy to type **:S** instead of **:s**.

Setting Breakpoints

By setting breakpoints, you can stop the program at any point during execution. The program will run until it reaches the breakpoint, then stop when it reaches the breakpoint instruction. To set a breakpoint, use the command **:b**, preceded by an address. To delete a breakpoint, use the command **:d**, preceded by an address. For example:

```
_fact_:b
```

sets a breakpoint at the location addressed by the symbol **_fact_**. When **adb** runs the program, it will stop before executing the instruction at this address. It prints a message telling you that you are at a breakpoint and reports the instruction it was about to execute:

```
:r
breakpoint     _fact_:              linkw     a6,#0
```

Preceding a breakpoint command with a count tells **adb** to run through the breakpoint *count* times before stopping. To print out all the current breakpoints, use the command:

```
$b
breakpoints
count   bkpt                command
1       _MAIN_+488
1       _fact_
```

This report shows that there are currently two breakpoints set at locations **_fact_** and **_MAIN_+488**. Both breakpoints have a count of 1; that is, **adb** will suspend execution each time it reaches either of these breakpoints. The *command* field supports an advanced feature of **adb** that won't be discussed here.

Before we said that the **:d** command deletes a breakpoint. For example, to delete the first breakpoint in this list, use the command **_MAIN_+488:d**. To delete the second breakpoint, use the command **_fact_:d**.

Working with Subroutines and Functions

The most important things you can do with a subroutine or a function are:

- Use a stack trace to find out how the routine was called (this is valid when you are in the routine or after an abnormal termination).

- Set a breakpoint at the beginning of the routine to find out what arguments are being passed to it.

- Set a breakpoint at the return from a function to find out what arguments are being passed back.

Stack Traces

When you are stopped within a routine, the command $c will produce a stack trace that lists the currently active procedures and the arguments with which they were called. Here is an example of a typical stack trace:

```
$c
_fact_ (11bef4,11bef8) _fmyexp_+384
_fmyexp_ (11becc,11bec4)  _MAIN_+60c
_MAIN_ () _main+484
_main(1,120f58,120f2c) __start_in_c+e04
__start_in_c() bstart+1f4
```

The first line reports that the subroutine currently executing begins at location **_fact_** (the beginning of the routine **FACT**). This call took place at location **_fmyexp_+384**. **FACT** was called by **FMYEXP**, which in turn was called by **_MAIN_** (the FORTRAN top-level routine). **_MAIN_** was called by **_main** and **__start_in_c**, which belong to the run-time initialization library; the names may be different, depending on your UNIX implementation.

The stack trace also shows the arguments with which these routines are called. **FACT** has two arguments: **11bef4** and **11bef8** (hex). FORTRAN passes arguments to subroutines by pointer. Therefore, these are the locations holding the values that were passed to this subroutine. To see the actual values of these arguments, inspect these locations in the core image. For example:

```
11bef4/D
__started+1e8: 5
```

shows that the decimal value 5 was passed to **_fact_** as its first argument. Remember, whether this report makes sense depends on what kind of an argument **_fact_** is expecting. Also, the value of any argument may not be what you expect; FORTRAN routines often modify their arguments during execution.

The second line shows the subroutine **FMYEXP**, which called **FACT**, was also called with two arguments (**11becc** and **11bec4**). We can use the same technique to inspect these arguments: treat these values as pointers, and use the / command to read the relevant location in the program's image. This technique is valid when you are stopped at a breakpoint and when the program has terminated abnormally. If a program quits with a core dump, you can run **adb** on the *core* file and use **$c** to find out exactly where it died.

Call tracing is one of **adb**'s most useful features. Note, though, that the arguments with which the object code calls assembly language routines may *not* correspond exactly to the arguments with which your FORTRAN code calls its subroutines. Discrepancies will occur in three situations: if any FORTRAN arguments to a subroutine have type **CHARACTER**, if a function returns a **CHARACTER** value, and if a function returns a **COMPLEX** value.

In all of these cases, the FORTRAN compiler needs to pass some arguments in addition to those explicitly requested in your program. For each **CHARACTER** argument, the compiler will add an additional argument containing the length of the character string. For example, consider the statement:

```
CALL PRINTER(TEXT,TOKEN)
```

where **TEXT** and **TOKEN** are of type **CHARACTER**. In this case, FORTRAN will call **PRINTER** with four arguments and **PRINTER**'s entry in a stack trace will look like this:

```
$c
_printer_(5678,37498,120,4) _caller_+b36
```

5678 is a pointer to **TEXT**, 37498 is a pointer to **TOKEN**, 120 is the length of **TEXT**, and 4 is the length of **TOKEN**.

If a function returns a **COMPLEX** variable, the compiler will add an additional argument prior to the function's other arguments. This is a pointer to a location where the function will write its returned value. For example, a function defined like this:

```
COMPLEX FUNCTION MKCPLX( X )
```

will appear with two arguments in a stack trace:

```
$c
_mkcplx_(d45a,23c8) _caller_+a20
```

The first argument, **d45a**, is a pointer to the returned value; the second argument, **23c8**, is a pointer to the function's real argument, **X**. The compiler treats functions returning **CHARACTER** variables similarly. In this case, the compiler will add two extra arguments before any other arguments: the first is a pointer to the **CHARACTER** variable being returned, and the second is the length of the variable that has been returned.

Arguments Passed to a Routine

Once you can get a stack trace, it is a simple step to read the arguments that were initially passed to a routine. All you need to do is set a breakpoint at any point before the routine has had a chance to modify its arguments, use **$c** to find out how the routine was called, and use **/** to pick apart its argument list.

Setting a breakpoint at the entry to a subroutine is simple. Use the command:

```
_name_:b
```

where *_name_* is the symbol name for the subroutine. However, 68000-based systems must execute the **link** instruction at the beginning of the routine before **adb** can read its arguments. Therefore, single step (**:s**) to execute the first instruction, then give the **$c** command. For example:

```
_fact_:b
:r
breakpoint      _fact_:              linkw     a6,#0
:s
stopped    at    _fact_+4:     addl #-0x2c,a7
$c
_fact_(0x21ddc,0x21de0)   + 4
_fmyexp_(0xefffde4,0x21dc8)  + 3c
_MAIN_() + dc
_main(0x1,0xefffe28,0xefffe30) + 54
21ddc/D=
5
```

As a shortcut, **_name_+4:b** will usually save you the trouble of single-stepping. This technique assumes that the first instruction is four bytes long, which may not be the case on some machines.

Inspecting Returned Values

Setting a breakpoint at the return from a subroutine is more difficult and depends on your compiler's calling sequence. On most 68000-based systems, this technique will work:

• Set a breakpoint at the entry point to the routine.

• Look at the contents of the link register (by convention, a6) and add four; this is an address within the program's stack.

- Look at the contents of this stack address; this is the subroutine's return location. Set a breakpoint at this location and continue.

For example, to set a breakpoint at the return from the FORTRAN subroutine **CASH**, do the following:

```
_cash_+4:b        Breakpoint at the entry to cash
:r                Execute until you reach the breakpoint
breakpoint...     Now you're stopped at the breakpoint
<a6+4?            Read the link register, add four to it, \
                  and report the contents of this location
0xefffd60:   21a0 Return address is 21a0
21a0:b            Breakpoint at the return address
:c                Continue executing
breakpoint...     Now you're stopped at the return from CASH
```

At this point, you can inspect the data returned by the subroutine or function. Most 68000-based systems place returned values in data register 0. Enter the command **<d0=** (with an appropriate modifier) to read the returned value:

```
<d0=f
          +2.6692967e+00    Returned value from CASH
```

FORTRAN subroutines don't return values per se; they either modify common blocks or modify their arguments. To inspect a subroutine's returned values, you would take a stack trace at the entry point, continue execution until the subroutine returns to its caller, and then use the / command to inspect the subroutine's arguments, which now contain the data the subroutine is passing back to its caller.

Remember that functions returning **COMPLEX** and **CHARACTER** values are exceptions: the compiler turns them into subroutines with additional arguments at the beginning of the argument list.

Examining Local Variables

There is no good way to examine local variables based on the variable names in the source program unless they are in common blocks. **adb** is an assembly language debugger; you will have to inspect the program's assembly language and figure out where the variables and arrays you care about are located.

NOTE

Many versions of **adb** claim that the notation *routine-entry-name.variable-name* will let you examine a local variable by name.

We aren't aware of any modern system for which this notation works. The developers of your system may have fixed this feature; please let us know if they have.

Working with Common Blocks

You can refer to the elements of a common block by knowing the offset of each element into the common block. The beginning of any common block is identified by a symbol. The name of this symbol is the name of the common block, converted to lowercase, with an underscore added before and after. Blank common has the special name __BLNK__.

For example, consider the common block defined by the statements:

```
DOUBLE PRECISION D
REAL F
INTEGER IN
COMMON /BOZ/D,F,IN
```

The command _boz_/F prints the value of **D** as a double precision floating-point number, _boz_+8/f prints the value of **F** as a single-precision floating-point number, and _boz_+12/D prints the value of **IN** as a decimal integer. Note that the offset of each element depends on the data type of the elements that precede it.

NOTE

The offset of any element into a common block may depend on whether the FORTRAN compiler automatically added padding to the common block. Most UNIX compilers never add padding; some provide options for padding.

Modifying Values

The four commands available for modifying or patching a program are described in the following table:

Command	Function	Size
/w	Write data into the data or stack segment.	2 bytes
?w	Write data into the text (executable) or stack segment.	2 bytes
/W	Write data into the data or stack segment.	4 bytes

Command	Function	Size
?W	Write data into the text (executable) or stack segment.	4 bytes

By themselves, these commands modify the program image on which you are working. They do not modify the executable file or the core dump itself. If you want to modify the executable (e.g., to "patch" it) or the core dump, invoke **adb** with the **-w** option. Any changes you make with /W or /w will become permanent as soon as you exit from **adb**. If you are patching a program, be sure to delete all breakpoints before you quit. Otherwise, they will remain in the executable permanently.

NOTE

adb -w should not let you execute a program. The **:r** command may appear to work, but its results will be unpredictable.

To modify the value stored in a register, use the command:

```
expression > register-name
```

where *expression* is any legal **adb** expression and *register-name* specifies one of the system's registers.

Some Hints

Following are some ideas and techniques we found useful when working with **adb**.

Listing the Symbol Table

The UNIX utility **nm** lists an object file's symbol table. You can list all the symbols in a program's symbol table with the command:

```
% nm filename
```

This is particularly useful for finding the symbol names for built-in functions and subroutines. The following symbols are always defined and are of special importance: _etext, which shows the end of the program's text segment, and _edata, which shows the end of the program's data segment.

Adding Symbols to Increase Clarity

You can simplify debugging by adding your own symbols to your assembly program at appropriate places, like locations where you will want to breakpoint. Use the **f77 -S** command to produce an assembly language file, and add labels in whatever syntax your assembler supports. Use the command **f77** *filename.s* to produce an object module for debugging.

Adding Breakpoints and Inspecting Variables

It is easy to set a breakpoint at the entrance to a subroutine. Therefore, if you want to set a breakpoint at an arbitrary point in your program, you can add a dummy subroutine at this point, recompile your code, and set a breakpoint at the subroutine's entrance.

If you are willing to go this far, you can also use this mechanism to inspect variables. Assume that you want to inspect the variables **A**, **I**, and **F** but do not want to poke through the assembly language output to find what locations they occupy. Add the following code to your program:

```
...
CALL DUMMYSUB(A,I,F)
...
SUBROUTINE DUMMYSUB(A,I,F)
END
```

Now set the breakpoint at **_dummysub_ +4** (even though the subroutine does nothing, it will have at least one instruction), get a stack trace with **$c**, and use the stack trace to inspect your variables. Beware, though: unlikely as it seems, it is possible for code like this to change the behavior of your program, especially if it is heavily optimized.

Miscellaneous

Windowing systems are extremely convenient for debugging. You can run **adb** in one window and look at assembly files or source listings in another. The X Window System (best described in the *X Window System User's Guide*, available from O'Reilly and Associates) provides this facility, as do the proprietary windowing environments available from vendors like Hewlett-Packard, Sun, Silicon Graphics, and others. If you don't have X or an equivalent facility, the **emacs** editor family allows you to split the screen of an ASCII terminal into several windows. If you don't have **emacs**, Berkeley UNIX Version 4.3 has a **window** command that lets you create windows on an ASCII terminal. You can run **vi** in one window and **adb** or **dbx** in another.

6

Automatic Compilation with make

Creating a makefile
Invoking make
make and RCS
A Note on Source Files
Error Messages
Some Final Notes

The **make** facility is one of UNIX's most useful tools. It is essentially a programming language for automating large compilations. When used properly, **make** significantly reduces the amount of time spent compiling programs because it eliminates many needless compilations. Using **make** properly also guarantees that programs will be compiled with the correct options and linked to the current version of program modules and libraries.

The idea behind **make** is that you need not recompile a source file if a current object file already exists. An object file is current if it was compiled more recently than the last change to the source file. For example, consider the following situation: We have just modified *program.F* and want to compile and link it to the modules *inputs.F* and *outputs.F*.
The command:

```
% f77 program.F inputs.F outputs.F
```

compiles and links all three modules correctly. If the object modules *inputs.o* and *outputs.o* exist, *and* if they are current (i.e., the source files have not been changed since the object modules were last compiled), we could compile *program.F* with the command:

```
% f77 program.F inputs.o outputs.o
```

In this case, **f77** will compile *program.F* alone and link it to the two object files. Because this command makes a single compilation instead of three, it will take much less time. However, this compilation places more demands on the programmer, who must remember (or check) when *input.F* and *output.F* were last compiled and determine whether their object modules are current. This introduces potential for confusion: while compiling *program.F* and linking it to pre-existing object modules is faster, it only saves work if the object modules are correct.

make automates this process, reducing the potential for incorrect compilations while minimizing the overall amount of compilation needed. It determines whether the relevant object files exist and whether they are current and then performs the smallest set of compilations needed to create the output file you want. To understand how **make** performs this task, we need to define some terms:

target   A task that needs to be performed. In many cases, a target will be the name of the file you want to create; often it will be a name assigned to a task (i.e., a target may be a filename, but it does not have to be).

dependency   A relationship between two targets: target A depends on target B if a change in target B produces a change in target A. For example, an object file *buzz.o* depends upon its source file, *buzz.f* and on any other file that is included within its source file during preprocessing (*buzz.h*). A change in any of these sources changes the contents of the object file when it is compiled.

up to date   A file which is more recent than any of the files on which it depends. For example, if *buzz.o* is more recent than *buzz.f* and *buzz.h*, it is up to date because it reflects the most recent changes to its source files. If *buzz.o* is older than *buzz.f*, then the source code has been modified since the last compilation, and *buzz.o* does not include the latest changes.

makefile   A file describing how to create one or more targets. It lists the files on which the targets depend and gives the rules needed to compile these targets correctly. For most applications, you will want a single makefile in each source directory, describing how to compile the code in that directory. By default, **make** looks first for a makefile named *makefile*, then it looks for *Makefile*.

make   A method of **make**ing a target means executing the commands from the makefile that describe how to create the target, plus any commands needed to bring the target's dependencies up to date. A makefile may list many targets; you can **make** any of them with a single UNIX command.

To use **make**, you need to create a makefile describing how to create a file correctly, then you need to enter the **make** command to execute the makefile. First, we describe how to create a makefile, which is by far the more difficult of the two topics. Second, we describe how to invoke **make**.

Creating a makefile

Any makefile, no matter how complex, is a set of instructions describing how to build a number of *targets*. Often the target is some file; however, a target can be any name describing some task. For example, the following code is a very simple makefile describing how to build production and debugging versions of *stimulate*:

```
# A very simple makefile.
# Lines beginning with # are comments.
# Targets begin at the left margin, followed by : .
# Shell command lines must begin with a tab.
stimulate:
#       One or more commands to create stimulate
        f77 -o stimulate -O stimulate.F input.F output.F
stimulate.db:
#       One or more commands to create stimulate.db
        f77 -DDEBUG -g -o stimulate.db stimulate.F \
                input.F output.F
```

This makefile does nothing more than list the commands required to create the two different versions of *stimulate*. It says that the command:

```
% f77 -o stimulate -O stimulate.F input.F output.F
```

is sufficient to compile *stimulate* correctly, that optimization is in effect, and that no additional debugging code is included. Similarly:

```
% f77 -DDEBUG -g -o stimulate.db stimulate.F \
                input.F output.F
```

will correctly compile the debugging version, *stimulate.db*. The symbol **DEBUG** is defined for the preprocessor, telling it to include any debugging code present in the FORTRAN source files. Optimization is disabled, and the compiler will generate the augmented symbol table needed for **dbx** debugging. However, this makefile does not use most of **make**'s features. In particular, this makefile does not eliminate extra compilations, but it executes the simplest (and slowest) command that will perform a correct compilation.

NOTE

The first character on a command line *must* be the tab character (CTRL-I). A command line may not begin with a space or a series of spaces. This is perhaps the most common error in makefiles; it is difficult to find because the makefile usually appears correct. If it occurs, the **make** command will display the message "Must be a separator on line *n*." Some compilers and linkers are squeamish about object modules whose name does not end in *.o*. We assume that your system accepts these names.

make generates a new shell for each UNIX command line that it executes. Consequently, commands that are executed directly by the shell may only be effective on a single UNIX command line. In particular, the **cd** command only affects the command line on which it appears.

For example, consider the following lines:

```
cd ../stimsource
f77 stimsource.F
```

The **cd** command is useless here; it is only effective on the line in which it appears. To change to the directory *stimsource* before compiling *stimsource.F*, use the command:

```
cd ../stimsource; f77 stimsource.F
```

in your makefile. Remember that you can use the continuation character (\) to extend a single UNIX command line over several physical lines. If you do this, the \ must not be followed by any further characters, including spaces and tabs.

In general, to invoke **make**, enter:

```
% make target
```

where *target* is the name of one of the targets defined in the makefile. If you omit *target*, **make** generates the first target. For example, our simple makefile can be invoked in three ways:

```
% make stimulate
```

or:

```
% make stimulate.db
```

or:

```
% make
```

The first command executes the commands needed to make the target *stimulate*, the second generates *stimulate.db*, and the third makes the first target listed in the makefile (which happens to be *stimulate*).

Dependencies

The previous makefile lists only the commands that will build the targets correctly and makes no attempt to minimize the amount of work it needs to do. Dependencies add the idea of conditional execution to a makefile. In the introduction, we said that a target *buzz.o* depends on a file *buzz.f* if a change in *buzz.f* results in a change to *buzz.o*. Using this idea, let's analyze the compilation needed to produce the target *stimulate* from the previous makefile.

Note that *stimulate* depends on the source files *stimulate.F*, *input.F*, and *output.F*. However, this fact is not particularly useful—by itself, it will not let us write an efficient makefile. *stimulate* really depends on the object files *stimulate.o*, *input.o*, and *output.o*. We could even say that stimulate does not depend on *stimulate.F* at all. A change to *stimulate.F* has no direct effect on *stimulate*; changing *stimulate.F* affects the object file, *stimulate.o*, which in turn affects *stimulate.F*. The f77 command hides this dependency by automatically running the UNIX linker; you must be aware of it when writing makefiles. To use these dependencies, we need to rewrite the compilation command to separate compilation and linking:

```
stimulate: stimulate.o input.o output.o
    f77 -o stimulate stimulate.o input.o output.o
```

The first line says that the target *stimulate* depends on the object files *stimulate.o*, *input.o*, and *output.o*. The second line uses the f77 command to link these files, assuming that they already exist. Together, these two lines say "The target *stimulate* is out of date if it is older than *stimulate.o*, *input.o*, or *output.o*. If this is the case, create a new version of *stimulate* by linking these object files." We use f77 to do the linking, rather than invoking the linker ld directly, even though no compilation is taking place. We could write two similar lines to correctly link the debugging version, *stimulate.db*. In general, a target line looks like this:

target-name: *list-of-dependencies*

This line says that *target-name* depends on all the files listed in the *list-of-dependencies*.

However, this does not account for compiling. The object files *stimulate.o*, *input.o*, and *output.o* have their own dependency relationships: the corresponding source files and any other files (e.g., header files that might be included within the source files). Therefore, if *stimulate.o* is older than *stimulate.F*, we need to compile a new object file before linking everything to create the target *stimulate*. The same logic applies to *input.o* and *output.o*. To express these secondary dependencies in a makefile, we list all three object files as targets, with their own dependencies, and provide a command to compile an optimized version of each object file:

```
stimulate:   stimulate.o input.o output.o
     f77 -o stimulate stimulate.o input.o output.o
stimulate.o: stimulate.F
     f77 -c -O  stimulate.F
input.o: input.F headerfile.F
     f77 -c -O input.F
output.o: output.F
     f77 -c -O output.F
```

In addition to the simple dependency relationship between the object file *input.o* and its source file, we have also stated that *input.o* depends on another file, *headerfile.F*. This could be a file providing some important definitions that the INCLUDE statement inserts into *input.F* during compilation. Obviously, a change to either *headerfile.F* or *input.F* will require *input.o* to be compiled anew. Remember to include such files as dependencies in your makefiles.

The previous example illustrates a crucial feature of makefiles: any target can depend on a file that is a target in its own right. In this case, **make** proceeds recursively by **make**ing the files on which the target depends, guaranteeing that they are up to date, before you **make**ing the original target. **make** will take the following steps to generate a target:

1. Check to see if the files on which a target depends are up to date with respect to their own sources.

2. Create a new version of any file that is out of date.

3. Check to see if the target is up to date with respect to the files on which it depends.

4. Create a new version of the target if it is out of date.

Because **make** is recursive, it continues checking dependencies until it can guarantee that all the files needed to generate a target are current. For example, if we change the file *output.F* and use this makefile to generate a new version of the target *stimulate*, **make** will take these steps:

1. Determines whether *stimulate.o*, *input.o*, and *output.o* are themselves targets.

2. Upon discovering that all three are targets, determines whether *input.o*, etc. are up to date relative to their sources.

3. Determines that *output.o* is older than *output.F*, and compiles a new version.

4. Checks *stimulate*'s date relative to *stimulate.o*, *input.o*, and the new version of *output.o*.

5. Determines that *stimulate* is now out of date with respect to *output.o*.

6. Creates a new version of *stimulate* by linking the object files.

By definition, a target is out of date if it does not exist as a file. Therefore, a target which is a task name, rather than a filename, is always out of date. The command **make** *task* will always execute the *task*.

We can easily create a similar set of lines describing how to build the debugging version of *stimulate*, *stimulate.db*. These would be identical, except they would specify some different command line options for the compilation. These lines should be included with the preceding example in the same makefile; one makefile should describe all useful ways of compiling a given project. There is no restriction on the number of targets that can be in a makefile, and you can enter a UNIX command to **make** any target listed in the makefile. For example, the following lines compile *stimulate.db* with the **-DDEBUG** and **-g** options i.e., define the name DEBUG for the preprocessor and augment the symbol table for **dbx**. This is shown in the following example:

```
stimulate.db:  stimulate.do input.do output.do
     f77 -o stimulate.db stimulate.do input.do output.do
stimulate.do: stimulate.F
     f77 -o stimulate.do -c -DDEBUG -g stimulate.F
input.do: input.F headerfile.F
     f77 -o stimulate.do -c -DDEBUG -g input.F
output.do: output.F
     f77 -o stimulate.do -c -DDEBUG -g output.F
```

This generates a separate set of object files for debugging versions of *stimulate.o*, *input.o*, and *output.o*. Presumably, these files have been compiled with additional debugging code which the preprocessor has included through conditional compilation.

Here is another feature we might want in the makefile: a special target to delete all of the object modules and start with a clean slate. In other words, when we enter the command **make clean**, we want to delete everything. To write this section of the makefile, we remember target names that aren't filenames are always out of date. When we enter the command **make clean**, **make** looks for a file named *clean*. If a file doesn't exist (and we'll agree: we'll never put a file with this name in our development directory), it will execute all of the commands listed for this target. Here is some typical code:

```
clean:
        rm *.o *.do stimulate stimulate.db
```

Targets such as these are very common. It is also common to see a target named **install**, which moves the finished executable to its final resting place and sets its access modes appropriately.

These are the basics you need to write useful makefiles. Abbreviations, macros, and default compilation rules (discussed in the next section) are advanced features to let you write shorter, simpler makefiles. At this point you should be able to write a correct makefile for a complex development project. **make** can eliminate many needless compilations while guaranteeing your programs are compiled correctly. It performs bookkeeping you would otherwise do yourself. If you use **make** properly, you will not have to worry about when your object files were compiled or when the source code was modified. Once you have described a target's dependencies accurately, **make** automates this task for you.

Abbreviations and Macros

To simplify writing commands, a makefile can define substitution macros and use several predefined abbreviations. Here are two useful abbreviations:

$@   Stands for the full name of the target.

$*   Stands for the name of the target with the suffix deleted.

To shorten the previous makefile, use the $@ and $* abbreviations as follows:

```
stimulate: stimulate.o input.o output.o
        f77 -o $@ $*.o input.o output.o
stimulate.db: stimulate.do input.do output.do
        f77 -o $@ $*.do stimulate.do input.o output.o
input.o: input.F inputdefs.H
        f77 -c -O $*.F
input.do: ...etc....
```

When compiling the target *stimulate*, $@ and $* both stand for the string "stimulate". When compiling the target *input.o*, $* stands for the string "input" and $@ stands for the string "input.o". These abbreviations are useful in many situations;

they are particularly important for writing default compilation rules (discussed below).

A macro definition begins at the left margin of the makefile and has the form:

macro-name = macro-body

When **make** is processing the makefile, it substitutes *macro-body* for the string $(*macro-name*). Therefore, we can shorten the preceding makefile even more by defining the macro abbreviations **DEPENDS** and **DBDEPENDS** (i.e., dependencies for the production and debugging versions) as follows:

```
DEPENDS = input.o output.o stimulate.o
DBDEPENDS = input.do output.do stimulate.do
stimulate: $(DEPENDS)
      f77 -o $@ $(DEPENDS)
stimulate.db:   $(DBDEPENDS)
      f77 -o $@ $(DBDEPENDS)
```

Macros are also useful for defining a set of compilation options. For example, the macro:

```
F66FLAGS = -onetrip -66 -w -O
```

is a collection of options for FORTRAN 66 compatibility. The makefile line:

```
f77 -c $(F66FLAGS) input.F
```

would therefore compile *input.F* in FORTRAN 66 compatibility mode with optimization. Remember that **make** requires a macro invocation to appear between the delimiters $(and) .

Search Directories

Normally, **make** looks for files in the current directory. Adding a **VPATH** line to the makefile allows **make** to find files in directories other than the current directory. A **VPATH** line has the following form:

VPATH=*dir1*:*dir2*: ... :*dirn*

That is, **VPATH** should be set equal to a list of directories, which are separated by colons. The previous line means that when **make** looks for a file, it will look first in the current directory, then in *dir1*, then in *dir2*, and so on until it has exhausted the directory list. This feature is useful if the source code for a large program is split among several directories or if many different executable programs use the same source code. In the latter case, the source code can be in a single directory, the object files and makefile for each executable program can be in a separate directory, and each makefile can use a **VPATH** line to point to the source code directory.

NOTE

VPATH does not work properly in some older versions of **make**.

Default Compilation Rules

Makefiles can become even more efficient if you use *default rules* to define how to build targets. With default rules, you do not need to specify how to build a target explicitly. Instead, you define some standard actions that **make** will use in most common situations.

To use this feature, you must define a set of significant suffixes. (Standard UNIX documentation refers to these suffixes as prerequisites. We consider this term obscure and do not use it; however, you should be aware of it.) The appearance of these suffixes in a target line will cause **make** to use a default rule to generate this target, if an appropriate rule exists. To specify the list of significant suffixes, use the **.SUFFIXES:** keyword, followed by the list of suffixes that will be involved in any default rules. By itself, **.SUFFIXES:** clears the suffix list. When it is followed by one or more suffixes, a **.SUFFIXES:** line adds the new suffixes to the list.

For example, the lines:

```
# Start by clearing the list of suffixes.
.SUFFIXES:
# We want to specify default rules for .F, .o, and
# .do files.
.SUFFIXES: .F .o .do
```

declare that any default rules in this makefile will involve the suffixes *.F*, *.o*, and *.do*.

To specify a default rule, list the suffixes that uniquely determine when the rule is applicable. The last suffix in the list must be the suffix of the target. Follow this list by a colon and a semicolon, then enter a UNIX command, stated in as general terms as possible. There must be no spaces in the suffix list for a default rule. For example, the statement:

```
.F.o:; f77 -c $@ -O $*.F
```

supplies a compilation rule that will be used by default whenever a target line states that a *.o* file depends on a *.F* file. When this is the case, **make** will use the FORTRAN compiler to compile the file named `target.F` with optimization, producing the object file `target.o`—provided, of course, that the makefile does not supply compilation instructions explicitly.

Similarly, the statement:

```
.F.do:; f77 -c $@ $(DEBUGFLAGS) $*.F
```

specifies a default rule for compiling debugging versions of object files. This compilation rule will be used when a target line lists a *.F* file as a dependency for a *.do* file and when no explicit compilation commands appear.

Putting this in context, consider the following makefile:

```
# Start by clearing the list of suffixes.
.SUFFIXES:
# We want to specify default rules for .F, .o, and
# .do files.
.SUFFIXES: .F .o .do
DEBUGFLAGS = -DDEBUG -g
PRODUCTFLAGS = -w -O
PRODUCTOBJS = program.o other.o
DEBUGOBJS = program.do other.do
EXECNAME = product
# A default rule to make a "production" .o file.
.F.o:; f77 -c $@ $(PRODUCTFLAGS) $*.F
# A default rule to make a .do file (debugging .o module).
.F.do:; f77 -c $@ $(DEBUGFLAGS) $*.F
# Generate executables:
production: $(PRODUCTOBJS)
        f77 -c $(EXECNAME) $(PRODUCTOBJS)
debug:  $(DEBUGOBJS)
        f77 -c $(EXECNAME) $(DEBUGOBJS)
# Target line to make some object modules.
program.o: program.F header.H
other.o: other.F
# Target lines to make some debugging object modules.
program.do: program.F header.H
other.do: other.F
clean:
        rm *.O *.do
        rm product
```

This is a complete makefile. The command **make program.o** checks the date of *program.F* and, if needed, uses the default rule for creating a *.o* file. This default rule leads to the compilation:

```
% f77 -c program.o -w -O program.F
```

which is compilation with optimization and with warning messages suppressed. Similarly, the command **make other.o** invokes the compilation:

```
% f77 -c other.o -w -O other.F
```

The commands **make other.do** and **make program.do** create debugging versions of these programs, as determined by the preprocessor variable **DEBUG**, with no optimization and debugging capabilities. The commands **make production** and

make debug generate production and debugging executable files by linking (and, if necessary, compiling) the appropriate object files. Finally, **make clean** deletes all object modules and executables. Note that the default rules for building *.o* and *.do* files work because they use abbreviations heavily. Abbreviations let you write generic compilation commands that can be used for many different compilations.

The **make** facility can take this a step further and provide its own default rules for compilation. For example, if you do not provide a default rule for FORTRAN compilation, **make** will supply its own default rule. Consequently, the following line is a complete makefile:

```
program.o: program.F
```

With this makefile, the command **make** executes the compilation:

```
% f77 -c program.F
```

make has its own default rules for FORTRAN, C, **lex, yacc,** and some other languages. In the extreme, a null makefile (i.e., a makefile that is 0 bytes long) is perfectly valid. With a null makefile, the command:

```
% make program.o
```

executes the command:

```
% f77 -c program.F
```

This is supplied completely by the **make**'s default rules. However, this is not a particularly good way to use **make**, because these internal default rules do not, and cannot, know anything about the options you want to use for compilation. Consequently, using them sacrifices much of the versatility that UNIX compilers offer.

Invoking make

To use the **make** facility, create a file named *makefile* in the directory where the source code on which you are working resides. After you have written the makefile, enter the command:

```
% make target-name
```

within this directory, where *target-name* is the name of the task you want to perform. In many cases, it will be the name of a file you wish to generate. Often, it will simply be the name of a task and will not correspond to any file. With the

make command, **make** reads the makefile in the current directory and executes whatever commands are needed to create the target you named successfully. If you omit *target-name*, **make** will create the first target described in the makefile.

Normally, there is a single makefile per directory. This makefile should govern all the compilations for the source code within the directory; of course, it may link this code to other modules that reside elsewhere. Ideally, you and your colleagues have coordinated software development in a way that lets you link your module to standard versions of other modules that have been released.

Convenient Flags

This section lists the most useful options for **make**. Others are described in the *UNIX Programmer's Reference Manual*.

-f *filename*

> Normally, the **make** command looks for a makefile within the current directory that is named either *makefile* or *Makefile*. This option tells **make** to use *filename* as a makefile, rather than the standard makefile. For example, the command:

```
% make -f othermake target
```

> looks in a file named *othermake* for instructions describing how to make *target*.

-n   Don't execute any commands. Instead, list the commands that would be executed under normal conditions. In other words, **make** lists the commands it would issue if it were to **make** a target now, without taking any action. This is useful for debugging. Remember that **make**'s behavior is time-dependent: since **make**'s behavior depends on the last time a file was modified, it will not necessarily take the same actions whenever you use it.

-i   Normally, **make** terminates immediately if a command returns a nonzero error code. When used with **make**, some UNIX commands return this error code incorrectly. The -i option forces **make** to ignore these error codes. (Equivalently, the makefile can include the special entry **.IGNORE**.) This is particularly useful because some UNIX programs return a nonzero exit code incorrectly when used with **make**.

-k   The -k option is similar to -i, except that **make** will not attempt to build the target in which the error occurs. It will continue to build any other targets required.

-q   Don't execute any commands. Instead, determine whether the target of this **make** is up to date. Return a zero status code if the target is up to date, and return a nonzero status code if the target is not.

-s   Normally, **make** prints all commands that it executes on the terminal. With this flag, **make** is silent and does not print any messages. (Equivalently, the makefile can include the special entry .SILENT.)

-t   Don't execute any commands found within the make file. Instead, "touch" all target files that are out of date, making them up to date without changing them.

make and RCS

The RCS source management system, described in the next chapter, lets a team of programmers store and check out source code in a controlled way. However, source files managed by RCS are not available at all times. Before they can be used, you must first check them out. Furthermore, their date reflects the time they were checked out, not the time they were modified. This may cause extra compilations.

If you use RCS, your makefiles should take these issues into account. The following example shows how RCS check-out can be integrated into a makefile:

```
# Guarantee that the program mod is current.
# mod depends on its object file, which depends
# on its FORTRAN source.  The FORTRAN source is
# under RCS management.
mod: mod.o
        f77 -o mod mod.o
mod.o: RCS/mod.F,v
        co mod.F ; f77 -c mod.F; rm -f mod.F
```

This makefile lists the RCS file *mod.F,v* (located within the subdirectory *RCS*), rather than the file *mod.F*, as the source on which *mod.o* depends. At any given time, *mod.F* may not exist; if it exists, its date may reflect the time it was checked out, not the last time it was modified. Describing the dependency in terms of *RCS/mod.F,v* eliminates this problem. If this RCS file is more recent than the object file, then someone has modified the source file *mod.F* and checked it in more recently than the last compilation. To get the an accurate version of the source file, **make** checks out the current version of *mod.F*, from which it generates the object file *mod.o*.

With this scheme, the suffix *.F,v*, rather than the suffix *.F*, would have to appear in any suffix list for default rules. In addition, modifying the source code will not cause a recompilation until the source has been checked in. Since you don't want to check in a source file for each new compilation (this defeats the purpose of RCS), you will want to define two targets for each program in your makefile: a standard target that compiles a new version using released sources (i.e., RCS sources) and an experimental target that uses unreleased source code that does not check out a new version from RCS. For more information about RCS, see Chapter 7, *Source Management with RCS*.

A Note on Source Files

make assumes that your source code is split into several different files. If it is not (i.e., if all the sources for your program are in one single file), there is no reason to use **make**. You will always compile the entire program every time, wasting a lot of time recompiling routines that have not changed. Unfortunately, many FORTRAN programmers like to put all their code into a single huge file. This is a bad practice for several reasons. As we have said, you cannot use **make** effectively; it is almost impossible for several programmers to work on the same program; and one large file is very unwieldly.

UNIX provides a program called **fsplit** which breaks a FORTRAN program into a group of files, one per subroutine or function. This is a good first try, but still not quite what you really want: working with several hundred files is not really much more convenient than working with one gigantic file. **fsplit** takes you to the other extreme. Ideally, you should collect groups of routines that perform related tasks into files. Each file is then a module that contains all the code for some well-defined part of the program. For example, you might have a set of I/O functions in one file, the core of the application in a second file, a preprocessor for input data in a third file, error handling routines in a fourth file, and so on. This approach, which you will have to implement by hand, allows you to take advantage of **make** and simplifies the task of working on your source code.

Error Messages

This section lists the most common error messages that **make** produces and their meanings. **make** implementations vary, so the messages may differ on your system.

Don't know how to make *target*

> The makefile does not contain any rules showing **make** how to construct the given *target* explicitly, and there are no default rules applicable to *target*.

Too many command lines for *name*

The makefile contains more than one explicit target line telling **make** how to create *name*. A makefile can only have one target line for each target.

target **not remade because of errors**

This message only appears if you invoke **make** with the -k option. It means that an error (i.e., a nonzero exist status code) occurred while **make** was building *target*. As a result, **make** gave up work on that target and continued to the next.

target **is up to date**

The *target* you specified on the command line is already up to date, and, therefore, **make** is taking no action.

Must be a separator on rules line *n*

In a makefile, each line following a target (i.e., each line describing how to build the target) must begin with a tab. This message informs you that line *n* should begin with a tab but doesn't.

No suffix list

make needs to use a default rule to make the target you specified; however, the suffix list is empty. This can only happen if your makefile includes the line .**SUFFIXES:** with no suffixes following it; **make**'s default suffix list will normally prevent this message from occurring.

Unknown flag argument *flag*

You have invoked **make** with a command line flag that it does not recognize.

No description argument after -f flag

You have invoked **make** with the -f flag but have not specified the name of a makefile with the flag.

Infinitely recursive macro

The makefile contains a macro which it cannot expand because the macro includes itself (e.g., **CFLAGS** = $(**CFLAGS**)).

Inconsistent rules lines for '*prefixes*'

You have specified default rules for the given suffixes, but the line specifying these rules is badly formed. You may have typed :: instead of :; after the suffixes to which the rule applies. Note that this message only appears if there are already default rules (possibly the implicit default rules built into **make**) applicable to these prefixes. In many cases, **make** will simply ignore the rule.

Warning: *macro* **changed after being used**

You changed the definition of a macro after the macro was used in the makefile. The consequences of this are difficult to predict, since **make**'s rules on when macros are expanded are complex and considerably beyond the scope of this book.

Some Final Notes

This chapter describes some important makefiles features. For more information, see the description of the **make** command in Section 1 of the *UNIX Programmer's Reference Manual* and to the Nutshell Handbook *Managing Projects with make*.

Both the standard UNIX documentation and this chapter have described **make** in terms of automating compilations. It can also be used for maintaining documentation, accounting, or any other task that involves a large number of files. **make** has been used to tailor on-line documentation to a system configuration by running editor scripts to include and delete sections from manuals.

Remember that makefiles are much more than command lists. They are programs with complicated rules for conditional execution, default actions, and other features. In short, **make** is one of UNIX's most versatile tools when used appropriately. The time you can save during compilation is worth the time you invest writing your makefile.

7

Source Management with RCS

Revision Trees
Basic Operations
More About Checking In
New and Old Generations
Other Features

RCS (the *Revision Control System*) is a source-code management tool designed to aid program development under UNIX. It is not a standard part of UNIX per se but is distributed with the rest of the system as part of the user-contributed software (along with the manual entries for the *UNIX Programmer's Reference Manual*). More recently, the Free Software Foundation has published a version of RCS. Many UNIX versions provide a collection of tools called SCCS. SCCS is functionally identical to RCS but has a completely different user interface. If your site uses SCCS, this chapter will still be a useful conceptual introduction; however, you will need to learn a different set of commands.

RCS meets an important need in managing large programming projects. It allows you to automate many of the tasks involved in coordinating a team of programmers. These tasks include maintaining all versions of a program in a recoverable form, preventing several programmers from modifying the same code simultaneously, helping programmers to merge two different development tracks into a single version, ensuring that a single program is not undergoing multiple simultaneous revisions, and maintaining logs for revisions and other changes.

Revision Trees

RCS maintains your revisions in a tree structure. The first version of a file under RCS control is the root of a tree. It is given number 1.1. Succeeding versions that descend linearly from this file are the trunk of the tree, and are numbered 1.2, 1.3, etc.

A new development branch can begin at any point on this tree. This branch consists of another chain of descent beginning from some other file. RCS gives the first "branch" beginning at Revision 1.3 the number 1.3.1, it numbers the second branch beginning at this point 1.3.2, etc. The first revision along the first branch is 1.3.1.1, the second is 1.3.1.2, etc. Branches can begin at any point, at any time and can start from other branches, from the root, etc. Just as the word root refers to the first element in a tree, we will use the word tip to refer to the last version of a file along a branch. Figure 7-1 shows an RCS tree containing eight versions of one file. The trunk of this tree consists of five versions; a branch (another develpment path) started from Version 1.3.

The tool **rcsmerge** exists to help you merge versions from different branches of development. This tool can be very useful if two developers have been working in different directions on the same program. One programmer might be fixing bugs in an old release, and another might be adding some new features. **rcsmerge** helps you to integrate both of their changes painlessly, so that you can produce a new version containing both the bug fixes and the new features. It will not be described further here.

Basic Operations

The two fundamental commands for using RCS are **ci** and **co**. These commands "check in" and "check out" software that RCS is maintaining. When you check a file in, RCS deletes your source file and creates or modifies a file called *source*, v, where *source* is the name of the original and , v is an extension that indicates an RCS file. By deleting *source*, RCS prevents you from doing any further editing without using **co** again. When you check out a file, RCS extracts a version of the file—usually the most recent version—from the corresponding RCS file.

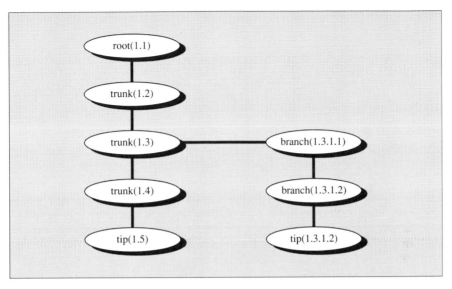

Figure 7-1. A simple RCS revision tree

To do a simple checkin, use the following command:

```
% ci filename
```

This creates a new RCS version of your file. If the file is not currently managed by RCS, this command places the file under RCS management, gives it the version number 1.1, and prompts for a description of the file. If the file is already being managed by RCS, this command will assign the next higher version number in the sequence (1.2 follows 1.1) and will prompt you for a description of the changes you have made since the last checkin. The following example shows what happens when you check in Revision 1.4 of a file called *test*:

```
% ci test
test,v  <--  test
new revision: 1.4; previous revision: 1.3
enter log message:
(terminate with ^D or single '.')
>> fixed a trivial error on the last line
>> .
done
%
```

The prompt ">>" indicates that RCS is waiting for a line of text. Typing a . (period) or pressing CTRL-D on an unused line terminates the log message. At this point, RCS enters the message in its file and prints the word "done". RCS will warn you if you check in a file that has not been modified since it was last checked out. You can force it to check the file in anyway by typing **y** in response to its warning message:

```
% ci test
test,v  <--  test
new revision: 1.8; previous revision: 1.7
File test is unchanged with respect to revision 1.7
check in anyway? [ny](n): y
done
%
```

Used by itself, the command **ci** deletes your working version of the file. If you want to retain a read-only version of the file, enter the command:

```
% ci -u filename
```

In this case, you retain a copy of *filename* for reference. You cannot modify the file, however, because it is no longer checked out.

In order to use a file that has been placed under the control of RCS, use the check-out command, **co**, as follows:

```
% co filename
```

where *filename* is either the name of the file you want to work on or the name of the RCS archive file for *filename* (i.e., the commands **co test** and **co test,v** are identical). This retrieves the latest version of your file from the RCS file in which it has been stored.

By itself, **co** is sufficient if you only want to read, compile, or otherwise use the file without changing it. However, **co** restores your source file with read-only access: you cannot edit it or make changes. If you want to modify the file, use the command:

```
% co -l filename
```

This not only creates a file that you can modify but also installs a lock. This means that no one else can modify the file until you return it to RCS with **ci**. Other programmers can still use **co**, getting a read-only version of the file. Conversely, if someone else has already locked the file, **co -l** will not let you check it out. If you try to check out a file that someone else has already locked, **co** will reply:

```
% co -l lockedfile
co error:  revision n already locked by someone-else
```

where *someone-else* is the username of whoever locked the file. If you see this message, negotiate with the lock's owner to find out when he or she will be finished.

If strict locking (explained below) is in effect, you cannot check in a new version of a file unless you have locked it first: unless you locked the file on check-out, you will only have a write-protected version which you cannot modify and which you don't need to check in. You can always use **co** to check a file out, no matter who has locked it. You can then read it, compile it, and do anything you want *except* change it.

NOTE

It is possible to circumvent this protection by using the UNIX commands for changing file access modes, etc. Please don't. If you do not want the protection that RCS gives, don't use RCS in the first place. One person who refuses to play by the rules can quickly confuse a large development effort.

RCS Directories and Files

Before checking a file in or out, RCS always looks for a subdirectory named *RCS* within the current directory. If this directory exists, RCS will keep all the files it creates within that directory, keeping your working directories free from extra clutter.

RCS creates a separate RCS file for every file under its management. This file stores a description of the file you are managing, the entire change log, the current version of the file, a list of users who are allowed to access the file, the file's date and time, and a list of changes that lets RCS reproduce any obsolete version of the file at will. Despite the information they maintain, RCS files are not substantially larger than the source files they manage. However, they do grow with time. If you need to reduce your disk requirements, you can use the **rcs** command to eliminate old versions of the file that are no longer needed. Do this with the command:

```
% rcs -orange filename
```

where *range* specifies the revision numbers you want to trim from your file. It can be a single revision number (e.g., **-o1.3** deletes Revision 1.3); two revision numbers separated by a dash (e.g., **-o1.1-1.3** deletes Revisions 1.1, 1.2, and 1.3); a revision number preceded by a dash (e.g., **-o-1.2.4.3** deletes all revisions on branch 1.2.4 up to and including 1.2.4.3); or a revision number followed by a dash (e.g., **-o1.4.3.3-** deletes all revisions from 1.4.3.3 to the tip of branch 1.4.3).

This command also deletes the messages for any discarded versions from the change log. It never deletes the initial description of the file, even if you delete Version 1.1. It never changes version numbering; for example, Version 1.78 remains Version 1.78, even if you delete all previous versions.

The Revision Log

Whenever you check in a file, RCS prompts you for a log message describing the changes you have made since the last revision. This log exists so that you can easily find out who changed the program, when, and why.

The command **rlog** displays the entire log for a file. For example:

```
% rlog test
rcs file:          test,v;   Working file:      test
head:              1.2
locks:
access list:
symbolic names:
comment leader:   "# "
total revisions: 2;      selected revisions: 2
description:
this is a simple test of rcs
to play with it
---------------------------
revision 1.2
date: 86/06/26 10:00:15; author: loukides; state: Exp;
lines added/del: 2/0
another revision to demonstrate the features of a log.
---------------------------
revision 1.1
date: 86/06/26 08:24:14;  author: loukides;   state: Exp;
This is the initial version of the program.
=========================================================
%
```

In addition to the revision number and the log of comments, this display shows the date and time at which each revision was checked in, the author of the modifications, the total number of lines added and deleted in this modification, and the file's current state. Note that RCS considers a modification to a line to be deleting the old line and adding the new line. The state field shows the file's status at each revision. By default, the state field will always be **Exp**, which stands for experimental. By using the command:

```
% rcs -s filename
```

you can give any revision any state you wish. This is described in the section "Other Features" later in this chapter.

Identification Strings

If you wish, RCS can put identification strings into your source code and object files. These strings contain information about the current revision number, the author, and the time the file was last checked in. Here is a typical identification string:

```
$Header: lindecomp.F,v 1.1 86/06/27 11:28:37 loukides Exp $
```

It shows the filename, the version number, the modification date and time, and the person who made the last modification to this version.

To include an identification string in a file, insert the marker:

```
$Header$
```

To let the program compile correctly, the marker should be within a comment statement. RCS will replace this marker with the identification string whenever you check out the file.

Alternatively, you can place this marker within an initialized **CHARACTER** variable that is not used elsewhere in the program. During compilation, the compiler will include the identification string within the object module. For example, RCS will place the identification string within the following **DATA** statement:

```
CHARACTER*128 RCSID
DATA RCSID /$Header$/
```

When this code is compiled, the identification string will be used as data to initialize the local variable **RCSID**. This string will therefore be preserved in the resulting object file and in all files to which this file is linked. You can then use the **ident** command described below (or another tool of your own design) to retrieve all the RCS headers in the object file. By doing so, you can determine at a later time which versions were used to produce an executable. Knowing exactly which source code was used to build any release of a program can be essential if you are debugging a large, widely used application. Note that RCS does not maintain the object modules themselves. It places its header in the source file; compilation propagates this string into the object file.

NOTE

This example assumes that the RCS header is fewer than 128 characters long. In practice, this should suffice for almost all cases. However, there is no restriction on its length.

RCS will replace the marker Log with the accumulated revision log messages. This marker should be contained within a comment. Since the standard FOR-TRAN comment must appear entirely on a single line, you must use a preprocessor comment; for example:

```
/*      $Log$       */
```

When you use such preprocessor comments, the filename for your FORTRAN program must end with the extension *.F*. In some versions, the RCS machinery contains its own mechanism for handling the multiline message produced by Log; it automatically reproduces the appropriate comment marker (for FORTRAN, a C) at the beginning of each line. If your version of RCS supports this feature, you don't need to wrap the Log marker with a preprocessor-style comment.

Other markers with similar functions are $Author$, $Date$, $Locker$, $Revision$, $Source$, and $State$. RCS replaces $Source$ with the complete pathname of the RCS file storing this version. The meanings of the other markers should be self-evident.

The utility program **ident** will search through any file, regardless of its type (i.e., text files, object files, even core dumps) and extract all identification strings. For example, the command **ident a.out** prints all the identification strings it finds in the executable file named *datamasher*:

```
% ident datamasher
$Header:lindecomp.F,v 1.3 86/06/27 11:28:37 mike Exp$
$Header:satman.F,v 1.7 86/09/21 15:29:38 mike Exp$
$Header:doggies.F,v 1.5 86/10/20 10:07:38 howard Exp$
```

If you produced *datamasher* by compiling many files under RCS control and linking them, this command would summarize all the modules and revisions from which *datamasher* is built. This can make it easier to discover whether an executable file was linked with the correct versions of all object modules, or it can help you to discover which versions of the source code are responsible for some bug. For example, after reading the previous report, you might remember that Version 1.5 of *doggies.F* had a numeric stability problem that was fixed in Version 1.6. A look at the RCS log for *doggies.F* would confirm this. You could then relink, do some testing, and send your customer a new version of *datamasher*.

Strict Access

By default, RCS is in the strict-access mode. This mode has two important features:

1. No one is allowed to check in a file without locking it first.
2. No one can modify a file unless it was checked out locked.

To take RCS out of the strict-access mode, use the command:

    % rcs -U *filename*

where *filename* is the name of a particular file under RCS management. It may be either the working filename or the RCS filename (i.e., the name with the *,v* extension). This places RCS in the open-access mode for this file. In this mode, the owner of *filename* can modify the file without locking it first. All other users must still lock a file before modifying it. Only use RCS in the "open-access" mode if you are the only programmer modifying this file. Otherwise, you risk multiple simultaneous modifications by different programmers and thus defeat one of RCS' primary aims.

Return RCS to strict access with the command:

    % rcs -L *filename*

More About Checking In

The **ci** command may refuse to let you check in a file, printing the message:

    ci error: no lock set by *your-name*

This can only occur under two circumstances:

1. If you did not lock the file upon check-out in the strict-access mode.
2. If someone locked the file after you checked it out in open-access mode.

ci will not tell you who locked the file. As far as it is concerned, you are the one who is at fault for not locking a file you intended to modify and replace. If this situation occurs, lock the file by using the following command:

    % rcs -l *filename*

At this point, two things can happen. In the first situation, where no one else locked the file, RCS retroactively locks the file so that you can check in your file normally with the **ci** command. In the second situation, RCS will print the warning:

    rcs error: revision *n* already locked by *someone-else*

where *someone-else* is the username of whoever has locked your file. You need to negotiate with him or her to reach a solution. Presumably, the two of you have been modifying the file at the same time and need to assess any damage. Tools like **rcsdiff** and **rcsmerge** will help you find out the differences between the two files and create a new version that incorporates the modifications to both files. Neither of these situations should occur unless you or your colleagues are playing "fast and loose" with file access. RCS does not eliminate the need for discipline and coordination. It only makes discipline and coordination easier to live with.

At times, you may want to do a checkin, followed immediately by a checkout. You may want to install a version reflecting the current state of your program (possibly as a backup), then continue editing immediately. Rather than using two operations, RCS lets you perform both with the command:

```
% ci -l filename
```

This updates the RCS file and gives you a lock without erasing your working file, allowing you to continue editing immediately.

New and Old Generations

At points in the development cycle, you will decide that your program has reached a decisively different stage. You may want your version numbering to reflect this new state: for example, by changing from Version 1.X to Version 2.1. To do this, use the **-r** option when you check in the program, as shown in the following example:

```
% ci -rn filename
```

This assigns the version number *n* to the most recent version of *filename*. For example, the command:

```
% ci -r2.3 makefile
```

checks in *makefile* with version number 2.3

If you want to check out an old version of this file, use the **-r** option with **co**. For example:

```
% co -l -r1.4 makefile
```

retrieves Version 1.4 of *makefile*, provided that it has not been declared obsolete. There are several reasons for retrieving an old version: nostalgia and recovering from disastrous modifications are only two of the more likely ones. You may also wish to start a different course of development from a pre-existing software base (e.g., to develop software for two different systems). When you again check in this file, by default RCS will, by default, create a new branch for development. It will give the first item in this branch the number *n*.1.1, where *n* is the number of the version you checked out.

Other Features

States

You can use the **rcs** command to assign a *state* to any version of a file. A state can be any string of characters, as long as the string has some meaning for you. For example, you can assign the state **Exp** for experimental software, **Stab** for stable software, **Rel** for released software, and **Obs** for obsolete software maintained for archival purposes only. To assign a state to a particular revision of a file, use the command:

```
% rcs -sstate:revision filename
```

where *state* is the state you want to assign and *revision* is a revision number. If you omit *revision*, RCS will assign this state to the last revision on the main branch of development.

Names

By using the command:

```
% rcs -n filename
```

you can assign a symbolic name to any revision. This name can be used in place of a revision number in all commands within the RCS system. For example, you can assign the name *betatest* to Version 2.4 of a program with the command:

```
% rcs -nbetatest:2.4 filename
```

After making this assignment, the two commands:

```
% co -rbetatest filename
```

and:

```
% co -r2.4 filename
```

are equivalent. Assign a symbolic name by entering a command of the following form:

```
% rcs -nname:revision filename
```

where *name* is the symbolic name you want to assign, *revision* is the version number of a specific version, and *filename* is the name of a file under RCS control. If you omit the version number, rcs will delete the symbolic name. A symbolic name can only be assigned to a single version in each file under RCS management. rcs will print an error message if you try to assign a symbolic name to two different revisions. For example:

```
% rcs -nworking:1.4 test        Name Version 1.4 "working"
rcs file: test,v
done
% rcs -nworking:1.5 test        Try to name Version 1.5 "working"
rcs file: test,v
rcs error: symbolic name working already bound to 1.4
test,v unchanged.               Error message; nothing happened
% rcs -nworking test            Delete the name "working"
rcs file: test,v
done
%
```

If you wish, you can assign several different symbolic names to the same version.

Changing a File's Description

If you need to change the description associated with a file, use the command:

```
% rcs -t filename
```

This will delete the current description from the RCS file for *filename* and prompt you for a new description. For example:

```
% rcs -t test
rcs file: test,v
enter description, terminated with ^D or '.':
NOTE:  This is NOT the log message!
>> This is a new description for the file.
>> .
done
%
```

This leaves all the logging messages unchanged.

You can do the same thing during checkin by using the -t option with the **ci** command. In this case, **ci** will prompt you for a new descriptive message first and then prompt you for a message for a revision log:

```
% ci -t test
test,v  <--  test
new revision: 1.10; previous revision: 1.9
enter description, terminated with ^D or '.':
NOTE:  This is NOT the log message!
>> A new description message
>> .
enter log message:
(terminate with ^D or single '.')
>> A new log message
>> .
done
%
```

Access Lists

An *access list* is a list of users who are allowed to use RCS to manipulate a file. In most cases, RCS will refuse to allow anyone not on the access list lock or otherwise modify a file. There are only three exceptions to this rule:

- The owner of a file can always access it.

- A superuser can always access any file.

- If the access list is empty, anyone can access the file.

Access lists apply to the RCS revision tree as a whole (i.e., to all revisions of a file). You either have access to all versions of a file or you do not have access to any.

When a file is first placed under the control of RCS, it has an empty access list. This means that anyone can access it, provided that it is not locked. To add names to the access list of any file, use the command:

```
% rcs -anames filename
```

where *names* is a list of login names separated by commas. This list cannot contain any spaces. For example, the command:

```
% rcs -aellen,john,james testfile
```

adds the users with login names **ellen**, **john**, and **james** to the file named *testfile*.

If many people are working on the project, it may be simpler to add names in batches rather than list them individually. Therefore, you may want to add all the names from one file access list to another. For example, you may wish to create an RCS file, then give it the same access list as other files in the same project. To do this, use the following **rcs** command:

```
% ci newfile              Put newfile under RCS management
% rcs -Aoldfile newfile   Give newfile the access list from oldfile
```

To delete names from a file access list, use the command:

```
% rcs -enames filename
```

Again, *names* is a list of names separated by commas; it may not contain spaces. For example, the command:

```
% rcs -eellen,john,james testfile
```

removes the names **ellen**, **john**, and **james** from the access list for *testfile*. Anyone who is allowed to access a file is allowed to edit its access list.

Any user can check out a read-only version of the file, whether they are on the access list. If you try to lock a file and are not on the access list, RCS will reply with the following error message:

```
co error:  user yourname not on access list
```

8

Program Timing and Profiling

Simple Timings
Introduction to Profiling
Generating a Profile with gprof
Profiling with prof

Most programs run in a time-critical environment, therefore, it is important to minimize execution time. However, varying system load and other conditions make it difficult to measure program execution time accurately. It is even more difficult to pinpoint the portions of a program that are performance problems. UNIX provides a group of timing and profiling utilities to help maximize the performance your programs achieve. In this chapter, we discuss the tools that help you get the best performance from FORTRAN programs.

There are many aspects of performance: total "wall clock" time, CPU time, the number of times any routine or code segment was executed, the percentage of the total time performing I/O, etc. Therefore, there are many different kinds of profilers, each adapted to a particular purpose. These profilers fall into two major classes:

- **Simple timers.** Simple timers measure the total time that the system spent executing a program, together with other statistics about the system's CPU usage. The results apply to the program as a whole; they are not broken down in any way. Two simple timers are available:

time   A simple timer built into the UNIX C shell.

/bin/time   Another version of *time* that is not built into the C shell. It is useful in situations where the C shell is not applicable (e.g., to time commands executed by **make**).

In addition, timing routines may be called from within the program itself.

- **Report-generating profilers.** Report-generating profilers produce a rather lengthy report analyzing program performance on a routine-by-routine basis. They help you discover which routines account for most of the program's execution time, helping you to direct your tuning efforts to the most important parts of the code. There are two report-generating profilers:

prof   A profiler that provides a *flat analysis* of your program's execution, counting the total time spent in each function and the number of calls to each function.

gprof   A profiler that provides a *call graph analysis* of your program. This profile counts the amount of time spent in each function, like **prof**. It also provides a much more detailed analysis of how functions call each other, how much time each function spends on behalf of each of its callers, etc.

The following table summarizes of the commands used to enable and produce results from the different kinds of profilers. For **prof** and **gprof**, generating raw data and using the results (either producing a readable report or producing an improved version of the program) are separate steps.

Generate Data	Produce Results	Explanation
time a.out	-	Simple profile.
/bin/time a.out	-	Simple profile.
f77 -p; a.out	prof	Flat profile; produces a report.
f77 -pg; a.out	gprof	Call graph profile; produces a report.

Simple Timings

Two programs, *time* and */bin/time*, provide simple timings. Their information is highly accurate, because no profiling overhead distorts the program's performance. Neither program provides any analysis on the routine or trace level. They report the total execution time, some other global statistics, and nothing more. You can use them on any program without special compilation **f77** options.

time and */bin/time* differ primarily in that *time* is built into the C shell. Therefore, it cannot be used in shell scripts or in makefiles. It also cannot be used if you prefer the Bourne shell (**sh**). */bin/time* is an independent executable file and therefore can be used in any situation. To get a simple program timing, enter either *time* or */bin/time*, followed by the command you would normally use to execute the program. For example, to time a program named **analyze**, enter the following command:

```
% time analyze inputdata outputfile
9.0u 6.7s 0:30 18% 23+24k 285+148io 625pf+0w
```

This indicates that the program spent 9.0 seconds on behalf of the user (user time), 6.7 seconds on behalf of the system (system time, or time spent executing UNIX kernel routines on the user's behalf), and a total of 30 seconds elapsed time. Elapsed time is the wall clock time from the moment you enter the command until it terminates, including time spent waiting for other users, I/O time, etc. By definition, the elapsed time is greater than your total CPU time and can even be several times larger.

The following example shows the CPU time as a percentage of the elapsed time (18 percent). The remaining data report virtual memory management and I/O statistics. They are the amount of shared memory used, the amount of nonshared memory used (**k**), the number of block input and output operations (**I/O**), and the number of page faults plus the number of swaps (**pf** and **w**) The memory management figures are unreliable in many implementations, so take them with a grain of salt.

/bin/time only reports the real time (elapsed time), user time, and system time. For example:

```
% /bin/time analyze inputdata outputfile
        60.8 real           11.4 user          4.6 sys
```

This reports that the program ran for 60.8 seconds before terminating, using 11.4 seconds of user time and 4.6 seconds of system time, for a total of 16 seconds of CPU time.

Introduction to Profiling

Now that we have discussed simple timings, we can move to the profiling tools. These tools provide timing information for individual routines within the program. First, we need to introduce some terminology. If routine **A** calls routine **B**, we call **A** the parent of **B** and we call **B** the child of **A**. We refer to all the routines that routine **C** calls directly as the children of **C**, and we refer to all routines that **C** calls, directly or indirectly, as the descendants of **C**. For example, consider the routines **A**, **B1**, **B2**, **C1**, **C2**, **C3**, and **D**. A calls **B1** and **B2**; **B1** calls **C1**, **C2**, and **C3**; and **D** calls **B2**. Figure 8-1 represents this graphically.

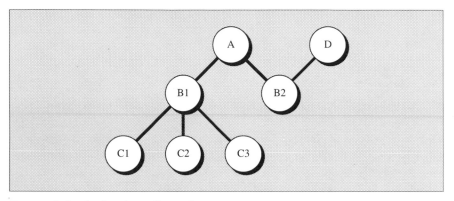

Figure 8-1. A simple call graph

B1 and **B2** are the children of **A**, and **B2** is the only child of **D**. **C1**, **C2**, and **C3** are all descendants of **A**, along with **B1** and **B2**. **A** is the only parent of **B1**, and both **A** and **D** are parents of **B2**.

The profilers produce two distinct kinds of output: a flat profile shows the total time that the program spent executing each routine and an extensive call graph profile analyzes execution time in terms of each routine's parents and children. For example, a flat profile for the previous routines shows the total time spent in **A**, **B1**, **B2**, and so on. The call graph profile provides more detail by splitting up the total execution time for each routine into several constituent parts. It shows how much of the total time spent executing any routine can be attributed to calls from each of its parents. It also shows how much of the total time spent executing any routine was spent executing each of the routine's children. This detailed information lets you determine which portions of the program are used heavily and, in addition, why they are used heavily: not just which procedure requires the most execution time, but which calls to this procedure (and which calls within the procedure) account for this time.

Preparing a Program for Profiling

A normal executable file cannot be profiled. Before you can profile a program, you must enable profiling. To enable profiling, relink the program's object modules use one of the following commands:

```
% f77 -pg -o myfile f1.o f2.o...    Enable gprof profiling for myfile
```

or:

```
% f77 -g -o myfile f1.o f2.o...    Enable prof profiling for myfile
```

f1.o, f2.o, etc. are the object modules that must be linked to generate the executable program *myfile*. Note that you could also generate *myfile* by recompiling your source code from scratch; however, this is inefficient. Why recompile (relatively slowly) when all you need to do is link (relatively quickly)?

Programs run significantly slower (roughly 30 percent) when profiling is enabled. Therefore, you should disable profiling (by relinking without **-p** or **-pg**) before releasing a production version.

Name Handling

In order to read a profile, you need to know how the compiler converts the name of a FORTRAN subprogram into a symbol name. Normally, the compiler generates a symbol name by converting the subprogram's name to lowercase and adding an _ (underscore) before and after. Because FORTRAN is normally case-insensitive, it does not need to distinguish between upper- and lower-case letters. Following are some typical conversions:

Subprogram Name	Symbol Name
XXX2	**_xxx2_**
mklo	**_mklo_**
miXEd	**_mixed_**

In a profile, the symbol **_xxx2_** identifies entries describing *XXX2*, etc.

If the compiler is invoked with the **-U** (case-sensitive) option, it does not convert the names to lowercase. For example:

Subprogram Name	Symbol Name
XXX2	**_XXX2_**
mklo	**_mklo_**
miXEd	**_miXEd_**

The main program is always assigned the name _MAIN_, regardless of the -U option.

Generating a Profile with gprof

Once you have enabled profiling, run the executable file with any reasonable data. This produces a file named *gmon.out*, in addition to any other output produced by your program. *gmon.out* is a collection of statistics in a form that is not readable by humans.

You must now use the UNIX utility **gprof** to interpret these statistics and present them in a usable form. **gprof** produces useful data from one or more *gmon.out* files. To create this table, use **gprof** as follows:

```
% gprof list-of-options executable-file stat-files > output
```

where *executable-file* is the name of the executable file that you are profiling and *stat-files* is a list of *gmon* files that have resulted from executing the program. This feature lets you generate a profile from several different program runs. If you want to generate the profile from a single file named *gmon.out*, you can omit *stat-files*. Similarly, you can omit *executable-file* if the name of the executable file is *a.out*. The output from **gprof** is sent to standard output, which is normally connected to your terminal. Because these tables are much too large to be viewed on a terminal, you should redirect standard output to a file.

list-of-options is a list of valid **gprof** options. The options relevant for profiling FORTRAN programs are:

-b   As part of its report, **gprof** normally prints several pages explaining the entries in the profile tables. This option suppresses these explanations.

-e *name* Do not include the routine *name* in the call graph profile. Similarly, do not include any of *name*'s descendants unless these routines are called via routines other than *name*. Time spent executing these rou-

tines is included in the totals. This option does not affect the flat profile, which includes all routines. The command line may contain any
number of **-e** options. For example:

```
-e _sub1_ -e _sub2_
```

leaves the FORTRAN routines **SUB1** and **SUB2** out of the call graph.

-E *name*   This is similar to **-e**, but time spent executing the omitted routines is
not included in the totals.

-f *name*   Print the call graph profile for *name* and its descendants only. This
report includes time from all routines in its totals, whether these routines appear in the profile. More than one **-f** option may be used. For
example:

```
-f _sub1_ -f _sub2_
```

prints the call graph for the FORTRAN routines **SUB1** and **SUB2** and
their descendants but omits entries for all other routines.

-F *name*   Similar to **-f**; however, it includes only the times attributable to *name*
and its descendants in total time and percentage computations.

-s   Merge all listed *stat-files* into a single file. This file will have the
name *gmon.sum*. It has the same format as other *stat-files* and, therefore, can be used in future **gprof** runs. It is a convenient way to collect data from many runs of an executable file.

-z   With this option, **gprof** generates a list of routines that are never
called.

For example, the command:

```
% gprof -s myprog statrun1 statrun2 statrun3 > profout
```

produces a profile which combines the data contained in the files *statrun1*,
statrun2, and *statrun3*. Each of these files was produced by an independent run of
the program **myprog**. The profile will be placed in the file *profout*. Furthermore,
the **-s** option tells **gprof** to merge the contents of *statrun1*, *statrun2*, and *statrun3*
into a file named *gmon.sum*. *gmon.sum* can then be used to merge these data into
future program runs.

Interpreting a Profile from gprof

The output from **gprof** consists of three sections. **gprof** first displays the call
graph profile, which analyzes the execution time for each routine in terms of its
parents and children. This is followed by the flat profile, which simply lists the
total time spent executing each routine. Finally, **gprof** includes an index that lists

all profiled routines in alphabetical order (note that all upper-case letters precede all lower-case letters and that the underscore character appears between upper- and lower-case letters in the collating sequence) and assigns an index number to each. This index number will help you to cross-reference routines in the call graph profile.

Both the call graph profile and the flat profile have a single entry per routine. Each routine in these profiles falls into one of the following classes:

- The routines **monitor, monstartup,** and **moncontrol** perform tasks on behalf of the profiler. In addition, routines whose names begin with the prefixes **_mon__, _fmon__,** and **_gmon__** perform tasks on behalf of the profiler. These also will not be part of a production program. You can subtract the time these routines contribute from the program's execution time. By default, these routines are not included in the call graph profile; they are always included in the flat profile. The actual names may vary, depending on your UNIX implementation, but it should be easy to pick out which routines represent profiling overhead.

- Routines whose names begin and end with underscores (e.g., **_comput_**) are routines found in your FORTRAN source program. The routine **_MAIN_** is your program's top-level routine (i.e., the point at which your program begins execution).

- Routines whose names begin with an underscore but do not end with an underscore (e.g., **_fstat** or **_t_runc**) are routines written in C. In virtually all cases, these will be system calls, I/O routines, math routines, or other routines within the UNIX execution environment. These may contribute significantly to the program's total execution time and may provide valuable information.

The Flat Profile

The *flat profile* provides a one-dimensional view of where your program is spending its time. It tells you how much of the program's total time was spent by each function, the average amount of time each function took per call, etc. There is no information about the interaction between subroutines. Often, you don't need this kind of information; it is usually good enough to know that your program spends 70 percent of its time executing the function **RUNFAST**. If this is all you need to know, you are better off looking at a simple flat report than the voluminous output produced by the call graph profiler.

Although it is more basic, the flat profile appears after the call graph profile in **gprof**'s output. There is a single line entry for each subroutine. These entries are sorted according to the amount of time spent executing the subroutine itself, not counting time spent executing the subroutine's descendants. Each entry in the flat profile contains the following information:

name   Name of the subroutine. This is followed by an index number that may make it easier to interpret the call graph. The index number is normally enclosed in [] (square brackets). If the index number is enclosed in () (parentheses), the routine it identifies will not be included in the call graph profile. For example, a subroutine named **AGAIN** may be listed as **_again_ [43]**, where the number 43 is the index number assigned to the routine.

%time   Percentage of the program's total execution time spent executing this subroutine. **gprof** does not include time spent executing the subroutine's descendants in this figure.

self seconds   Total number of seconds spent executing this subroutine, not including time spent executing the subroutine's descendants.

cumulative seconds
                     Total number of seconds spent executing this subroutine and all the subroutines previously appearing it in the flat profile.

calls   Total number of calls to this subroutine that occurred while the program was executing. This figure is not printed for profiler routines.

self ms/call   Average amount of time in milliseconds spent executing this subroutine each time it was called. For example, a subroutine that contributed 1000 seconds to the program's total execution time and was called 10000 times averaged 100 milliseconds (0.1 seconds) per call. This figure counts only the time spent executing this subroutine itself and excludes any time spent executing any of this subroutine's descendants. This figure is not printed for profiler routines.

total ms/call   Average amount of time in milliseconds spent executing this subroutine and its children each time it was called. For example, if **_factor_** averages 2 milliseconds per call but calls other subroutines in a way that averages 27 milliseconds per call, the total ms/call for **_factor_** is 29 and the self ms/call for **_factor_** is 2. This figure is not printed for profiler routines.

For example, here are a few lines from the output of a typical **gprof** profile:

% time	cumulative seconds	self seconds	calls	self ms/call	total ms/call	name
25.9	21.23	21.23				monitor (302)
17.4	35.47	14.23	1200000	0.01	0.01	_pow_ri [4]
16.2	48.75	13.28	1200000	0.01	0.01	_fact_ [5]
10.4	57.23	8.48	100000	0.08	0.36	_fmyexp_ [3]
. . . .						
0.6	75.08	0.50	1	500.00	36566.67	_MAIN_ [3]
. . . .						
0.0	81.93	0.00	1	0.00	0.00	_wrt_F [244}

This shows that the program required a total of 81.93 seconds of execution time. The routine **_wrt_F** is the last entry in the profile and shows a cumulative time of 81.93. However, this includes 21.23 seconds from monitor and additional time from other routines in the profiler; the actual time required by a production run would be roughly 60 seconds. By itself the program's main procedure, _MAIN_, only accounts for 0.5 seconds of the execution time. This is because _MAIN_ spends most of its time calling other functions; in itself, _MAIN_ is relatively simple and fast.

The most heavily used subroutine called by the program is **_pow_ri**; it accounted for more than 14 seconds of execution time (17.4 percent of the total) and was called 1.2 million times. This routine is part of the mathematical library; it is used to raise a REAL number to an INTEGER power. This fact may help you to improve your algorithm; if you can reduce the number of calls to **_pow_ri** by eliminating exponentiations, you will improve the program's performance. However, you cannot change **_pow_ri** itself, because it is a library routine.

The next most heavily used routines, **FACT** and **FMYEXP**, are FORTRAN subroutines from the program itself (their names begin and end with underscores). An average call to **FMYEXP** requires 0.36 milliseconds, of which 0.08 milliseconds are spent executing **FMYEXP**. The rest are spent executing subroutines that **FMYEXP** invokes. An average call to **FACT** requires 0.01 seconds. Because **FACT** and **FMYEXP** are called so often, improvements to these algorithms will have a marked effect on the performance of the program as a whole.

Improvements to other routines will not affect the program as much. If the program only spends 5 percent of its time executing a given subroutine, you can improve the program's performance by 5 percent at most by modifying the subroutine. This may be a lot of work for very little return. Applying this principle to our example, we see that there is nothing to be gained by optimizing the main routine.

In general, the most important subroutine calls (the calls in which the program spends most of its time) appear at the top of the flat listing. Three strategies are available for improving the performance of the program by looking at these subroutines:

1. Improve the algorithms used in these subroutines so they execute more quickly.

2. Improve the calling routine, so the subroutines are not called as often.

3. Eliminate the routines most often called by rewriting them within their callers.

The last strategy is called inline substitution. It can be very effective for subroutines and functions that are called many times and do virtually no work (i.e., routines for which the procedure call overhead are large compared to the actual computation they perform). Some very advanced compilers may do this as part of optimization.

The Call Graph Profile

In some situations, the one-dimensional information provided by a flat profile is not enough. You need a two-dimensional display that shows why every routine was called: which routines called it, which routines it called, and what the total running time comprised. If several parts of the program call the same routine, you may want to know which calls account for most of the routine's time. Maybe some calls have worst-case arguments that could be better served by a different kind of function, or maybe one part of the program is calling the routine many times when it isn't really necessary. This is the kind of information that a *call graph profile* provides.

The call graph profile has a complex multiline entry for each routine. Different entries are separated by dashed lines. The column labeled **name**, toward the right side of the report, shows the routine under analysis in each section. **gprof** lists the routine's parents above and to the right of the routine's name; it lists the routine's children below and to the right of the routine's name. Each name is followed by the index number that **gprof** assigned. For example, the first entry in a call graph profile looks something like this:

```
                                  called/total      parents
       index  %time  self  descendents   called+self  name          index
                                  called/total      children
       ---------------------------------------------------------------------
       Data about FRED and JOE   (parent)                    _joe_   [23]
       Data about FRED and MARY   (parent)                   _mary_  [30]
       Data regarding FRED                                 _fred_  [15]
       Data about FRED and ETHEL (child)                     _ethel_  [10]
       Data about FRED and BOB (child)                       _bob_   [3]
       ---------------------------------------------------------------------
```

This shows, in abstract form, the call graph entry for **FRED**, a FORTRAN routine. Two routines, **JOE** and **MARY**, are listed above **FRED**; these are **FRED**'s parents. In turn, **FRED** calls **ETHEL** and **BOB**; **FRED**'s children. The line labeled **_fred_** shows data about **FRED** alone, the line labeled **_joe_** shows data about **JOE** in relation to **FRED**, and so on. Note that this entry does not contain complete information about **JOE**, **MARY**, **ETHEL**, and **BOB**; it only contains information about their relation to **FRED**. For complete information about **JOE**, look for the entry that lists **_joe_** as the function's name.

The data to the left of these names consist of several columns. The first two columns, **index** and **%time,** show the index number for the routine that this entry describes and the percentage of the total running time that was spent executing this routine and its descendants. This figure ignores overhead profiling and procedure call overhead.

The remaining three columns contain separate data for the routine being analyzed, its parents, and its children. These columns are labeled **self, descendants,** and **called+self**.

Self

This column analyzes the total time spent executing the routine. The **self** entry for the routine under analysis shows the total amount of time spent executing this routine, excluding any time spent executing its children. For example, the following chart shows that **FRED** spent a total of 30 seconds in execution:

```
                                     parents
          . . . self . . .           name          index
                                     children
      -------------------------------------------------------------------
                    10.00            _joe_    [23]
                    20.00            _mary_   [30]
                    30.00           _fred_    [15]
                    14.00            _ethel_   [10]
                    38.00            _bob_    [3]

      -------------------------------------------------------------------
      Other columns have been omitted for clarity.
```

The parent lines in this chart show the amount of time that **FRED** spent executing on behalf of each of its parents. This chart shows that **FRED** spent a total of 10 seconds running when it was called by **JOE** and 20 seconds when it was called by **MARY**. These total 30 seconds: **FRED**'s total contribution to the program's overall running time. The child lines show how much time each child spent running when it was called by **FRED**. This shows that **ETHEL** spent 14 seconds running when it was called by **FRED** and **BOB** spent 38 seconds running when it was called by **FRED**. Note that **FRED**'s self time of 30 does not include time spent executing **ETHEL** or **BOB**; therefore, **BOB**'s self time of 38 seconds is not inconsistent with the other data in this display.

Descendants

This column shows the total amount of time the function being analyzed spent executing its descendants. Again, we will use a simplified profile entry to explain the significance of the data in this column:

```
                                          parents
         . . . self descendants . . .     name        index
                                            children
    ------------------------------------------------------------
                  10.00    22.33            _joe_    [23]
                  20.00    44.66            _mary_   [30]
                  30.00    67.00          _fred_     [15]
                  14.00    13.00            _ethel_    [10]
                  38.00     2.00            _bob_    [3]
    ------------------------------------------------------------
```
Other columns have been omitted for clarity.

The entry in the descendants column for the routine under analysis shows the total amount of time this routine spent waiting for its descendants to execute. This table shows that **FRED** spent 67 seconds waiting for its descendants, **ETHEL** and **BOB**, and any routines that these call. The total time spent executing **FRED** is its self time (30 seconds) plus its descendants time (67 seconds), or 97 seconds. The two lines above **_fred_** report the amount of time **FRED** spent waiting for descendants on behalf of its two parents. This profile shows that **FRED** spent 22.33 total seconds executing **ETHEL** and **BOB** when it was called by **JOE** and 44.66 seconds executing **ETHEL** and **BOB** when it was called by **MARY**. Note that these add up to 67, the total number of seconds **FRED** spent executing its descendants.

Finally, the table shows the number of seconds from **BOB** and **ETHEL**'s descendants time that can be attributed to calls from **FRED**. (The total time **BOB** and **ETHEL** spend executing their descendants does not appear here.) **ETHEL** spent 13 seconds executing its descendants on behalf of **FRED**, for a total of 27 seconds of execution time on behalf of **FRED** (self seconds plus dependents seconds). **BOB** spent 2 seconds executing its descendants when it was called by **FRED**. This accounts completely for the 67 seconds **FRED** spent executing its descendants: 14 seconds executing **ETHEL** itself, 13 seconds executing **ETHEL**'s descendants, 38 seconds executing **FRED** itself, and 2 seconds executing **FRED**'s descendants.

Called

The column with three headings, **called/total**, **called+self**, and **called/total**, reports how many times each routine was called. We will call this column the **called** column, ignoring the separate labels. Here is a portion of a call graph entry focusing on the **called** column:

```
                    called/total          parents
            . . .   called+self       name        index
                    called/total          children
    -----------------------------------------------------------
                    9000/10000            _joe_  [23]
                    1000/10000            _mary_  [30]
                    10000            _fred_  [15]
                    323/700               _ethel_  [10]
                    600/600               _bob_  [3]

    -----------------------------------------------------------
```

Other columns have been omitted for clarity.

For **FRED**, the routine under analysis in this entry, this column reports a total of 10000 calls. This means that **FRED** was called 10000 times while the program was executing. (This figure includes only nonrecursive calls. If **FRED** is called recursively, an additional figure will report the number of recursive calls. FORTRAN does not support recursive subprogram calls.) Above the line for **FRED**, the **called** column reports the number of calls each parent made to **FRED**, followed by the total number of calls to **FRED**. **JOE** made 9000 calls to **FRED** (out of the total 10000 calls); **MARY** made the remaining 1000 calls. Below the line for **FRED**, this column reports the number of calls **FRED** made to each of its children, followed by the total number of calls to its children. So **FRED** made 323 out of a total 700 calls to **ETHEL**. **FRED** made 600 out of 600 calls to **BOB**, showing that **FRED** is the only routine called **BOB**.

Putting the Pieces Together

Here is an entry from an actual profile describing the FORTRAN procedure **FMYEXP**, its parents, and its children:

```
                               called/total     parents
       index  %time   self  descendents  called+self  name          index
                                          called/total     children
       ------------------------------------------------------------------
                       6.35      23.00   100000/100000    _MAIN_   [1]
                       6.35      23.00   100000           _fmyexp_  [3]
       [3]    56.3   12.25       0.00  1200000/1200000    _pow_ri  [4]
                      10.75       0.00  1200000/1210000    _fact_   [5]
       ------------------------------------------------------------------
```

This display shows, in detail, how **FMYEXP** interacts with its parents and children. This routine **FMYEXP** has a single parent, _MAIN_ (the program's main procedure), and two children, _pow_ri (a library routine written in C) and the FORTRAN routine **FACT**.

A single line describes **FMYEXP** itself. Together with its descendants, it accounts for 56.3 percent of the program's total execution time. It spends 6.35 seconds executing, not including any time spent executing its two children. It spends 23 seconds executing these children, **FACT** and _pow_ri. **FMYEXP** is called 100000 times, including recursive calls (of which there are none). All of these calls come from _MAIN_; furthermore, this is the only routine _MAIN_ calls.

The following lines _fmyexp_ describe the relationship between this routine and its children. Of the total 23 seconds that **FMYEXP** spent executing its children, 12.25 seconds were spent executing _pow_ri on behalf of **FMYEXP** and 10.75 seconds were spent executing **FACT** on behalf of **FMYEXP**. Neither _pow_ri nor **FACT** has any children, so they spend 0 seconds executing their descendants. Note that this does not include time spent executing either _pow_ri or **FACT** on behalf of other routines. To find out whether other procedures call _pow_ri and the amount of time it spent executing on behalf of these procedures, you must look up the _pow_ri's entry in the profile. **FMYEXP** called _pow_ri 1200000 times; this accounts for all of the calls to this routine. **FMYEXP** made 1200000 calls to **FACT**, and **FACT** was called a total of 1210000 times. This indicates that other routines call **FACT**.

The previous lines _fmyexp_ describe the relationship between this routine and its parents. Because **FMYEXP** has a single parent, only one entry appears here; therefore, this entry is not a particularly good example. The following example describes **FACT**, which is called by both **FMYEXP** and _MAIN_:

				called/total	parents	
index	%time	self	descendents	called+self	name	index
				called/total	children	
		0.10	0.00	10000/1200000	_MAIN_	[2]
		12.25	0.00	1200000/1200000	_fmyexp_	[3]
[4]	23.7	12.35	0.00	1210000	_fact_	[4]

The routine **FACT** has no children and two parents. _MAIN_ calls **FACT** directly 10000 times, and **FMYEXP** calls **FACT** 1200000 times; this accounts for all 1210000 calls to **FACT**. **FACT** accounts for 12.35 seconds: 23.7 percent of the program's total running time. Of this, calls to **FACT** from _MAIN_ account for 0.1 seconds and calls to **FACT** from **FMYEXP** account for 12.25 seconds. This suggests that the program's performance would be helped significantly by substituting **FACT** in-line in the routine **FMYEXP**. Calls to **FACT** from _MAIN_ are relatively infrequent and do not contribute a lot to the total execution time; therefore, substituting these calls inline will not improve performance significantly.

Profiling with prof

The **prof** profiler produces a flat profile similar to the flat profile at the end of **gprof**'s output. In this respect, the flat profile is redundant; you don't really need **prof**. However, its output is less unwieldly, and because the report is much simpler, distortion from timing overhead is significantly less.

To enable profiling with **prof**, compile or link the program with the **-p** option, then execute the program. This will produce monitor file named *mon.out*. This file is similar to the *gmon.out* produced for **gprof**. It is a collection of raw statistics about program execution and is not readable by humans. After generating this file, enter the command:

```
% prof list-of-options executable stat-files > output
```

where *executable* is the name of the executable file you are profiling and *stat-files* is a list of *mon* files that have resulted from executing the program. This features lets you generate a profile that combines the results from several different program runs. If you want to generate the profile from a single file named *mon.out*, you may omit *stat-files*. Similarly, you may omit *executable-file* if the name of the executable file is *a.out*. Output from **prof** is sent to UNIX standard output. It is usually more convenient to redirect the data to a file (as shown previously) than to view it on the terminal.

The *list-of-options* is optional; it may consist of options chosen from the following list:

-s   Produce a summary file named *sum.out*. This is the *stat-file* formed by combining all *stat-files* listed on the command line.

-z   Report functions that are never called. Normally, these are suppressed.

-n   Sort the output by the number of calls to the function. Normally, the output is sorted by time, with the function or trace consuming the most time listed first.

The report produced by **prof** is a series of lines, each of which has the following form:

```
%time   cumsecs    #call   ms/call   name
```

%time   The percentage of the program's total running time spent executing the trace identified by *name*.

cumsecs   The total number of seconds spent executing the routine identified by *name* and all routines preceding it on the list.

#call   The total number of times the routine was called.

ms/call   The average number of milliseconds spent in the routine *name* each time it was called.

name   The name of a subprogram (subroutine, function, or library routine). Function names are equivalent to the original FORTRAN function names, converted to lowercase, with an underscore added before and after; this is the same convention used by **gprof**.

Here are a few selected lines from a typical **prof** profile:

```
%time       cumsecs       #call    ms/call   name
 10.6        7.30         1000      7.30     _myexp_
  7.2       12.24         3000      1.64     _modf_
  6.4       16.67         8000      0.55     _loc_pow_
  6.1       20.85         8000      0.52     _fact_
```

This report shows that the routine **MYEXP** occupied 10.6 of the total execution time, for a total of 7.3 seconds. It was called 10000 times and required (on the average) 7.3 milliseconds whenever it was called. **_modf_** (a library function) took 7.2 percent of the total time, accounting for 4.94 seconds and averaging 1.64 milliseconds per call. **FACT** accounted for roughly 4.2 seconds of the total running time (6.1 percent); it was called 8000 times and averaged 0.52 milliseconds per call. By default, the **prof** profile omits entries describing the profiling overhead functions.

A

Extensions and Oddities: UNIX Compatibility Issues

UNIX FORTRAN Compilers
UNIX Extensions
Quirks

UNIX FORTRAN Compilers

A FORTRAN 77 compiler is a standard part of Berkeley UNIX. In this section, we'll discuss the compiler, the extensions that have been added to it, and a few of its quirks. Knowing about the compiler's features and misfeatures will make it much easier to port programs from other operating systems to UNIX.

Before the scientific programming community began moving to UNIX, there was a single UNIX FORTRAN compiler: the Feldman and Weinberger compiler. Today there are many. To serve the scientific programming market, many UNIX system manufacturers have developed their own FORTRAN compilers. For the most part, these compilers are descendants of the Feldman and Weinberger compiler. They differ primarily in that they offer much more comprehensive optimization and provide many compatibility options (typically to provide compatibility with VMS FORTRAN). To gain some common ground, we'll discuss the standard UNIX compiler. Be aware that the compiler you are using may be different from (and probably better than) the compiler described here. As we discuss the standard compiler, we will point out the areas that are most likely to be different. The one thing most likely to change is the compiler's name. The standard Berkeley compiler is called **f77**; on your system, it may be called **fortran** or **fc**.

At the end of this chapter, we'll discuss some of the nonstandard features we have seen in UNIX FORTRAN compilers. We'll give some opinions on how useful (and how common) these features are. In general, it's a bad idea to get too comfortable with nonstandard features. Good as an extension may be, it will not help you when you need to port your code to some other system.

UNIX Extensions

Feldman and Weinberger added a number of extensions to the FORTRAN 77 language. Several of these (e.g., the **DOUBLE COMPLEX** data type) are common to virtually all FORTRAN compilers. Others are unique to UNIX and add interesting new features to the language. A third group of extensions is better left unmentioned, but we will at least tell you what to avoid. In this section, we'll run down the list of UNIX extensions.

Data Types

UNIX FORTRAN supports two additional data types. These data types are found in virtually all FORTRAN compilers:

- The **DOUBLE COMPLEX** data type, also known as **COMPLEX*16**, represents double-precision complex numbers. The real and imaginary parts of the complex number are represented by 64-bit (**DOUBLE PRECISION**) quantities.
- The **INTEGER*2** data type uses 16 bits to represent an integer. If the compiler is invoked with the **-i2** option, all **INTEGER** quantities are **INTEGER*2**, unless specified otherwise.

The **-i2** option makes all **INTEGER** and **LOGICAL** data into two-byte quantities, unless you explicitly request four bytes. This option may help you to port very old FORTRAN code coming from 16-bit systems. We do not recommend using **-i2** except as a convenience when porting. Do not use **-i2** to reduce a program's memory requirements, even if you have large integer arrays. Many modern systems are optimized for 32-bit operations, so **-i2** may actually make your program run slightly slower.

Normally FORTRAN assumes that all variables whose names begin with the letters "I" through "N" have type **INTEGER** and that all others have the type **REAL**. The **IMPLICIT** statement, which is defined in the ANSI standard, allows you to change the default typing. Under UNIX, FORTRAN provides an **IMPLICIT UNDEFINED** statement. Placing this statement in the declaration portion of a FORTRAN subroutine or function suspends implicit data typing. With an **IMPLICIT UNDEFINED** statement, you must have an explicit declaration for every variable. This is completely contrary to typical FORTRAN style, but it is a good idea: turning off implicit typing makes it much easier to detect misspelled variable names and other nuisances. (You can achieve the same effect by compiling the program with the **-u** option).

Constants

UNIX provides a notation for binary, octal, and hexadecimal constants. These constants may be used in **DATA** statements to initialize variables. The general form is:

c' constant'

where the character *c* is **B** for a binary constant, **O** for an octal constant, and **X** for a hex constant. For example, the following data statement initializes three elements from the array **IA**:

```
DIMENSION IA(3)
DATA IA /B'101',O'200',X'FF'/
```

The first constant represents the value 5, the second represents the value 128 (in octal), and the third represents 255 (in hexadecimal).

There is also a standard UNIX notion for the common nonprinting character string constants. These are called the "backslash escape sequences" because they all begin with a \ (backslash):

Sequence	Character
\n	Newline (CTRL-J)
\t	Tab (CTRL-I)
\b	Backspace (CTRL-H)
\f	Form-feed (CTRL-L)
\0	Null (0)
\'	Apostrophe (never terminates a string)
\"	Double quotation mark (never terminates a string)
\\	Backslash
\c	Any single character *c*

FORTRAN programs can use these escape sequences to insert special characters into character strings. Remember that each of these sequences represents a single (one-byte) character.

The UNIX FORTRAN compiler provides Hollerith constants but only in a very restrictive sense. Hollerith constants may be used instead of character constants (i.e., in situations where a character constant would be legal) and in data statements. At least one common FORTRAN construction is illegal on most compilers: you cannot assign a Hollerith constant to a noncharacter variable. For example:

```
      CHARACTER*10 CSTR
      INTEGER I
C  legal Hollerith constants
      DATA I/4Habcd/
      CSTR = 10Hefghijklmn
C  illegal Hollerith usage (sometimes allowed)
      I = 4Habse
```

For compatibility purposes, many UNIX compilers now allow you to assign a Hollerith constant to a non-**CHARACTER** variable.

Tab Formatting

Like most modern FORTRAN compilers, the UNIX compiler allows considerably more flexibility in line format than the ANSI standard. UNIX allows tab-formatted lines, in which a tab character is used to separate the statement label field from the statement itself. If a tab occurs anywhere within the first six characters on the line, the characters to the left of the tab, if there are any, are the statement label and the characters to the right are the statement itself. The maximum length of the statement varies depending on your implementation but is always long (several hundred characters).

UNIX also provides a less restrictive format for continuation lines, in addition to the standard format. If the first character on a line is an & (ampersand), the remainder of the line is considered a continuation.

If a line is not tab-formatted, the FORTRAN compiler enforces the standard column-formatting rules: columns 1 through 5 are the statement label, columns 7 through 72 are the statement, and columns 73 through 80 are ignored. A character in column 6 indicates a continuation line.

File Inclusion

UNIX provides two ways of including another file within a program:
• By using the C preprocessor **#include** directive.

- By using a FORTRAN statement of the form:

  INCLUDE *"filename"*

Many non-UNIX compilers implement the **INCLUDE** statement.

I/O Extensions

The UNIX extensions to FORTRAN I/O are generally undistinguished. However, there are one or two worth knowing about:

- You can specify:

  ```
  FORM="PRINT"
  ```

  when opening a file for output. This means that the I/O library will interpret the first character of each line as an old-style carriage control character. If the first character is a 0, it will be replaced by a newline character. If the first character is a 1, it will be replaced by a form-feed. All other initial characters are ignored.

- During formatted input, you can use commas to separate values. Commas override the explicit field widths specified in **FORMAT** statements, *provided that* the comma-separated fields are shorter than the **FORMAT** specification. For example, the following line is valid input for three integers and a floating-point number:

  ```
  program prompt:> 3,42,345,-2.564D3
  ```

Intrinsic Functions

The UNIX compiler supports several additional intrinsic functions:

Function	Definition
OR(A,B)	Bitwise OR of the operands A and B
AND(A,B)	Bitwise AND of the operands A and B
XOR(A,B)	Bitwise exclusive OR of the operands A and B
NOT(A)	Bitwise negation of the operand A

Many manufacturers interested in the scientific programming market have also added the so-called **MIL-STD** intrinsic functions (many additional bitwise operations, including arithmetic and logical shifts).

Extensions to Avoid

There are a few extensions that should have been banished:

- Many compilers claim to allow recursion, but few implement it correctly. Your compiler may have fixed this problem, but don't assume that recursion works without some careful experimentation. The FORTRAN standard does not require recursion, and few FORTRAN compilers outside of the UNIX world try to support it. Along with recursion, don't trust the **STATIC** and **AUTO-MATIC** keywords.

- UNIX FORTRAN allows direct access I/O on internal files. This is a rather strange idea that can lead to some strange bugs. We recommend that you stay away from it. While direct access internal I/O will probably work, it is not a good idea.

Quirks

Let's face it: the standard compiler does not have a good reputation among FORTRAN programmers. Its ill-repute isn't really deserved, however: the most annoying features arise from obeying the ANSI standard more strictly than most older compilers. The UNIX compiler is not as forgiving as many others. (As you can imagine, UNIX developers complain about the need to match other FORTRAN compilers "bug for bug.") The following sections list some things to watch out for.

Save Status and Zero Initialization

Many FORTRAN programs assume that variables will retain their values from one invocation of a subprogram to the next (i.e., programs assume that all variables implicitly have **SAVE** status). Under UNIX, variables do not have **SAVE** status unless they are listed in a **SAVE** statement. For example, consider the routine **COUNTER**. This routine increments a variable each time it is called. The version on the left will not work correctly under UNIX; the value **ICNT** will not be preserved from call to call. The version on the right will work correctly.

```
C you often see code like this:    C good UNIX code below:
        FUNCTION ICOUNT()                  FUNCTION ICOUNT()
        INTEGER ICNT                       INTEGER ICNT/0/
                                           SAVE ICNT
        ICNT = ICNT+1                      ICNT = ICNT+1
```

```
ICOUNT=ICNT                    ICOUNT=ICNT
END                            END
```

It is small consolation to note that the program on the left violates the ANSI standard. It still will not work, and in practice, it may be a problem to find out which variable actually needs to be saved. Some UNIX FORTRAN compilers have command line options that request SAVE status for all variables in the program. If your compiler has an option like this, the code on the left will work correctly. This can make porting a lot easier, but you should note that SAVE status often interferes with some important optimizations.

This example illustrates another quirk of the UNIX compiler. The code on the right explicitly initializes ICNT to 0. Again, this is correct code. According to the ANSI standard, the code on the left has no basis for assuming that ICNT is initially 0, despite the fact that it happens to work on many compilers. Under UNIX, this is often a bad assumption; ICNT may have some completely random value. Some UNIX compilers have command line options that request automatic zero initialization. If your compiler does, the code on the left will work correctly.

Common Block Padding

Padding means adding null space to common blocks so that the data within the common block is aligned correctly. Alignment refers to the position of data within memory. Virtually all computers have some kind of optimal alignment which you must obey for optimal performance. By far the most common set of alignment restrictions is:

Data Item Size	Alignment
CHARACTER	No restrictions (any address).
INTEGER*2 **LOGICAL*2 (if available)**	Base address must be a multiple of two (half-word alignment).
INTEGER **REAL** **COMPLEX**	Base address must be a multiple of four (word alignment).
DOUBLE PRECISION **DOUBLE COMPLEX**	Base address must be a multiple of eight (even word alignment).

Padding a common block means adding space between elements where necessary to observe the system's alignment rules.

The problem with padding is that some compilers do it and some don't. There is no general agreement; IBM compilers pad, VAX/VMS compilers don't. UNIX compilers don't add any padding. When you move code from a padding system to a nonpadding system, you are faced with these problems:

- The code probably will not obey the new system's alignment rules and may run slowly (nonaligned memory operations take more time than aligned operations).

- The size of the common block may change. Assumptions that your program makes about common block size may be wrong.

- The offset of any variable or array within a common block may change. Any assumptions your program makes about the position of data within a common block may be wrong.

Programs that define the same common block in different ways (unfortunately, a common programming practice) almost always make assumptions about the size and offsets of common block elements.

Some UNIX compilers provide a padding option for compatibility. If you are moving code from a padding system to UNIX, using this option will minimize your problems. If your compiler does not have such an option, you may need to reorganize your common blocks. It is a good practice to organize common blocks according to the size of the data items, putting the largest data types first (i.e., **DOUBLE PRECISION** variables and arrays first, followed by **REAL, INTEGER,** and **LOGICAL**, followed by **INTEGER*2** and **LOGICAL*2**, followed by **CHAR-ACTER**). Common blocks with this structure will be immune to padding problems and will obey all known alignment restrictions.

Argument Matching

Many older FORTRAN implementations allow you to omit some arguments when you are calling a subroutine (i.e., these compilers allow you to write subroutines with optional arguments). UNIX FORTRAN has no conception of optional arguments. When you call a subroutine or a function, you must always supply all of its arguments.

Along the same lines, the FORTRAN 77 standard requires the type of all actual arguments to match the type of the program's dummy arguments. Compilers typically have no way of enforcing this rule, and the UNIX compiler is no exception; you can get away with a lot. However, there is one practice you cannot get away with. On some computers, short data types are prefixes of long data types; (i.e., a **DOUBLE PRECISION** number is a **REAL** number with additional low-order bits). On these systems, it is a common practice to pass a **DOUBLE PRECISION** number to a routine expecting a **REAL** argument and vice versa. Most modern UNIX hardware platforms follow the IEEE 754 floating-point standard. With this floating-point representation, **REAL** numbers are not a prefix for **DOUBLE**

PRECISION numbers. Therefore, if a subroutine has **REAL** arguments, you must pass **REAL** data to it; if a subroutine has **DOUBLE PRECISION** arguments, you must pass **DOUBLE PRECISION** data to it.

NOTE

This is not a restriction imposed by UNIX; rather, it is imposed by the hardware on which you run UNIX. You might get away with it on some systems, but it is very bad programming practice.

Capitalization

The FORTRAN compiler's treatment of capitalization is a persistent annoyance. UNIX is almost always case-sensitive; upper- and lower-case letters are considered different. By definition, FORTRAN is not case-sensitive, and FORTRAN programs are traditionally written in uppercase. The UNIX compiler handles this situation by translating the FORTRAN program into lowercase, except for character strings and Hollerith constants. You will find that you have to type variable names and function names in lowercase when you are debugging.

Listings

The standard UNIX compiler does not provide program listings, cross-reference listings, and other amenities. Some manufacturers have added these facilities, but you will probably have to do without them. You can use the **grep** utility to create your own cross-reference listings on the spot. For example, to find all occurrences of the variable **MYBIGCOUNT**, use the command:

```
% grep -n MYBIGCOUNT *.[fF]
dot.f:1:        SUBROUTINE MYBIGCOUNT(X,Y,Z,T, N)
matm.f:10:      CALL MYBIGCOUNT(A, B, C, D, 100000)
```

The **grep** command looks for all occurrences of the string "MYBIGCOUNT" in the FORTRAN source files in the current directory. The report reveals that "MYBIGCOUNT" is the name of a subroutine which begins on line 1 of the file *dot.f*; it is called once, on line 10 of *matm.f*. The **-n** option tells **grep** to print the line number and filename with every occurrence. Another useful option is **-i**, which makes the search case-insensitive.

If you are working on a very large program and have distributed the source code into several different directories, you can combine **grep** and **find** to search the entire directory tree:

```
% grep -n MYBIGCOUNT `find . -name "*.[Ff]" -print`
```

The **find** command produces a list of filenames. It is one of UNIX's most complicated commands, but the simple **find** here can be used as a template for most useful searches. It means "look through the current directory (.) and all its subdirectories, find files whose names match *.[*Ff*], and print their names on standard output." Surrounding the **find** command with left single quotes allows **grep** to use the output from **find** as an argument list. Don't forget **-print**. If you omit it, **find** will do nothing.

In many ways, a **grep** search is preferable to a cross-reference listing. **grep** gives filenames and source line numbers and only shows the variables that are important. You don't have to search through many pages of cross references to find the one item you want. Furthermore, this listing shows all occurrences of **MYBIGCOUNT**, even if the program is broken into many files; traditional program listings can only cross reference a single file. Because tools like **make** and RCS can only be used effectively if the program is broken into several files, a traditional cross-reference listing is of little use.

The utility **nm** produces a symbol table listing. This is an indispensable tool if you want to debug your program at the assembly level. To get a sorted symbol table listing, you may want to pipe the output from **nm** into the **sort** utility.

Miscellaneous

The following points are relatively minor details that do not fit cleanly into any other categories. For most programs, they should be inconsequential. But you may be the lucky one who runs into a problem.

- UNIX FORTRAN compilers do not allow **REAL** numbers to be used as array subscripts. Array subscripts must be **INTEGER** (or **INTEGER*2**) quantities, as required by the standard.

- The UNIX FORTRAN compiler automatically truncates floating-point constants to single precision, unless the constant explicitly specifies otherwise (e.g., 2.718281828345687444D0). This behavior may be a problem in computations for which numerical accuracy or stability is an issue. One can imagine better ways of interpreting constants.

B

Programs Mixing FORTRAN and C

Calling C Procedures from FORTRAN
C Programs Calling FORTRAN
Compilation

This chapter discusses how a FORTRAN routine can call code that is written in C and vice versa. Therefore, we're going to break the promise we made in the preface: we will assume that you understand both C and FORTRAN.

Calling C Procedures from FORTRAN

First, we will discuss how to call C functions from FORTRAN programs. Essentially, this section discusses how to write a C procedure so that a FORTRAN program can call it successfully.

Naming

By default, the FORTRAN program converts function and subroutine names to lowercase and appends an _ (underscore). The C compiler never performs any case conversion and does not append an underscore. Therefore, if a FORTRAN program calls a C procedure with the statement:

```
CALL PROCNAME()
```

the C procedure must be named **procname_**. The C procedure may or may not return a value (i.e., its type may be **void**); any returned value will be ignored. If a FORTRAN program calls a C function with the statement:

```
X = FNNAME()
```

then the C procedure must be named **fnname_**. The C procedure must return a value (i.e., its type must not be **void**).

Unfortunately, the additional underscore makes it impossible for FORTRAN programs to call most UNIX system functions directly. FORTRAN equivalents for the most common system functions are available; they are described in Section 3F of the *UNIX Programmer's Reference Manual*. In the more general case, you will have to write your own FORTRAN binding for the system functions that interest you; that is, you will have to write a C routine (with a name ending in an underscore) that calls the system function you want. For example, if you want to make the low-level **write** system call from FORTRAN, you will have to write an intermediate function in C (for example, **c_write_**) that passes its arguments along to **write** appropriately.

Remember that names appearing in FORTRAN programs are converted to lowercase by default. If the compiler is invoked with the -U option, this conversion does not take place. Capitalization of the function's name in C must match the capitalization used in FORTRAN. Therefore, if the C function's name has capital letters, you must compile the FORTRAN program with the -U option.

Arguments to Procedures

Scalars

FORTRAN routines pass arguments by reference; they pass a pointer to the actual argument, rather than the value of the argument themselves. When a FORTRAN program calls a C function, the C function's arguments must be declared as pointers to the appropriate data type. For the FORTRAN scalar data types **INTEGER**, **INTEGER*2, REAL, DOUBLE PRECISION**, and **LOGICAL**, there is a simple correspondence between the type of the FORTRAN actual argument and the type of the argument in the C procedure. The following table shows this correspondence:

FORTRAN Type	C Type
INTEGER I	**int *i**
INTEGER*2 N	**short *n**

FORTRAN Type	C Type
REAL Z	float *z
DOUBLE PRECISION D	double *d
LOGICAL LO	int *lo

For example, the FORTRAN statements:

```
INTEGER I
INTEGER*2 J
REAL X
DOUBLE PRECISION D
LOGICAL L
CALL VEXP ( I, J, X, D, L )
```

can call a C procedure defined as:

```
void vexp_ ( i, j, x, d, l )
int *i;
short *j;
float *x;
double *d;
int *l;
{
...Program text...
}
```

The arguments to the C procedure are declared as pointers because FORTRAN programs pass their arguments as pointers (i.e., by reference) by default and C programs pass arguments by value. Therefore, an argument passed to a C procedure from a FORTRAN program must be declared as a pointer explicitly. Note that there is not a simple correspondence between **CHARACTER** data and any C type; procedure calls that pass **CHARACTER** data are a special case, which we will explain later.

Arrays

For the FORTRAN arrays of types **INTEGER, INTEGER*2, REAL, DOUBLE PRECISION**, and **LOGICAL**, there is a simple correspondence between the type of the FORTRAN actual argument with which a C procedure is called and the type of the argument in the C procedure. The following table shows this correspondence:

FORTRAN Type	C Type
INTEGER X( )	int x[ ]
INTEGER*2 X( )	short x[ ]
REAL X( )	float x[ ]
DOUBLE PRECISION X( )	double x[ ]
LOGICAL X( )	int x[ ]

FORTRAN Type	C Type
LOGICAL*2 X( )	short x[ ]

For example, consider the following FORTRAN call:

```
DIMENSION I(100), X(150)
CALL ARRAY( I, 100, X, 150 )
```

The C procedure **array** may be defined as follows:

```
array_( i, isize, x, xsize );
int i[ ];
float x[ ];
int *isize, *xsize;
{
...Program text...
}
```

The C procedure should take these factors into account:

- FORTRAN and C access arrays differently. FORTRAN organizes arrays in column-major order (i.e., the first dimension of a multiple-dimensioned array varies the fastest). C organizes arrays in row-major order (i.e., the last dimension varies the fastest).

- FORTRAN array indices start at 1, by default; C indices start at 0. Unless you declare the array otherwise, the FORTRAN element **X(1)** corresponds to the C element **x[0]**.

- Array arguments to the C procedure do not need to be declared as pointers. Arrays are always passed by reference.

CHARACTER Types

If you pass a **CHARACTER** argument to a C procedure, the called procedure must be declared with an extra integer argument at the end of its argument list. This argument will be the length of the character variable. An additional integer argument will be added for each **CHARACTER** argument that is passed to the called procedure. The C type corresponding to **CHARACTER** is **char**. For example, consider the following FORTRAN call:

```
CHARACTER* (*) C1
CHARACTER*5 C2
REAL X
CALL CHARMAC( C1, X, C2 )
```

The C procedure corresponding to this call must be declared:

```
charmac_(cl, x, c2, n1, n2);
integer n1, n2;
char *cl, *c2;
float *x;
{
...Program text...
}
```

where **n1** and **n2** are the lengths of the character strings **c1** and **c2**, respectively. These additional arguments are passed by value, not by reference.

COMPLEX Types

To pass an argument of type **COMPLEX** or **DOUBLE COMPLEX** to a C procedure, the corresponding argument in the C procedure must be declared as follows:

```
struct { float  real, imag; } *complex;
```

or:

```
struct { double  real, imag; } *dcomplex;
```

depending on whether the FORTRAN actual argument is **COMPLEX** or **DOUBLE COMPLEX**. For example, the FORTRAN statements:

```
DOUBLE COMPLEX DC
COMPLEX C
CALL COMPL( DC, C)
```

call a C routine declared as:

```
compl_( dc, c );
struct { double real, imag; } *dc;
struct { float  real, imag; } *c;
{
...Program text...
}
```

Structures

FORTRAN does not normally have any structured data types. Therefore, it is (strictly speaking) impossible to pass a structure to a C routine. By default, C passes structures by value, which is also something FORTRAN cannot do. There is, however, a workaround that can handle the most important cases. Relatively few C routines actually pass structures by value; most pass a pointer to a structure. Therefore, you can define a common block that matches the structure you want to pass and then use the first element of the common block (which is the base address of the common block) as an argument. For example, the FORTRAN statements:

```
COMMON /STRUCT/A,I,F,N
CALL CFUNCT(A)
```

can be used to call **cfunct_**, defined as:

```
void cfunct_(s)
struct s_ {
      float a;
      int i;
      float f;
      int n;
      } *s;
{
/* text of cfunct_ */
}
```

Returned Value

For all types except **CHARACTER, COMPLEX,** and **DOUBLE COMPLEX,** a C procedure called as a function must return a value of the C type corresponding to whatever type the FORTRAN program expects. The following table shows this correspondence:

FORTRAN Type	C Type
INTEGER*2	**short**
INTEGER	**int**
LOGICAL	**int**
REAL	**float**
DOUBLE PRECISION	**double**

For example, consider these FORTRAN statements:

```
INTEGER IRET, CFUNCT
IRET = CFUNCT()
```

The C routine **cfunct_** should be declared as:

```
int cfunct_();
```

Functions Returning Character Data

If a FORTRAN program expects a function to return data of type **CHARACTER**, the FORTRAN compiler adds two additional arguments to the beginning of the called procedure's argument list. The first of these arguments is a pointer to the location in which the called procedure should store the result. The second is the maximum number of characters that should be returned. The called routine should have type **void**, which means that its returned value is ignored. It is the called procedure's responsibility to copy its result through the address specified in the first argument.

For example, consider the code:

```
CHARACTER*10 CHARS, MAKECHARS
DOUBLE PRECISION X, Y
CHARS = MAKECHARS( X, Y )
```

The C routine **makechars_** must be written as follows:

```
void makechars_( result, length, x, y );
char *result;
int length;
double *x, *y;
{
...Program text, producing returnvalue...
        for (i = 0; i < length; i++ ) {
                result[i] = returnvalue[i];
        }
}
```

Note that:

- The arguments **length** and **result** *do not* appear in the FORTRAN statement calling **MAKECHARS**; they are added by the compiler.
- It is the responsibility of the called routine to copy the result string into the location specified by **result**. The called routine must not copy more than **length** characters.
- The called procedure has type **void.**

Functions Returning Complex Data

If a FORTRAN program expects a procedure to return a **COMPLEX** or **DOUBLE COMPLEX** value, the FORTRAN compiler adds an additional argument to the beginning of the called procedure's argument list. This additional argument is a pointer to a location at which the called procedure must store its result. The called procedure's returned value will be ignored. For example, consider the code:

```
COMPLEX BAT, WBAT
REAL X, Y
BAT = WBAT ( X, Y )
```

The C routine **wbat_** must be written as follows:

```
void wbat_(location, x, y);
struct {float real, imag; } *location;
float *x, *y;
{
float realpart;
float imaginarypart;
...Program text, producing realpart and imaginarypart...
        *location.real = realpart;
        *location.imag = imaginarypart;
}
```

Again, note that the argument **location** to **wbat_** does not appear in the FORTRAN call to **WBAT**; it is added by the compiler. It is the responsibility of the C subroutine to copy the result's real and imaginary parts correctly into the location specified by the argument **location**.

If this were a function returning a **DOUBLE COMPLEX** value, the type **float** would be replaced by the type **double** in the definition of **wbat_**.

C Programs Calling FORTRAN

When a C routine calls a FORTRAN procedure, it must:

- Convert the procedure's name to lowercase (unless the FORTRAN code was compiled with the **-U** option, in which case the capitalization in C and FORTRAN must match).
- Append an _ (underscore) to the FORTRAN procedure's name.
- Pass all arguments as pointers.

For example, consider the following C code:

```
main()
{
extern float ftnfn_();
int in
float flo
```

```
x = ftnfn_(&in, &flo);
}
```

This program calls the function **FTNFN**, which must be defined as:

```
REAL FUNCTION FTNFN(I,F)
INTEGER I
REAL F
...
FTNFN = returned-value
END
```

The following table shows the correspondence between C data types and FORTRAN data types:

C Data Type	FORTRAN Data Type
int *x	INTEGER*4 x
short *x	INTEGER*2 x
float *x	REAL*4 x
double *x	REAL*8 x
struct {float real,imag;}; *x	COMPLEX*8 x
struct {double real,imag;}; *x	COMPLEX*16 x

Arrays in C are always passed by reference. The corresponding dummy argument in a FORTRAN subprogram should be an array of the corresponding type.

FORTRAN generally does not have data structures, although some manufactures obsessed with VAX/VMS compatibility may have added them. In general, a C routine cannot return a structure to a FORTRAN caller, nor can C call a FORTRAN program with a structure as an argument. If you need to do this and cannot modify the C program, you must write an intermediate C procedure to handle the transition between C and FORTRAN.

Compilation

The C and FORTRAN compilers can be invoked via either the **f77** or the **cc** command. There is one crucial difference between **cc** and **f77**: the two programs invoke the linker, **ld**, in different ways. Use **cc** to invoke the linker if the program's main, or top-level, routine is written in C; use **f77** if the main routine is written in FORTRAN. Using the proper compilation command links the program to the correct initialization and run-time support routines.

If the main program is written in C (and you therefore compile with **cc**), you must also take the following steps:

- **If FORTRAN routines call intrinsic or math functions,** you must add the options **-lF77** and **-lm** to the **cc** command line when you link. These options explicitly request linking to the math library. **f77** links programs to these libraries by default; **cc** does not.

- **If a FORTRAN routine performs I/O,** you must add the option **-lI77** to the **cc** command when you link. You may need some other libraries if your system has significant extensions to standard UNIX I/O. Prior to calling any FORTRAN routine that performs I/O, the C main program must call the routine **f_init** for I/O initialization. **f_init** has no returned value and no arguments.

- **If a FORTRAN routine makes any system calls** (i.e., if a FORTRAN routine calls any routines in the FORTRAN system call library, described in Section 3F of the *UNIX Programmer's Reference Manual*), you must add the option **-lU77** to the **cc** command line when you link.

For example, the following C program calls the FORTRAN subroutine **FORTIO**:

```
main()
{
extern void fortio_();
extern void f_init();

f_init();  /*initialize the FORTRAN I/O library*/
fortio_(); /*perform FORTRAN I/O*/
}
```

The following command compiles the FORTRAN and C source files **main.c** and **fio.f**, links them with the proper libraries, and generates an executable (*a.out*) file:

```
% cc main.c fio.f -lI77
```

The program's main procedure is written in C; therefore, **cc** must be used to link the object modules and produce the executable file. The additional **-l** option ensures the FORTRAN I/O library will be present.

C

Data Representations

Data Representations
Storage Layout
Integer Representation
Logicals
Floating-Point Numbers

Data Representations

Properly speaking, data representation is neither a FORTRAN language issue nor a UNIX issue. Data representation is defined by the hardware. However, because FORTRAN programmers are often vitally concerned with the details of data representation and because data representations are gradually standardizing, we will devote some time to data representation issues.

Storage Layout

Like Gulliver's Lilliputia, the computer world is divided into two factions: systems that place the most significant byte of any quantity at the lowest address in memory and systems that place the least significant byte at the lowest address. Borrowing Swift's nomenclature, these are often referred to as *Big-endian* and *Little-endian* systems. The split goes something like this:

Little Endian	Big Endian
Least significant bit at lowest address	Most significant bit at lowest address
DEC (VAX series)	IBM (370 series and successors)
Intel (8086 series systems)	Motorola (68000 series systems)

Some processors (in particular, the MIPS R2000 series) have a "mode bit" so they can handle both formats. However, that doesn't concern you. Users usually don't have access to this configuration bit. If you are using this kind of processor, it is set up to work in one mode or the other.

Regardless of the byte ordering, manufacturers generally refer to the least significant bit as bit 0. The most significant bit is therefore bit 7, 15, or 31 (depending on whether you are referring to a byte, a half-word, or a word).

Integer Representation

INTEGER*2 and **INTEGER** quantities are usually represented as signed, twos complement numbers of two or four sequential bytes, respectively. The most significant bit of this number (bit 15 or 31) is the sign. For example, the hexadecimal number FFFFFFFF represents -1 as an **INTEGER** quantity.

An **INTEGER*2** quantity can represent any integer value between -32768 and 32767. An **INTEGER** quantity can represent any integer value between -2147483648 and 2147483647.

Some systems (notably CRAY) support 64-bit integers (**INTEGER*8**). These are rare exceptions to the rule. If your program uses 64-bit integers, you are probably in trouble. However, you should note that very few programs use 64-bit integers because they actually need a 64-bit representation. You can often get away with 32-bit integers, although you may need to add padding to common blocks.

Logicals

LOGICAL variables are four-byte quantities that can have the value .TRUE. or .FALSE.. Under UNIX, the value 0 represents .FALSE.. Nonzero values represent .TRUE..

Floating-Point Numbers

Until recently, every manufacturer had its own way of representing floating-point numbers. This presented tremendous problems when moving programs from one system to another: porting any but the simplest algorithm to another system generally introduced problems with numerical stability and round-off error. In the last few years, the IEEE standard for floating-point representation (IEEE 754) has come a long ways toward eliminating these problems. This standard is particularly widespread in the UNIX world; most manufacturers of UNIX systems adhere to it.

Single Precision (REAL, REAL*4)

Single-precision floating-point numbers have FORTRAN type **REAL*4 (REAL)**.

In the IEEE 754 representation, a single-precision floating-point number is a 32-bit (single-word) quantity in which bit 31 is the *sign*, bits 30 through 23 are the *biased exponent*, and bits 22 through bit 0 are the *fraction*. That is, the exponent field is 8 bits wide and the fraction field is 23 bits wide, as shown below.

31	30 23	22 0
Sign	Biased Exponent	Fractional Part
1 bit	8 bits	23 bits

The *sign* is 0 for a positive number, 1 for a negative number.

The *biased exponent* is the number's *binary exponent* plus a *bias* of 127. The bias guarantees that all exponents are positive, simplifying the problem of representing negative exponents. The *binary exponent* may have any value between -126 and +127 (1 <= biased exponent <= 254). The values -127 and +128 are reserved for exception handling.

The *fraction* represents the fractional part of the mantissa of a floating-point number. The integer part of this mantissa is always one and is not represented.

The value of any single-precision floating-point number is therefore:

(-1)**sign * (1+fraction) * 2**(biased_exponent-127)

REAL numbers can have values in the range of -3E38 < x < 3E38. The minimum magnitude of a floating-point number is 1.2E-38.

Double Precision

Double-precision floating-point numbers have FORTRAN type **REAL*8** (**DOUBLE PRECISION**).

In the IEEE 754 representation, a double-precision floating-point number is a 64-bit (eight-byte) quantity in which bit 63 is the *sign*, bits 62 through 52 are the *biased exponent*, and bits 51 through bit 0 are the *fraction*. That is, the exponent field is 11 bits wide and the fraction field is 52 bits wide, as shown below.

63	62 52	51 0
Sign	Biased Exponent	Fractional Part
1 bit	11 bits	52 bits

The *sign* is 0 for a positive number, 1 for a negative number.

The *biased exponent* is the number's *binary exponent* plus a *bias* of 1023. The bias guarantees that all exponents are positive, simplifying the problem of representing negative exponents. The *binary exponent* may have any value between -1022 and 1023 (1 <= biased exponent <= 2055). The values -1023 and +1024 are reserved for exception handling.

The *fraction* represents the fractional part of the mantissa of a floating-point number. The integer part of this mantissa is always one and is not represented.

The value of any double-precision floating-point number is therefore:

(-1)**sign * (1+fraction) * 2**(biased_exponent-1023)

DOUBLE PRECISION numbers can represent values in the range $-1.7E308 < x < 1.7E308$. The minimum magnitude of a **DOUBLE PRECISION** number is 2.3E-308.

COMPLEX

COMPLEX*8 (**COMPLEX**) and **COMPLEX*16** (**DOUBLE COMPLEX**) data types are represented by two consecutive floating-point numbers of single or double precision, respectively. These should be aligned on boundaries appropriate for single- or double-precision numbers. The first number (i.e., the lower address) represents the real part of the quantity; the second number (i.e., the higher address) represents the imaginary part. Single- and double-precision complex data types are shown below.

Real Part	(Single Precision)	*Addr* + 0
Imaginary Part	(Single Precision)	*Addr* + 4
Real Part	(Double Precision)	*Addr* + 0
Imaginary Part	(Double Precision)	*Addr* + 8

Error Conditions

The IEEE 754 floating-point representation introduced three new quantities to floating-point arithmetic: positive and negative infinity (written Inf and -Inf) and "not-a-number" (written NaN). The infinities represent positive or negative overflow. NaN represents an indeterminate or impossible result. For example, **arccos(1.3)** is NaN; it is neither an overflow nor an underflow but an impossible result.

A computation that produces an infinity or a NaN may generate an arithmetic exception. Equivalently, a function may return an error code and set the **errno** variable to **EDOM** or **ERANGE** (these concepts are described in Chapter 4, *FORTRAN Working Environment*. The details of exception handling are subtle and depend heavily upon the system's implementation. There are many situations in which operations involving infinities or even NaNs are legal; the design of IEEE 754 explicitly allows programs to propagate infinities and NaNs through further calculations, if desired. When infinities and NaNs appear in computations, they behave the way you would expect them to. An infinity plus, minus, or times any nonzero finite number is still an infinity; infinity minus infinity is NaN (indeterminate); infinity times zero is NaN; any operation on a NaN produces another NaN; etc.

D

UNIX Error Numbers and Signals
General UNIX Error Numbers
FORTRAN-Specific Error Numbers
Signals

General UNIX Error Numbers

When an error occurs during a UNIX system call, the system call writes a standard error number (called a *condition code* on many operating systems) into the global variable **errno**. In Chapter 4, *FORTRAN Working Envoronment*, we discussed the techniques FORTRAN programs could use to find out about **errno**. Error conditions fall into two broad classes:

- Operations that are illegal to UNIX (e.g., attempting to write a read-only file). These are handled with standard UNIX error codes, described in the introduction to Section 2 of the *UNIX Programmer's Reference Manual*.

- Illegal FORTRAN-specific operations that cannot be detected during compilation (e.g., an illegal run-time format statement). These are handled with error codes listed in the reference page for the **PERROR** system call in Section 3 of the *UNIX Programmer's Reference Manual*.

The following two tables summarize the different error conditions. Table D-1 summarizes the errors UNIX generates that are not specific to FORTRAN programs. Each error condition is associated with an identification number, a symbolic constant, and an explanatory text string (shown in italics). The symbolic names for these codes are primarily of interest to C programmers. FORTRAN programmers should also be familiar with them. The standard UNIX documentation and much of the secondary literature uses these constants as generic names for the error conditions. You do not need to know what **ENOTDIR** means off the top of your head, but you do need to know that **ENOTDIR** is a standard system error represented by a constant in *errno.h*.

Table D-1: Standard UNIX Error Codes

ID	Symbol	Meaning
1	**EPERM**	*Permission error*. The program does not have the authority to access the file.
2	**ENOENT**	*No such file or directory*. Attempt to access a nonexistent file.
3	**ESRCH**	*No such process number*. The program referred to another process using a nonexistent process identification (PID) number. This may mean that the other process died.
4	**EINTR**	*Interrupted system call*. The program received a signal while a system call was in progress.
5	**EIO**	*I/O error*. A physical I/O error occurred during read or write.
6	**ENXIO**	*No such device or address*. Nonexistent I/O device.
7	**E2BIG**	*Arg list too long*. The program attempted to execute another program and tried to pass more than 10240 arguments.
8	**ENOEXEC**	*Exec format error*. Attempt to execute a file with an incorrect format (e.g., an incompatible binary).
9	**EBADF**	*Bad file number*. Attempt to read/write a file only opened for write/read or a file that that not been opened.

Table D-1: Standard UNIX Error Codes (con't)

ID	Symbol	Meaning
10	ECHILD	*No children.* The program attempted to wait for any subprocesses to complete; however, there were no subprocesses still in existence.
11	EAGAIN	*No more processes.* User or system process table is full.
12	ENOMEM	*Not enough memory.* Insufficient virtual memory or swap space.
13	EACCESS	*Permission denied.* Illegal file access (i.e., insufficient permission).
14	EFAULT	*Bad address.* An address fault occurred while processing system call arguments.
15	ENOTBLK	*Block device required.* An I/O operation requested a character interface when the block interface was appropriate.
16	EBUSY	*Device busy.* Attempt to access a device that is busy (e.g., a tape drive that is in use).
17	EEXIST	*File exists.* Inappropriate use for an existing file (e.g., file used as a link).
18	EXDEV	*Cross-device link.* Attempt to create a hard link across two file systems.
19	ENODEV	*No such device.* Nonexistent I/O device.
20	ENOTDIR	*Not a directory.* A directory operation specified for a file (e.g., a filename appearing in the middle of a path specification).
21	EISDIR	*Is a directory.* A file operation (i.e., a write) requested for a directory.
22	EINVAL	*Invalid argument.* Bad argument passed to a system call.
23	ENFILE	*File table overflow.* Too many files open system-wide.
24	EMFILE	*Too many open files.* This process has more files open than the system allows.

Table D-1: Standard UNIX Error Codes (con't)

ID	Symbol	Meaning
25	ENOTTY	*Inappropriate ioctl.* Illegal terminal control operation.
26	ETXTBSY	*Text file busy.* Attempt to execute a file open for writing or write a file open for execution.
27	EFBIG	*File too large.* Exceeded maximum file size.
28	ENOSPC	*No space left on device.* A disk (or another device) is full.
29	ESPIPE	*Illegal seek.* A attempt to seek on a pipe.
30	EROFS	*Read-only file system.* A attempt to write a read-only file system.
31	EMLINK	*Too many links.* Too many hard links to a file (more than 32767).
32	EPIPE	*Broken pipe.* Attempt to write to a pipe with no readers.
33	EDOM	*Argument too large.* Illegal argument to or result from math function.
34	ERANGE	*Result too large.* Transfinite result from math function.
35	EWOULDBLOCK	*Operation would block.* A nonblocking system call would have blocked if allowed to complete.
36	EINPROGRESS	*Operation now in progress.* "Long" operation requested on a nonblocking resource.
37	EALREADY	*Operation already in progress.* Operation attempted on a nonblocking resource that was in use.
38	ENOTSOCK	*Socket operation on nonsocket.* Network error.
39	EDESTADDREQ	*Destination address required.* Network error.
40	EMSGSIZE	*Message too long.* Network error.
41	EPROTOTYPE	*Protocol wrong type for socket.* Network error.

Table D-1: Standard UNIX Error Codes (con't)

ID	Symbol	Meaning
42	ENOPROTOOPT	*Option not supported by protocol.* Network error.
43	EPROTONOSUPPORT	*Protocol not supported.* Network error.
44	ESOCKTNOSUPPORT	*Socket type not supported.* Network error.
45	EOPNOTSUPP	*Operation not supported.* Network error.
46	EPFNOSUPPORT	*Protocol family not supported.* Network error.
47	EAFNOSUPPORT	*Address family not supported.* Network error.
48	EADDRINUSE	*Address already in use.* Network error.
49	EADDRNOTAVAIL	*Can't assign requested address.* Network error.
50	ENETDOWN	*Network is down.* The network is unavailable.
51	ENETUNREACH	*Network is unreachable.* The network is inaccessible.
52	ENETRESET	*Network dropped connection.* The remote host crashed or was rebooted during a network operation.
53	ECONNABORTED	*Software caused connection abort.* Network error.
54	ECONNRESET	*Connection reset by peer.* The remote host rebooted during a network operation, or the operation timed out.
55	ENOBUFS	*No buffer space available.* Network error.
56	EISCONN	*Socket is already connected.* Network error.
57	ENOTCONN	*Socket is not connected.* Network error.
58	ESHUTDOWN	*Can't send after socket shutdown.* Network error.
60	ETIMEDOUT	*Connection timed out.* Network error. Remote host probably down.

Table D-1: Standard UNIX Error Codes (con't)

ID	Symbol	Meaning
61	ECONNREFUSED	*Connection refused.* Remote host refused network connection.
62	ELOOP	*Too many levels of symbolic links.* Symbolic links may be at most eight layers deep.
63	ENAMETOOLONG	*File name too long.* Maximum length of a filename is 255 characters; maximum length for the entire file specification is 1023 characters.
64	EHOSTDOWN	*Host is down.* Attempt to reach a host that is down via the network.
65	EHOSTUNREACH	*Host is unreachable.* Attempt to reach a host that is inaccessible via the network.
66	ENOTEMPTY	*Directory not empty.* Directories may not be deleted unless empty.
69	EDQUOT	*Disk quota exceeded.* Attempt to allocate disk space when over quota.
70	ESTALE	*Stale NFS file handle.* Network error.
71	EREMOTE	*To many levels of remote.* Attempt to nest remote file system mounting.

FORTRAN-Specific Error Numbers

Table D-2 describes the errors that are specific to FORTRAN programs. They are also identified with error codes but do not have a symbolic name assigned. All of these errors are caused by I/O operations.

Table D-2: FORTRAN Error Codes

ID	Meaning
100	*Error in format.* An illegal I/O format was evaluated during execution.
101	*Illegal unit number.* The program used a logical unit number outside the range 0 to 99.
102	*Formatted I/O not allowed.* The program attempted formatted I/O on a file opened as **UNFORMATTED**.
103	*Unformatted I/O not allowed.* Unformatted I/O attempted on file opened as **FORMATTED**.
104	*Direct I/O not allowed.* Direct I/O attempted on file opened as **SEQUENTIAL**.
105	*Sequential I/O not allowed.* Sequential I/O attempted on file opened as **DIRECT**.
107	*Can't backspace file.* A backspace was attempted on a unit for which seek operations are illegal (e.g., a terminal).
108	*Off beginning of record.* Attempt to tab left past the start of a record.
109	*No * after repeat count.* A repeat count for list-directed input was improperly formed.
110	*Off end of record.* Attempt to read or write past the end of a record.
112	*Incomprehensible list input.* The input for list directed I/O did not match the data in the I/O list.
113	*Out of free space.* UNIX could not allocate buffer space for an I/O operation.
114	*Unit not connected.* The program attempted an operation on a logical unit that had not been opened.
115	*Invalid data for integer format term.* Input data for an integer item illegal.
116	*Invalid data for logical format term.* Input data for a logical item illegal.
117	*Status='new', file exists.* If a file is declared 'new', the file must not exist.
118	*Status='old', file does not exist.* If a file is declared 'old', it must already exist.
119	*Opening too many files or unknown system error.* The program opens too many files. The number of files process may have open at one time is system-dependent.
120	*Requires seek ability.* The I/O operation requested a seek, which is impossible on this unit (e.g., terminals cannot seek).

Table D-2: FORTRAN Error Codes (con't)

ID	Meaning
121	*Illegal argument.* The argument for an I/O keyword was illegal.
122	*Negative repeat count.* The repeat count for list-directed input was negative.
123	*Illegal operation for unit.* The logical unit could not perform the operation.

The FORTRAN library routine subroutine **PERROR** can be used to print the text associated with the last error that occurred. **PERROR** handles both regular UNIX errors and FORTRAN-specific errors. There may be some variation in these messages from system to system.

Signals

Table D-3 includes the names of all UNIX signals, the signal's number, the action that any program will take by default upon receiving the signal, and a short description of the signal's standard meaning.

Table D-3: Berkeley UNIX Signals

Signal Name	No.	Default Action	Meaning
SIGHUP	1	Terminate	Hangup. Sent to the program when you are working from a modem and hang up. Terminates the program gracefully.
SIGINT	2	Terminate	Interrupt. Sent to the program by typing CTRL-C.
SIGQUIT	3	Core dump	Quit.
SIGILL	4	Core dump	Illegal instruction.
SIGTRAP	5	Core dump	Trace trap. Used to implement breakpoints.

Table D-3: Berkeley UNIX Signals (con't)

Signal Name	No.	Default Action	Meaning
SIGIOT	6	Core dump	Corresponds to an obscure PDP-11 instruction; abort.
SIGEMT	7	Core dump	Corresponds to an obscure PDP-11 instruction; abort.
SIGFPE	8	Core dump	Floating-point exception.
SIGKILL	9	Terminate	Kill. The program is stopped as quickly as possible. You cannot change the default action for this signal. It is normally used to destroy runaway processes.
SIGBUS	10	Core dump	Bus error. The program attempted to access memory illegally.
SIGSEGV	11	Core dump	Segmentation violation. The program attempted to access memory illegally.
SIGSYS	12	Core dump	Bad argument to system call.
SIGPIPE	13	Terminate	The program attempted to write on a pipe, but the pipe had no reader.
SIGALRM	14	Terminate	Alarm clock. Used to implement sleep.
SIGTERM	15	Terminate	Software termination signal. Some other program asked this program to stop.
SIGURG	16	Ignored	Urgent condition present on socket.
SIGSTOP	17	Stop	Stop (cannot be caught or ignored). The program will resume operation upon receiving a **CONTINUE** signal.

Table D-3: Berkeley UNIX Signals (con't)

Signal Name	No.	Default Action	Meaning
SIGTSTP	18	Stop	Stop signal generated from keyboard (normally by entering CTRL-Z). Identical to the previous **STOP** command, except generated from a keyboard.
SIGCONT	19	Ignored, if running; Continue, if stopped	Continue execution after the program has been stopped. This signal is sent by entering the commands **fg** or **bg**.
SIGCHLD	20	Ignored	A process generated by this program changed status. It either stopped, terminated, or resumed running after being stopped.
SIGTTIN	21	Stop	The program attempted to read from a terminal while it was in the background. Programs are only allowed to read from the terminal in the foreground. This signal stops the program; once it has been stopped, you can bring it into the foreground with the **fg** command and enter data when it is convenient.
SIGTTOU	22	Stop	The program attempted to write to a terminal while it was in the background. This is normally legal; however, under some circumstances it isn't allowed.
SIGIO	23	Ignored	I/O is possible on a descriptor. (See the entry for **fcntl** in Section 2 of the *UNIX Programmer's Reference Manual*.)

Table D-3: Berkeley UNIX Signals (con't)

Signal Name	No.	Default Action	Meaning
SIGXCPU	24	Terminate	The program's CPU time limit has been exceeded. CPU time limits are not normally in effect but may be enforced at your site; facilities like NQS use this signal to notify a process that is out of time. By catching this signal and responding appropriately, a program may be able to terminate gracefully and save some information from the run.
SIGXFSZ	25	Terminate	The program's maximum file size limit has been exceeded. Like CPU size limits, these limits may be enforced by facilities like NQS.
SIGVTALRM	26	Terminate	Virtual time alarm. (See the entry for **setitimer** in Section 2 of the *UNIX Programmer's Reference Manual*.)
SIGPROF	27	Terminate	Profiling timer alarm. (See the entry for **setitimer** in Section 2 of the *UNIX Programmer's Reference Manual*.)
SIGWINCH	28	Ignored	Window size change.
	29		Undefined.
SIGUSR1	30	Terminate	User-defined signal 1.
SIGUSR2	31	Terminate	User-defined signal 2.

The actions listed in Table D-3 are only defaults (i.e., the table shows what happens when the program receives a given signal, provided that you have not specified some custom action to be taken). FORTRAN programs can use the system function **SIGNAL** to change the default action for all signals except 9 and 17 (**SIGKILL** and **SIGSTOP**).

Index

Colophon

Our look is the result of reader comments, our own experimentation, and distribution channels.

Distinctive covers complement our distinctive approach to UNIX documentation, breathing personality and life into potentially dry subjects. UNIX and its attendant programs can be unruly beasts. Nutshell Handbooks help you tame them.

The animal featured on the cover of *UNIX for FORTRAN Programmers* is a mammoth.

Edie Freedman designed this cover and the entire UNIX bestiary that appears on other Nutshell Handbooks. The beasts themselves are adapted from 19th-century engravings from the Dover Pictorial Archive.

Linda Lamb designed the page layout for the Nutshell Handbooks. The text of this book is set in Times Roman; headings are Helvetica®; examples are Courier. Text was prepared using SoftQuad's *sqtroff* text formatter. Figures are produced with a Macintosh™. Printing is done on an Apple LaserWriter®.